Everyman, I will go with thee,
and be thy guide

THE EVERYMAN
LIBRARY

*The Everyman Library was founded by J. M. Dent
in 1906. He chose the name Everyman because he wanted
to make available the best books ever written in every
field to the greatest number of people at the cheapest possible
price. He began with Boswell's 'Life of Johnson';
his one-thousandth title was Aristotle's 'Metaphysics',
by which time sales exceeded forty million.*

*Today Everyman paperbacks remain true to
J. M. Dent's aims and high standards, with a wide range
of titles at affordable prices in editions which address
the needs of today's readers. Each new text is reset
to give a clear, elegant page and to incorporate the latest thinking
and scholarship. Each book carries the pilgrim logo,
the character in 'Everyman', a medieval mystery play,
a proud link between Everyman
past and present.*

Edith Wharton

A BACKWARD GLANCE

Edited by
CANDACE WAID
Yale University

Consultant Editor for this volume
CHRISTOPHER BIGSBY
University of East of Anglia

'Je veux remonter le penchant de mes belles années . . .'
Chateaubriand: *Mémoires d'outre-tombe*

'Kein Genuss ist vorübergehend'
Goethe: *Wilhelm Meister*

EVERYMAN
J. M. DENT · LONDON

First published in Everyman in 1993

© Introduction, chronology and other critical apparatus
J. M. Dent 1993

Photoset by Deltatype Ltd, Ellesmere Port

Printed in Great Britain by
The Guernsey Press Co. Ltd
Guernsey, Channel Islands

J. M. Dent
Orion Publishing Group
Orion House
5 Upper St Martin's Lane, London WC2H 9EA

British Library Cataloguing-in-Publication Data
is available upon request.

ISBN 0 460 87402 0

CONTENTS

To the friends
who every year on All Souls' Night
come and sit with me
by the fire

NOTE ON THE AUTHOR

EDITH WHARTON was born in 1862 into a privileged New York family. As a child, she spent six years in Europe with her parents, returning to New York at the age of ten. She was privately educated, and read widely in French, German and Italian as well as English. From early childhood she had a passion for 'making up', and in her teens she wrote a novella and poems some of which her mother had privately printed.

At twenty-three she married Teddy Wharton, an older friend of one of her brothers, but the marriage was not fulfilling emotionally or intellectually. With her inherited wealth the Whartons were able to travel freely and live comfortably in New York where Edith began to publish her stories in magazines. A nervous breakdown in her early thirties interrupted her work, but in 1899 her first volume of stories was published. Houses were always of great importance to her, and in 1901 she built The Mount, a country mansion in Massachusetts where she was able to write for the next ten years. Her first full-length novel, a historical romance, was sent by her sister-in-law to Henry James, and she received his advice to 'stick to the New York subject'. In 1905 *The House of Mirth* (the New York subject *par excellence*) became her first bestseller.

In 1907 the Whartons established a permanent residence in Paris, spending the summers at her New England home The Mount until it was sold in 1911. Their marriage suffered from Edith Wharton's's deep dissatisfaction and Teddy Wharton's unstable behaviour and ended in divorce in 1913. Edith's own three-year affair with the Paris journalist Morton Fullerton, which began in 1908, seems to have given new feeling to her fiction, and she invested much energy in her deep and long friendships with Henry James, Sara Norton, Walter Berry and others. During World War One, she flung herself into war work in France for which she received both French and Belgian honours.

After the War, Edith established two much loved homes, one

near Paris and one on the Riviera, between which she divided the year. She continued to write steadily, winning a Pulitzer Prize in 1921 for *The Age of Innocence*, and to exchange visits with her friends. She visited America only once after 1913 to receive an honorary degree from Yale in 1923. She published twenty-two works of fiction, both novels and novellas, and many stories as well as non-fiction and an autobiography. She died in 1937 and was buried at Versailles near the grave of her lifelong friend Walter Berry.

NOTE ON THE EDITOR

CANDACE WAID is the author of *Edith Wharton's Letters from the Underworld: Fictions of Women and Writing*, as well as numerous essays on Wharton and an edition of Wharton's short fiction *The Muse's Tragedy and Other Stories*. Associate Professor of English and American Studies at Yale University, she also writes on Faulkner, Welty and other writers of the American South.

CHRONOLOGY OF EDITH WHARTON'S LIFE

Year	Age	Life
1862		24 Jan: born in New York into wealthy social elite, only daughter of Lucretia Rhinelander and George Frederic Jones: two much older brothers
1866–72	4–10	Travels with family in Europe to avoid post-Civil War inflation: Rome, Spain, Paris, Florence
1872	10	Returns to US. Lives at Newport in summer, New York in winter. Privately educated
1877	15	Completes novella 'Fast and Loose'
1878	16	Poems privately printed by her mother
1880	18	Family returns to Europe for father's health: London, Riviera
1881	19	Visits Venice, Florence
1882	20	Spring: father dies. Returns with mother to Newport. Autumn: takes up residence in New York. Brief engagement to Harry Stevens
1883	21	Meets Walter Berry (whom she described after his death as 'the love of my life')

CHRONOLOGY OF HER TIMES

Year	Artistic Events	Historical Events
1860		US Civil War begins
1863	Kingsley, *The Water Babies*	
1864		Civil War ends First Pullman car
1866	Elizabeth Gaskell, *Wives and Daughters*	
1868	Louisa Alcott, *Little Women*	
1870	Rossetti, first sonnets of 'The House of Life'	Franco-Prussian War
1871	George Eliot, *Middlemarch* Meredith, *The Adventures of Harry Richmond* MacDonald, *The Princess and the Goblin*	
1872	Spencer, *The Study of Sociology*	Banking scandal in New York
1873	Merimée, *Lettres à une inconnue*	
1875	Symons, *Renaissance in Italy* (1875–86)	
1876	Meredith, *Beauchamp's Career* Carroll, *The Hunting of the Snark*	Telephone invented
1879	James, *Daisy Miller* Ibsen, *A Doll's House*	Edison's incandescent lamp
1880		Bicycle invented
1881	James, *Portrait of a Lady* Rossetti, further 'House of Life' sequence	
1882		Combustion engine invented
1883		Metropolitan Opera founded Brooklyn Bridge completed
1884	Huysmans, *A rebours* Adams, *Esther*	

Year	Age	Life
1885	23	Marries Edward Robbins Wharton ('Teddy'), 13 years her senior, intimate friend of one of her brothers. They live at Newport in the summers and travel for 4 months (Feb–May) mostly in Italy. Begins friendship with Egerton Winthrop who 'directs and systematises her reading'
1887–9	25–7	First early meetings with Henry James (not remembered by him)
1888	26	Mediterranean cruise – 4 months in the Aegean. Inherits large bequest
1889	27	Rents a house in New York. Four poems published in *Scribner's*, *Harper's* and *Century* magazines
1891	29	First story published in *Scribner's*
1893	31	Buys Land's End Newport. Decorates it with collaboration of architect Ogden Codman. Buys a small house in New York. Meets the Bourgets; eventually they will become friends
1894–5	32–3	Nervous breakdown, after three years of recurring depression
1897	35	*The Decoration of Houses* with Ogden Codman. Walter Berry helps her with the style
1899	37	*The Greater Inclination* best of early tales, selected with help of Walter Berry. She and Teddy visit London, then Italy. Begins friendship with Sara Norton, daughter of Harvard professor Charles Eliot Norton
1900	38	First novella, *The Touchstone*. Further depressive illness
1901	39	*Crucial Instances*, 2nd collection of stories. Builds and decorates country estate, The Mount near Lenox, Mass., providing solace and refuge for writing. Mother dies
1902	40	*The Valley of Decision* is sent to James

Year	Artistic Events	Historical Events
1886	James, *The Bostonians*	
1887	Bourget, *André Cornelis*	
1888		International Council of Women
1891	Morris, *News from Nowhere* Hardy, *Tess of the D'Urbervilles*	
1892	Deaths of Tennyson and Whitman	
1893	Meynell, *Poems* Heredia, *Les Trophées*	
1894	Berenson, *Italian Painters of the Renaissance* (1894–1907) Sargent elected to Royal Academy	
1895	Hardy, *Jude the Obscure* James, *Guy Domville* Wilde, *An Ideal Husband*	New York Public Library opened
1897	Glasgow, *The Descendant*	
1898	Goncourt dies Charlotte Gilman, *Women and Economics*	Discovery of radium
1899	Kate Chopin, *The Awakening*	Boer War (1899–1902)
1900	Ruskin dies Isadora Duncan's solo recitals in Paris	
1901		Theodore Roosevelt president (till 1909) First transatlantic radio
1902	Gide, *L'Immoraliste* James, *The Wings of the Dove* Gertrude Stein moves to Paris	

Year	Age	Life
1903	41	*Sanctuary* (novella). Meets James in London. Travels in Italy to work on *Italian Villas and Their Gardens* (published 1904), text accompanied by Maxfield Parrish watercolours. Sells Newport home
1904	42	Spring: visits James in Rye. Oct: James visits The Mount, takes motoring trips in surrounding countryside
1905	43	*Italian Backgrounds* (travel book). First bestseller, *The House of Mirth*. James revisits The Mount
1907	45	*Madame de Treymes* (novella), *The Fruit of the Tree*. She and Teddy take flat in Paris; Wharton based in rue de Varennes for next 13 years, returning to The Mount for summers until 1911. James visits the Whartons in Paris, they tour in France. Meets Morton Fullerton, American journalist in Paris
1908	46	*The Hermit and the Wild Woman and Other Stories*. *A Motor-flight through France* (travel book). Friendship with Henry Adams begins. Begins passionate affair with Morton Fullerton
1909	47	*Artemis to Actaeon and Other Verse*. Affair with Fullerton reaches its height
1910	48	*Tales of Men and Ghosts* (short-story collection). Visits Bernard Berenson in Florence. Secretly subsidises Fullerton. Their affair starts to subside into 'companionship'
1911	49	*Ethan Frome*. Separates from Teddy. The Mount sold. Visits England
1912	50	*The Reef*. Motor-tours in England with James
1913	51	*The Custom of the Country*. Tours in Sicily. Divorce. Unsuccessful campaign for Nobel Prize for James. Friendship with Geoffrey Scott begins. Travels with Berenson through Germany and Luxembourg. Travels to US for a brief visit; will return only once more
1914	52	Spring: travels in N. Africa. Moves to England when war breaks out, then returns to Paris. Becomes involved in war work with refugees, orphans, workshops, fundraising
1915	53	*Fighting France: From Dunquerque to Belfort* (unusual travel book describing her many trips to the French Front). Receives Cross of the Légion d'Honneur for war work. Edits *The Book of the Homeless* to raise money for refugees. Begins friendship with André Gide, fellow relief worker
1916	54	*Xingu and Other Stories*

Year	Artistic Events	Historical Events
1903		Wright brothers make first powered aircraft flight
1904	Sturgis, *Belchamber* Freud, *The Psychopathology of Everyday Life*	Rutherford's discovery of radioactivity
1905	James, *The Golden Bowl*	
1907	William James, *Pragmatism* Gosse, *Father and Son* Kipling receives Nobel Prize for literature	
1908	Sinclair, *The Metropolis* Lee, *The Sentimental Traveller*	
1909	Gertrude Stein, *Three Lives* Diaghilev launches Ballets Russes in Paris	Model-T Ford inaugurates motor mass-production
1910		Edward VII dies, accession of George V
1911	*Kismet* produced in London and New York	
1912	Bourget, *Pages de critique et de doctrine*	
1913	Proust, *Du Côté de chez Swann* Sargent portrait of James	
1914		First World War breaks out
1916	James dies	

Year	Age	Life
1917	55	*Summer*. Travels in Morocco.
1918	56	*The Marne*. Buys Pavillon Colombe, north of Paris
1919	57	*French Ways and their Meaning* (cultural essays)
1920	58	*The Age of Innocence* becomes bestseller. *In Morocco* (travel book). Takes medieval monastery of Ste Claire, Hyères, on the coast; moves into Pavillon Colombe near Paris; divides life between the two as summer and winter homes
1921	59	Pulitzer Prize for *The Age of Innocence*
1922	60	*The Glimpses of the Moon*
1923	61	Travels in Spain. Makes last trip to US to receive Yale Doctorate of Letters. *A Son at the Front. Glimpses of the Moon* filmed with screenplay by F. Scott Fitzgerald
1924	62	*Old New York* (comprised of four novellas). Gold medal from National Institute of Arts and Letters (first woman novelist)
1925	63	*The Writing of Fiction. The Mother's Recompense*
1926	64	*Here and Beyond* (short-story collection). *Twelve Poems*. Mediterranean cruise
1927	65	*Twilight Sleep*. Walter Berry dies
1928	66	*The Children*. Teddy Wharton dies. *The Age of Innocence* successfully dramatised on Broadway
1929	67	*Hudson River Bracketed*. Seriously ill with pneumonia. Gold medal from American Academy of Arts and Letters
1930	68	Elected to American Academy of Arts and Letters. *Certain People* (short-story collection)
1932	70	*The Gods Arrive*
1933	71	*Human Nature* (short-story collection)
1934	72	*A Backward Glance* (autobiography)
1935	73	*The Old Maid* (novella) dramatised by Zoë Atkins; wins Pulitzer Prize for drama
1936	74	*Ethan Frome* dramatised. *The World Over* (short-story collection)

Year	Artistic Events	Historical Events
1917	Pulitzer Prizes first awarded Valéry, *La Jeune Parque*	US enters War
1918	Jekyll, *Colour in the Flower Garden*	Nov: armistice
1919	Milhaud, *Le Boeuf sur le toît*	
1922	Eliot, *The Waste Land* Joyce, *Ulysses*	
1923	Rilke, *Sonnets to Orpheus*	
1924	Forster, *A Passage to India*	
1925	Fitzgerald, *The Great Gatsby* Freud, *The Ego and the Id*	
1926	Gide, *Les Faux-Monnayeurs* Rilke dies	General Strike in England
1927	Deaths of Isadora Duncan and Walter Berry	Lindbergh flies the Atlantic
1929	Virginia Woolf, *To the Lighthouse* Museum of Modern Art founded in New York	US stock market crash
1932	Berenson, *Italian Pictures of the Renaissance* Huxley, *Brave New World*	
1933	George Moore dies Wells, *The Shape of Things to Come*	US recognises USSR
1935	Bourget dies	
1936	Margaret Mitchell, *Gone with the Wind* Faulkner, *Absalom, Absalom!*	Death of George V, Edward VIII abdicates, accession of George VI

Year	Age	Life
1937	75	11 August: dies at Pavillon Colombe. Buried at Versailles near the grave of Walter Berry. *Ghosts* (short-story collection) published posthumously
1938		*The Buccaneers* (unfinished) published posthumously

Year	Artistic Events	Historical Events
1939		Second World War begins

INTRODUCTION

In one of the most striking statements in the history of American autobiography, Henry Adams urged his friend Henry James to write his own life story, warning: 'I advise you to take your own life, to prevent biographers from taking it in theirs'.[1] As early as 1923, Edith Wharton, then sixty-one, expressed her concern about the need to compose her story in order 'to avoid having it inaccurately done by some one else after my death, should it turn out that my books survive me long enough to make it worth while to write my biography'. Advising her publisher about 'a plan which has been vaguely floating through my mind for some time', Wharton proposes writing about her 'own early memories, from 1865 to 1885 or 1890, in which I should like to interweave the recollections of my childhood and the beginnings of my literary life'. 'My original idea,' she explains, 'was to jot down these remembrances, and put them away for use after my death; but as they would be concerned only with the picture of my family life as a child and young girl, and with my literary development, I see no particular reason for keeping them back.'[2]

During the years after the Great War, Wharton had been thinking about the New York society of her youth. Looking backward, she composed her first novel set in the 1870s, the Pulitzer Prize-winning *Age of Innocence*. Continuing in this historical vein, she completed the four novellas that were gathered together under the title *Old New York*. In these works – *False Dawn (The 'Forties), The Old Maid (The 'Fifties), The Spark (The 'Sixties)*, and *New Year's Day (The 'Seventies)* – Wharton considered life in New York during the decades prior to her birth and the decades of her youth, an era which concluded with her debut into society in 1878 when she was nearly seventeen. Although she occasionally would claim that she had exhausted the story of old New York in these works of fiction, her memory seems to have been primed by their composition; it is at this point that she began to write her childhood memoir. Indeed, by the time she had begun to discuss the possibility of publishing an autobiography, Wharton may already have begun 'Life and I', a lively manuscript three chapters in length providing a more private confession of her childhood experiences and fears. This manuscript, which describes her early years and tells the story of the author as a young girl, was never completed and was published for the first time only in 1990.

It is not surprising that in the 1920s Wharton would contemplate a more public autobiography or think of herself as someone who might be worthy of a biographical assault. Wharton had been recognised as one of the finest American novelists. She was the first woman to win the Pulitzer Prize (1921) and the first woman to receive an honorary doctorate from Yale (1923). In 1924 she received the Gold Medal for 'distinguished service' from the National Institute of Arts and Letters, to which she was elected in 1926. The American Academy of Arts and Letters awarded her a Gold Medal for 'special distinction in literature' in 1929 and made her a member in 1930. An English review of her first bestseller, *The House of Mirth* (1905), the novel which was seen as her critical breakthrough, had called Wharton 'the Mrs Humphry Ward of the United States'. She eventually became identified as the 'female Henry James', a more flattering yet still frustrating categorisation that indicated the difficulty the critical establishment had in placing women writers. Wharton had become a nationally-known writer when she first began to publish stories in *Scribner's*. The 1899 publication of her first collection of stories, *The Greater Inclination* (which Wharton refers to in *A Backward Glance* as her 'own first born'), brought her international recognition. Eventually in her career she published over thirty-five books, including twenty-two novels and novellas, eleven collections of short fiction (comprised of many of her eighty-six stories), poetry, criticism and a variety of non-fiction works, including books about interior design and gardens, unusual travel books about France and French culture during the First World War —and her 1934 autobiography, *A Backward Glance*.[3]

Towards the end of 'Life and I', Wharton describes how she put aside her life as a debutante and eagerly returned to Europe with her parents: 'Without a pang I gave up the prospect of a "gay" winter, & turned my back on the various pretendants who had occupied my leisure without stirring my heart. I was going to see pictures & beautiful things again, & odd contradictory creature that I was, I went without a backward glance!'[4] Ten years after Wharton had put aside 'Life and I', she began the retrospective enterprise of *A Backward Glance* – a perspective which in many ways characterises much of the fiction she wrote after taking up permanent residence in France in 1913. Wharton's title, as the first of the four epigraphs suggests, is taken from the title of Whitman's memoir 'A Backward Glance O'er Travell'd Roads', the concluding essay composed by the poet for his 'death bed edition' when he had reached his 'three-score-and-ten-years'. Beginning her own *Backward Glance* at the age of seventy, Wharton had many reasons to identify with Whitman, whom she had memorialised in her novella about the 1860s, *The Spark* (written around the time that she was composing 'Life and I'). Both Whitman and Wharton ventured beyond the realm of literature to help people suffering from the violence of war. These wars, the Civil War for Whitman and the Great War for Wharton, marked turning points for these authors, a dramatic change in the lives recorded in their 'Backward Glances'.

Wharton's chapter about the war only briefly touches upon her extensive work with refugees in wartime Paris – for which she was made a Chevalier of the Legion of Honour – and her six trips to the French front which provided the background for *Fighting France*. Her autobiography returns repeatedly to the war not to call attention to her own exhausting labours but rather to acknowledge the cataclysmic event that severed the past from the present. Indeed, she relates the war and its repercussions to her decision to write her memoirs: 'If anyone had suggested to me, before 1914, to write my reminiscences, I should have answered that my life had been too uneventful to be worth recording.' She claims that 'not until the successive upheavals which culminated in the catastrophe of 1914 had "cut all likeness from the name" of my old New York, did I begin to see its pathetic picturesqueness'. In her fiction Wharton described the rituals of what she called 'old New York' in increasingly anthropological terms, and she came to see her autobiographical enterprise in terms of an archaeological expedition.

> The compact world of my youth has receded into a past from which it can only be dug up in bits by the assiduous relic-hunter; and its smallest fragments begin to be worth collecting and putting together before the last of those who knew the live structure are swept away with it.

Following the conventions of autobiography, Wharton devotes a portion of the opening chapter to a description of her ancestry, yet as she recovers these shards of knowledge Wharton reminds the reader of the stories that she herself cannot know – particularly the silent generations of women who are represented by 'a few shreds of anecdote, no more than the faded flowers between the leaves of a great-grandmother's *Bible*'. Here she speaks as a member of a vanished world, a world whose memory will soon join the ruins of Troy. Disclaiming any belief in the immortality of her own literary accomplishments and adopting a conventional tone of modesty, Wharton tells the story of old New York and the old world of Europe before both were destroyed and supplanted by what she would call a 'roaring and discontinuous universe'.[5] *A Backward Glance,* like *The Age of Innocence* and the unfinished *Buccaneers*, contains some of the most confident and lucid prose that Wharton composed during the period of great change from the end of the First World War to her death in 1937. Her novels from the 1920s seemed to suffer from her distance from contemporary American culture; she had returned home only once since her brief visit during the year of her divorce in 1913. However, the works which she set in the past or which, like her autobiography, required her to evoke the past, have the clarity of prose and purpose which is characteristic of her most powerful writing.

In 'Life and I', Wharton tells a more intimate story of her life. Like the unfinished novels 'Disintegration' (which she laid aside to write *The House of Mirth*) and 'Literature' (which was begun in 1913 and interrupted by the advent of the Great War in Europe), 'Life and I' reveals an isolated child who found solace in books and the sounds of words. Wharton describes 'making up', the narrative ritual of her childhood in which she would hold a book, often upside down, and tell stories in a loud and rapid voice while turning the pages as if she were reading. This crucial story about her childhood obsession with narration appears in 'Life and I' and in her unfinished fiction, 'Literature', before finding its place in the carefully-crafted *Backward Glance*. In 'Life and I' Wharton describes 'the sensuous rapture produced by the sight & sound' of words, which call her to mysterious and seductive regions.

[Words] were visible, almost tangible presences, with faces as distinct as those of the persons among whom I lived. And, like the Erlkönig's daughters, they sang to me so bewitchingly that they almost lured me from the wholesome noonday air of childhood into some strange supernatural region, where the normal pleasures of my age seemed as insipid as the fruits of the earth to Persephone after she had eaten of the pomegranate seed.[6]

Wharton also presents a severe portrait of her mother, Lucretia Jones, whom she describes in A Backward Glance as possessing 'all the dim impersonal attributes of a mother'. In one of the most revealing parts of 'Life and I', Wharton claims that she did not know where babies came from until several weeks after her marriage at the age of twenty-four, believing 'that married people "had children" because God saw the clergyman marrying them through the roof of the church'. She describes how she 'summoned up courage to appeal to my mother, & begged her, with a heart beating to suffocation, to tell me "what being married was like"'. Her handsome face at once took on the icy look of disapproval which I most dreaded. "I never heard such a ridiculous question!" she said impatiently; & I felt at once how vulgar she thought me'. When Wharton persists, her mother says, ' "You've seen enough pictures & statues in your life. Haven't you noticed that men are – made differently from women? . . . Then for heaven's sake don't ask me anymore silly questions. You can't be as stupid as you pretend!" '[7]

In A Backward Glance, Wharton constructs a more public persona. Like Henry Adams, who failed to mention in his autobiography that his wife took her own life, Wharton leaves out some of the most intimate and difficult passages of her life. Wharton mentions her marriage to Edward Wharton, a sportsman whose interests she did not share, but she does not tell the story of their divorce. Although she refers to her 'husband' and occasionally speaks from the perspective of the marital 'we', Teddy Wharton remains a vague figure. Described as 'a Bostonian by birth' and 'by blood a Virginian', the travelling companion of her youth with his 'boyish enjoyment of life' gives way to the disturbed figure who suffers from what she calls 'the creeping darkness of neurasthenia' (a detail which seems to have been included as a partial justification for the unmentioned divorce). Elsewhere, in a defensive gesture, Wharton inaccurately blames Teddy for the decision to sell her American home, the place she describes in A Backward Glance as her 'first real home'[8]. If this

accusation is not really fair – Wharton had agreed to sell the home
– it is revealing in its unspoken association of her failed marriage
and the severing of a more powerful and perhaps even more
ambivalent tie: her final separation from America. Wharton,
whom Henry James had called 'the great and glorious pendulum'
because of her yearly crossings of the Atlantic, describes a gentle
drifting apart in the chapter 'Widening Waters', but her reference
to the sale of The Mount, blaming Teddy's illness and his inability
to take care of the place, suggests that Wharton on some level had
to experience her departure from her native land as an
involuntary and even violent rupture. Although one must read her
fiction (especially *Ethan Frome*) to understand Wharton's fears
about what her life would have been like without the divorce, *A
Backward Glance* does tell a crucial part of the story, the story of
a woman who seized her life and was saved from what she saw as
a living death by the creation of art and the recognition she
received as an artist.

Wharton's *Backward Glance*, like Whitman's, is meant to tell
the story of a writer and her books. The beautiful descriptions of
the memoir gain their sharp perspective from their self-portrait of
the artist as a young girl. The history of Wharton's early efforts to
satisfy her literary yearnings in a society which was not known for
producing artists among its men, much less its women, gives the
account its poignancy. Whereas each of the three chapters that
comprise 'Life and I' closes with a reference to sexuality, the
opening chapters of *A Backward Glance* conclude with what was
for Wharton a related passion: her desire to become an artist, a
writer of scenes and a teller of tales. The title of her first book of
fiction, *The Greater Inclination*, suggests the place of fiction in her
life. In some ways Wharton's autobiography resembles
Wordsworth's *Prelude*, which claimed to represent 'The Growth
of a Poet's Mind'. Wordsworth also describes 'A backward glance
. . . by distance ruralised' before the poet took 'The road that
pointed toward the chosen Vale'. Yet the examples of both
Whitman and Wordsworth suggest that the song of the self is
more likely to be told in poetry. Wharton's *Backward Glance*, like
Whitman's, is not meant to be a revelatory document. This story
of her life, the story of a woman who lived for twenty-six years in
a marriage which may have remained unconsummated and who
discovered erotic love at the age of forty-six in a relationship with

a younger and more experienced lover (Morton Fullerton, the Paris correspondent of the London *Times*), does not appear in her autobiography. The most intimate story that Wharton ever tells (including the passages from her 'Love Diary' and the love letters to Morton Fullerton which she more than once begged him to return so that she could burn them) is found in her poetry and her fiction.

In its passionate and often violent first-person monologues, Wharton's volume of poems, *Artemis to Actaeon*, is perhaps her most intensely autobiographical work. (This is technically her second volume of poems; her first was the anonymous *Verses* that her mother had printed privately when Wharton was only sixteen.) However, these historical and mythological poems are told from the point of view of seemingly distant figures such as Artemis; Vesalius, the surgeon who was accused of cutting open a woman's body while she was still living; and the most lustful Saint, Margaret of Cortona. The often erotic and violent images of these poems describe a love of knowledge and a response to beauty which like the knife of Vesalius or the hounds of Artemis threaten to pierce and rend the beloved, either the object of mystery or the mortal who has dared to lift the veil of the goddess. Written in 1902, describing the almost disintegrating force of aesthetic, scientific and even spiritual knowledge, these poems seem prophetic in the wake of Wharton's later passionate awakening. In depicting the experience of the forbidden fruit of knowledge through the intensity of these historical characters, Wharton anticipated the experience of erotic passion. 'Life', written to Morton Fullerton around the time of the publication of the volume in 1909, is a wildly erotic poem about art written from the point of view of a reed who is given voice. It is a paeon to penetration and with each piercing of its 'flank', the reed discovers a whole range of heretofore hidden notes: experience and pain wound but they are also the basis for a deeper knowledge and a more profound art. This poem contains the phrase 'Life and I', which she later adopted for her private autobiography.[9]

Wharton's autobiographies, even the more revealing 'Life and I', seem mild when read next to this poetry about eroticism and violation and other works such as the ghost stories in which Wharton depicted strangled, abandoned and imprisoned women, and the novel *Ethan Frome*, in which Wharton describes a similarly terrifying narrative of entrapment. Like the poems,

Ethan Frome is one of Edith Wharton's rare compositions told in the first person and the tale seems to exorcise her worst fears in a 'vision' of the life she might have had if she had not escaped from her marriage and the life that accompanied it. Casting herself as the crippled Ethan, Wharton presents the weak men in her life (both her mentally disturbed husband and her vacillating lover) as the demanding women who trap the potentially noble Ethan in a life of caretaking.[10] Here and elsewhere in her fiction repeated motifs, preoccupations and characters provide insights into deep psychic structures. Writing about her ghost stories, Wharton insists that the best stories are those which frighten the teller of the tale. Wharton's work is most autobiographical not so much in its use of facts, details, characters or plots from her own life story but rather in the ways that she puts it to work through her own fears and obsessions. One must read between the lines of Wharton's autobiographies (both public and private) to detect such deep and painful stories.

Wharton's fiction is also autobiographical in its life-long concern with the story of the artist. In unfinished fictions like 'Disintegration' and 'Literature', Wharton tells the story of her own childhood loneliness and her intense engagement with words. 'Disintegration' would be rewritten in the 1920s as *The Mother's Recompense*, a novel which centres on the experience of a mother rather than a motherless child; 'Literature' would be replaced by a two-volume work, *The Gods Arrive* and *Hudson River Bracketed*, an account focussing on the adult life of another writer, Vance Weston. As Janet Goodwyn suggests, the transformation of these works from unfinished stories about childhood to novels about adults suggests the importance of the writing of 'Life and I' to the mature and accomplished woman who presents herself in *A Backward Glance*.[11] 'Literature', Wharton's first attempt to describe the childhood of a writer, was never completed, and Wharton always claimed that the Great War had changed the world so much that she had lost her sense of what a contemporary writer like Dickie Thaxter would write. Yet had it been completed its intimate use of scenes from her own early life might have precluded the writing of either 'Life and I' or *A Backward Glance*. (It is also possible that Wharton did not complete a highly autobiographical work such as 'Literature' because she had become aware that she herself was an historical personage who would be called on to tell the story of her life.) In her most erotic work *Summer*, the sequel to the chilling tale *Ethan*

Frome, Wharton presents the character of a young girl who is approaching sexual maturity and in the novel she was working on at the time of her death, *The Buccaneers*, she presents a heroine at a similar juncture. Charity Royall and Nan St George are the youngest of her central characters. Indeed, only rarely does Wharton try to enter into the minds of children. Through her writing, she managed to overcome her native shyness and to speak in the voice of a mature and confident woman. Any return to the vulnerable voice of childhood, particularly in a narrative which (whether it was called autobiography or fiction) was based on her own early years, was perhaps too painful to be countenanced.

Even where she is not representing or transfiguring a portrait of herself as a young artist, Wharton is preoccupied with the activity of the writer, especially the woman writer. In works as varied as *The House of Mirth, Ethan Frome* and *Summer*, Wharton is concerned with the relation of female figures to art and in particular to problems of writing. In her ghost stories, more than one woman leaves an account of her life and only long after her death finds at last a sympathetic reader for both her story and her life. While Wharton wrote of successful women writers in such works as her first novella, *The Touchstone,* and in an early story, 'Copy', the writers who are central figures in her autobiographical works such as 'Literature', and the Vance Weston novels – *Hudson River Bracketed* and *The Gods Arrive* – are men. Taken together, these works suggest Wharton's strong ambivalence about the woman writer and the lonely and loveless life that she imagines for this figure in the early works. In *The House of Mirth*, Lily Bart spends the last night of her life writing, but she dies because (whether accidentally or not) she takes her life rather than taking control of the plot and creating a story which will allow her to live. In *The Custom of the Country*, the would-be poet Ralph Marvell is destroyed by his alliance with a destructive female muse. For Wharton, who felt that she lacked a 'real personality . . . and was not to acquire one till my first volume of short stories was published', these characters are dead before they commit suicide: they are dead when they put their heads in their hands and cease to write. Yet in Wharton's fictions the woman writer is often already dead or claims to have 'died years ago'. Obsessed with the figure of Persephone from almost her first to her last works, Wharton repeatedly imagined the woman writer writing letters from the underworld where she had tasted pomegranate seed.[12]

In 1932 as she sat down to write the official account of her life, Wharton had to cast her gaze back to the America of her youth and the life that she had acquired – 'taken' – for herself through her reading, and ultimately through the practice of her art.

If *A Backward Glance* displays the reticence which was characteristic of Wharton's personality, it offers brilliant evocations of the places of her past. Even if *A Backward Glance* were not the autobiography of a gifted novelist, it would still be a fascinating document of the experience of Americans abroad in the nineteenth century as they travel by train and coach to the exotic land of Spain, and as the account of a young girl from the New York elite in the capitals of Europe. However, this work is so compelling precisely because Wharton is a powerful novelist. Her descriptions of her life in Europe – for instance when she walks along the Palatine collecting the shining shards of the past in the form of lapis lazuli and other stones to decorate souvenir tables at home – evoke remarkable scenes of a past era. Among the novelistic descriptions of old New York, there are wonderfully redolent accounts of menus and feasts with Roman punches which were prepared by the black cooks whom Wharton refers to by name and characterises as 'artists'. Describing the customs of the New York elite as they travel in Europe or summer in Newport, Wharton offers a sympathetic view of the exclusive society which spawned her. *A Backward Glance* in many ways serves as an ancillary guide to the novels for which Wharton is best known, her insider critiques and analyses of the fashionable elite, most notably *The House of Mirth*, *The Custom of the Country* and *The Age of Innocence*.

A Backward Glance devotes four chapters to the story of Wharton's ancestors, the personalities of her parents, the family's years in Europe, and her early reading and writing. The death of her father at the close of her final chapter about childhood, 'Unreluctant Feet', and the advent of her marriage at the beginning of the next chapter, 'Friendships and Travels', mark the moment of transformation which suggests the beginning of her adult life. Except for a single chapter which bears the name of 'Henry James' and another called 'The War', Wharton presents the story of her life through a series of chapters taking their titles from places. These places – 'New York and The Mount', 'London, "Qu'acre" and "Lamb"', 'Paris', and the more descriptively named 'Widening Waters' – all might be said to describe the process of 'widening waters'. Increasingly, as Wharton takes her place as a respected literary figure, she gravitates from her exile in her native land to 'the land of letters', which she associates with the most private of places given a chapter in the autobiography, her 'Secret Garden', as well as with her intimate circles of literary friends in England and France.

From the gatherings at her own home in New England, to the fine conversations at 'Qu'acre', the home of the delightful eccentric Howard Sturgis, and visits to James's 'Lamb House' and finally her entry through the Bourgets into the Parisian salon of Rosa Fitz-James, Wharton describes in anecdotes and carefully-drawn portraits some of the most interesting literary figures and most notorious hostesses of her time. *A Backward Glance* tells, among other things, the story of a shy woman who after trying to attract Henry James's attention with a new hat and dress finally met him through her writing. The descriptions of people include portraits of her friends, including Henry James, who is pictured in a New England heat wave as he sits next to a pile of sucked oranges, suffering from his swaddling girth and seeking comfort from an electric fan. In her depictions of his humour, his critical wit, as well as the less easily described textures of his speech and his gifts as a narrator and teller of family tales, Wharton has penned a complex portrait of James, what R. W. B Lewis has called 'the most attractive and persuasive sketch of Henry James ever recorded'.[13]

A Backward Glance is, of course, most compelling as a self-portrait of Edith Wharton. Although there is only one chapter devoted to telling the story of her writing, the volume as a whole describes not only the circumstances in which Wharton composed works like *Ethan Frome* and its seasonal sequel *Summer* (which she calls 'the hot Ethan') but more importantly many of the crucial events that marked her emergence as a writer. In a letter to her friend Sara Norton, who was then devoting her life to her aged and ill father, Wharton said she felt like shouting from the housetop to everyone in similar situations: 'Take your own life, every one of you!'[14] The leap that Wharton advises here is neither Henry Adams's admonition to write one's autobiography nor a call to suicide. It is rather a call to seize one's own life. In this sense it is related to the decision to write one's autobiography since it represents a decision to take control of one's life story. *A Backward Glance* is in a sense both book and monument; it tells the story of a woman who repeatedly seized her life by and through writing, stopping only to look back.

CANDACE WAID

Note on the Text

A Backward Glance was first published in New York by Charles Scribner's Sons in 1934. The first British edition was published in 1972 by Constable and Co. The subtitle 'An Autobiography' has been added by Everyman as a clarification for the modern reader.

Notes to the Introduction

1 Henry Adams, *The Education of Henry Adams*, ed. Ernest Samuels, appendix A, letter from Adams to James, 6 May 1908 (Boston: Houghton Mifflin Co. 1974), pp. 512–13.
2 Letter to Rutger B. Jewett, 21 February 1923, *The Letters of Edith Wharton*, ed. R. W. B. Lewis and Nancy Lewis (New York: Charles Scribner's Sons, 1988), pp. 462–3.
3 An edited, serialised version of *A Backward Glance* appeared in *The Ladies' Home Journal* between October 1933 and April 1934.
4 'Life and I', in *Novellas and Other Writings*, with notes by Cynthia Griffin Wolff (New York: The Library of America, 1990), p. 1094.
5 Preface to *Ghosts* (New York: Appleton-Century, 1937), p. x.
6 'Life and I', pp. 1075–6.
7 'Life and I', pp. 1087–8.
8 See R. W. B. Lewis, *Edith Wharton: A Biography* (New York: Harper and Row, 1975), especially pp. 305–13, for an extensive discussion of the complex reasons for the sale of The Mount and other aspects of the divorce.
9 *Artemis to Actaeon and Other Verse* (New York: Scribner's, 1909), p. 7.
10 For related discussions, see Lewis, pp. 309–10.
11 Janet Goodwyn, *Edith Wharton: Traveller in the Land of Letters* (London: Macmillan, 1990).
12 See Candace Waid, *Edith Wharton's Letters from the Underworld: Fictions of Women and Writing* (Chapel-Hill: University of North Carolina Press, 1991).
13 Lewis, p. 522.
14 17 October 1908, *Letters*, p. 163.

A FIRST WORD

Years ago I said to myself: 'There's no such thing as old age; there is only sorrow.'

I have learned with the passing of time that this, though true, is not the whole truth. The other producer of old age is habit: the deathly process of doing the same thing in the same way at the same hour day after day, first from carelessness, then from inclination, at last from cowardice or inertia. Luckily the inconsequent life is not the only alternative; for caprice is as ruinous as routine. Habit is necessary; it is the habit of having habits, of turning a trail into a rut, that must be incessantly fought against if one is to remain alive.

In spite of illness, in spite even of the arch-enemy sorrow, one *can* remain alive long past the usual date of disintegration if one is unafraid of change, insatiable in intellectual curiosity, interested in big things, and happy in small ways. In the course of sorting and setting down of my memories I have learned that these advantages are usually independent of one's merits, and that I probably owe my happy old age to the ancestor who accidentally endowed me with these qualities.

Another advantage (equally accidental) is that I do not remember long to be angry. I seldom forget a bruise to the soul – who does? But life puts a quick balm on it, and it is recorded in a book I seldom open. Not long ago I read a number of reviews of a recently published autobiography. All the reviewers united in praising it on the score that here at last was an autobiographer who was not afraid to tell the truth! And what gave the book this air of truthfulness? Simply the fact that the memorialist 'spared no one', set down in detail every defect and absurdity in others, and every resentment in the writer. That was the kind of autobiography worth reading!

Judged by that standard mine, I fear, will find few readers. I have not escaped contact with the uncongenial; but the antipathy they aroused was usually reciprocal, and this simplified and

restricted our intercourse. Nor do I remember that these unappre-
ciative persons ever marked their lack of interest in me by
anything more harmful than indifference. I recall no sensational
grievances. Everywhere on my path I have met with kindness and
furtherance; and from the few dearest to me an exquisite
understanding. It will be seen, then, in telling my story I have had
to make the best of unsensational material; and if what I have to
tell interests my readers, that merit at least will be my own.

Madame Swetchine, that eminent Christian, was once asked
how she managed to feel Christianly toward her enemies. She
looked surprised. '*Un ennemi? Mais de tous les accidents c'est le
plus rare!*'

So I have found it.

Several chapters of this book have already appeared in the
'Atlantic Monthly' and 'The Ladies' Home Journal.' I have also to
thank Sir John Murray for kindly permitting me to incorporate in
the book two or three passages from an essay on Henry James,
published in 'The Quarterly Review' of July 1920 and the Editor
of 'The Colophon' for the use of a few paragraphs on the writing
of 'Ethan Frome.'

E.W.

A Backward Glance

'A backward glance o'er travelled roads.'
Walt Whitman

Chapter One
The Background

Gute Gesellschaft hab ich gesehen; man nennt sie die gute
Wenn sie zum kleinsten Gedicht nicht die Gelegenheit giebt.
GOETHE: *Venezianische Epigrammen*

I

It was on a bright day of midwinter, in New York. The little girl
who eventually became me, but as yet was neither me or anybody
else in particular, but merely a soft anonymous morsel of
humanity – this little girl, who bore my name, was going for a
walk with her father. The episode is literally the first thing I can
remember about her, and therefore I date the birth of her identity
from that day.

She had been put into her warmest coat, and into a new and
very pretty bonnet, which she had surveyed in the glass with
considerable satisfaction. The bonnet (I can see it today) was of
white satin, patterned with a pink and green plaid in raised velvet.
It was all drawn into close gathers, with a *bavolet* in the neck to
keep out the cold, and thick ruffles of silky *blonde* lace under the
brim in front. As the air was very cold a gossamer veil of the finest
white Shetland wool was drawn about the bonnet and hung down
over the wearer's round red cheeks like the white paper filigree
over a Valentine; and her hands were encased in white woollen
mittens.

One of them lay in the large safe hollow of her father's bare
hand; her tall handsome father, who was so warm-blooded that in
the coldest weather he always went out without gloves, and
whose head, with its ruddy complexion and intensely blue eyes,
was so far aloft that when she walked beside him she was too near
to see his face. It was always an event in the little girl's life to take a
walk with her father, and more particularly so today, because she
had on her new winter bonnet, which was so beautiful (and so
becoming) that for the first time she woke to the importance of
dress, and of herself as a subject for adornment – so that I may
date from that hour the birth of the conscious and feminine *me* in
the little girl's vague soul.

The little girl and her father walked up Fifth Avenue: the old

Fifth Avenue with its double line of low brown-stone houses, of a desperate uniformity of style, broken only – and surprisingly – by two equally unexpected features: the fenced-in plot of ground where the old Miss Kennedys' cows were pastured, and the truncated Egyptian pyramid which so strangely served as a reservoir of New York's water supply. The Fifth Avenue of that day was a placid and uneventful thoroughfare, along which genteel landaus, broughams and victorias, and more countrified vehicles of the 'carry-all' and 'surrey' type, moved up and down at decent intervals and a decorous pace. On Sundays after church the fashionable of various denominations paraded there on foot, in gathered satin bonnets and tall hats; but at other times it presented long stretches of empty pavement, so that the little girl, advancing at her father's side was able to see at a considerable distance the approach of another pair of legs, not as long but considerably stockier than her father's. The little girl was so very little that she never got much higher than the knees in her survey of grown-up people, and would not have known, if her father had not told her, that the approaching legs belonged to his cousin Henry. The news was very interesting, because in attendance on Cousin Henry was a small person, no bigger than herself, who must obviously be Cousin Henry's little boy Daniel, and therefore somehow belong to the little girl. So when the tall legs and the stocky ones halted for a talk, which took place somewhere high up in the air, and the small Daniel and Edith found themselves face to face close to the pavement, the little girl peered with interest at the little boy through the white woollen mist over her face. The little boy, who was very round and rosy, looked back with equal interest; and suddenly he put out a chubby hand, lifted the little girl's veil, and boldly planted a kiss on her cheek. It was the first time – and the little girl found it very pleasant.

This is my earliest definite memory of anything happening to me; and it will be seen that I was wakened to conscious life by the two tremendous forces of love and vanity.

It may have been just after this memorable day – at any rate it was nearly at the same time – that a snowy-headed old gentleman with a red face and a spun-sugar moustache and imperial gave me a white Spitz puppy which looked as if its coat had been woven out of the donor's luxuriant locks. The old gentleman, in whose veins ran the purest blood of Dutch Colonial New York, was called Mr Lydig Suydam, and I should like his name to survive till this page has crumbled, for with his gift a new life began for me. The owning of my first dog made me into a conscious sentient person, fiercely possessive, anxiously watchful, and woke in me that long ache of pity for animals, and for all inarticulate beings, which nothing has ever stilled. How I loved that first 'Foxy' of mine, how I cherished and yearned over and understood him! And how quickly he relegated all dolls and other inanimate toys to the region of my everlasting indifference!

I never cared much in my little-childhood for fairy tales, or any appeals to my fancy through the fabulous or legendary. My imagination lay there, coiled and sleeping, a mute hibernating creature, and at the least touch of common things – flowers, animals, words, especially the sound of words, apart from their meaning – it already stirred in its sleep, and then sank back into its own rich dream, which needed so little feeding from the outside that it instinctively rejected whatever another imagination had already adorned and completed. There was, however, one fairy tale at which I always thrilled – the story of the boy who could talk with the birds and hear what the grasses said. Very early, earlier than my conscious memory can reach, I must have felt myself to be of kin to that happy child. I cannot remember when the grasses first spoke to me, though I think it was when, a few years later, one of my uncles took me, with some little cousins, to spend a long spring day in some marshy woods near Mamaroneck, where the earth was starred with pink trailing arbutus, where pouch-like white and rosy flowers grew in a swamp, and leafless branches against the sky were netted with buds of mother-of-pearl; but on the day when Foxy was given to me I learned what the animals say to each other, and to us . . .

2

The readers (and I should doubtless have been among them) who twenty years ago would have smiled at the idea that time could transform a group of *bourgeois* colonials and their republican descendants into a sort of social aristocracy, are now better able to measure the formative value of nearly three hundred years of social observance: the concerted living up to long-established standards of honour and conduct, of education and manners. The value of duration is slowly asserting itself against the welter of change, and sociologists without a drop of American blood in them have been the first to recognize what the traditions of three centuries have contributed to the moral wealth of our country. Even negatively, these traditions have acquired, with the passing of time, an unsuspected value. When I was young it used to seem to me that the group in which I grew up was like an empty vessel into which no new wine would ever again be poured. Now I see that one of its uses lay in preserving a few drops of an old vintage too rare to be savoured by a youthful palate; and I should like to atone for my unappreciativeness by trying to revive that faint fragrance.

If any one had suggested to me, before 1914, to write my reminiscences, I should have answered that my life had been too uneventful to be worth recording. Indeed, I had never even thought of recording it for my own amusement, and the fact that until 1918 I never kept even the briefest of diaries has greatly hampered this tardy reconstruction. Not until the successive upheavals which culminated in the catastrophe of 1914 had 'cut all likeness from the name' of my old New York, did I begin to see its pathetic picturesqueness. The first change came in the 'eighties, with the earliest detachment of big money-makers from the West, soon to be followed by the lords of Pittsburgh. But their infiltration did not greatly affect old manners and customs, since the dearest ambition of the newcomers was to assimilate existing traditions. Social life, with us as in the rest of the world, went on with hardly perceptible changes till the war abruptly tore down the old frame-work, and what had seemed unalterable rules of conduct became of a sudden observances as quaintly arbitrary as the domestic rites of the Pharaohs. Between the point of view of my Huguenot great-great-grandfather, who came from the French Palatinate to participate in the founding of New Rochelle, and my own father, who died in 1882, there were fewer differences than between my father and the post-war generation of Americans. That I was born into a world in which telephones, motors, electric light, central heating (except by hot-air furnaces), X-rays, cinemas, radium, aeroplanes and wireless telegraphy were not only unknown but still mostly unforeseen, may seem the most striking difference between then and now; but the really vital change is that, in my youth, the Americans of the original States, who in moments of crisis still shaped the national point of view, were the heirs of an old tradition of European culture which the country has now totally rejected. This rejection (which Mr Walter Lippmann regards as the chief cause of the country's present moral impoverishment) has opened a gulf between those days and these. The compact world of my youth has receded into a past from which it can only be dug up in bits by the assiduous relic-hunter; and its smallest fragments begin to be worth collecting and putting together before the last of those who knew the live structure are swept away with it.

3

My little-girl life, safe, guarded, monotonous, was cradled in the only world about which, according to Goethe, it is impossible to write poetry. The small society into which I was born was 'good' in the most prosaic sense of the term, and its only interest, for the generality of readers, lies in the fact of its sudden and total extinction, and for the imaginative few in the recognition of the moral treasures that went with it. Let me try to call it back . . .

Once, when I was about fifteen, my parents took me to Annapolis for the graduating ceremonies of the Naval Academy. In my infancy I had travelled extensively on the farther side of the globe, and it was thought high time that I should begin to see something of my own half.

I recall with delight the charming old Academic buildings grouped about turf and trees, and the smartness of the cadets (among whom were some of my young friends) in their dress uniforms; and thrilling memories of speeches, marchings, military music and strawberry ice, flutter pleasingly about the scene. On the way back we stopped in Baltimore and Washington; but neither city offered much to youthful eyes formed by the spectacle of Rome and Paris. Washington, in the days before Charles McKim had seen its possibilities, and resolved to develop them on Major L'Enfant's lines, was in truth a doleful desert; and it was a weary and bored little girl who trailed after her parents through the echoing emptiness of the Capitol, and at last into the famous Rotunda with its paintings of Revolutionary victories. Trumbull was little thought of as a painter in those days (Munkacsky would doubtless have been preferred to him), and when one great panel after another was pointed out to me, and I was led up first to the 'Surrender of Burgoyne' and then to the 'Surrender of

Cornwallis', and told: 'There's your great-grandfather,' the tall thin young man in the sober uniform of a general of artillery, leaning against a cannon in the foreground of one picture, in the other galloping across the battlefield, impressed me much less than the beautiful youths to whom I had just said goodbye at Annapolis. If anything, I was vaguely sorry to have any one belonging to me represented in those stiff old-fashioned pictures, so visibly inferior to the battle-scenes of Horace Vernet and Detaille. I remember feeling no curiosity about my great-grandfather, and my parents said nothing to rouse my interest in him. The New Yorker of that day was singularly, inexplicably indifferent to his descent, and my father and mother were no exception to the rule.

It was many years later that I began to suspect that Trumbull was very nearly a great painter, and my great-grandfather Stevens very nearly a great man; but by that time all who had known him, and could have spoken of him familiarly, had long been dead, and he was no more than a museum-piece to me. It is a pity, for he must have been worth knowing, even at second hand.

On both sides our colonial ancestry goes back for nearly three hundred years, and on both sides the colonists in question seem to have been identified since early days with New York, though my earliest Stevens forbears went first to Massachusetts. Some of the first Stevens's grandsons, however, probably not being of the stripe of religious fanatic or political reformer to breathe easily in that passionate province, transferred their activities to the easier-going New York, where people seem from the outset to have been more interested in making money and acquiring property than in Predestination and witch-burning. I have always wondered if those old New Yorkers did not owe their greater suavity and tolerance to the fact that the Church of England (so little changed under its later name of Episcopal Church of America) provided from the first their prevalent form of worship. May not the matchless beauty of an ancient rite have protected our ancestors from what Huxley called the 'fissiparous tendency of the Protestant sects', sparing them sanguinary wrangles over un-comprehended points of doctrine, and all those extravagances of self-constituted prophets and evangelists which rent and harrowed New England? Milder manners, a greater love of ease, and a franker interest in money-making and good food, certainly distinguished the colonial New Yorkers from the conscience-searching children of the 'Mayflower'. Apart from some of the old Dutch colonial families, who continued to follow the 'Dutch Reformed' rite, the New York of my youth was distinctively Episcopalian; and to this happy chance I owe my early saturation with the noble cadences of the Book of Common Prayer, and my reference for an ordered ritual in which the officiant's personality is strictly subordinated to the rite he performs.

Colonial New York was mostly composed of merchants and bankers; my own ancestors were mainly merchant ship-owners, and my great-grandmother Stevens's wedding-dress, a gauzy Directoire web of embroidered 'India mull', was made for her in India and brought to New York on one of her father's merchant-men. My mother, who had a hearty contempt for the tardy discovery of aristocratic genealogies, always said that old New York was composed of Dutch and British middle-class families, and that only four or five could show a pedigree leading back to the aristocracy of their ancestral country. These, if I remember rightly, were the Duers, the Livingstons, the Rutherfurds, the de Grasses and the Van Rensselaers (descendants, these latter, of the original Dutch 'Patroon'). I name here only families settled in colonial New York; others, from the southern states, but well known in New York – such as the Fairfaxes, Carys, Calverts and Whartons – should be added if the list included the other colonies.

My own ancestry, as far as I know, was purely middle-class; though my family belonged to the same group as this little aristocratic nucleus I do not think there was any blood-relationship with it. The Schermerhorns, Joneses, Pendletons, on my father's side, the Stevenses, Ledyards, Rhinelanders on my mother's, the Galantins on both, seem all to have belonged to the same prosperous class of merchants, bankers and lawyers. It was a society from which all dealers in retail business were excluded as a matter of course. The man who 'kept a shop' was more rigorously shut out of polite society in the original Thirteen States than in post-revolutionary France – witness the surprise (and amusement) of the Paris solicitor, Moreau de St Méry, who, fleeing from the Terror, earned his living by keeping a bookshop in Philadelphia, and for this reason, though his shop was the meeting-place of the most blue-blooded of his fellow émigrés, and Talleyrand and the Marquis de la Tour du Pin were among his intimates, yet could not be invited to the ball given for Washington's inauguration. So little did the Revolution revolutionize a society at once middle-class and provincial that no retail dealer, no matter how palatial his shop-front or how tempting his millions, was received in New York society until long after I was grown up.

My great-grandfather, the Major-General Ebenezer Stevens of the Rotunda, seems to have been the only marked figure among my forbears. He was born in Boston in 1751 and, having a pronounced tendency to mechanical pursuits was naturally drafted into the artillery at the Revolution. He served in Lieutenant Adino Paddock's artillery company, and took part in the 'Boston tea-party', where, as he told one of his sons, 'none of the party was painted as Indians, nor, that I know of, disguised; though,' (he adds a trifle casuistically) 'some of them stopped at a paint-shop on the way and daubed their faces with paint.' Thereafter he is heard of as a house-builder and contractor in Rhode Island; but at the news of the battle of Lexington he abandoned his business and began the raising and organizing of artillery companies. He was a first lieutenant in the Rhode Island artillery, then in that of Massachusetts, and in 1776 was transferred as captain to the regiment besieging Quebec. At Ticonderoga, Stillwater and Saratoga he commanded a division of artillery, and it was he who directed the operations leading to General Burgoyne's surrender. For these feats he was specially commended by Generals Knox, Gates and Schuyler, and in 1778 he was in command of the entire artillery service of the northern department. Under Lafayette he took part in the expedition which ended in the defeat of Lord Cornwallis; his skilful manoeuvres are said to have broken the English blockade at Annapolis, and when the English evacuated New York he was among the first to enter the city.

The war over, he declined further military advancement and returned to civil life. His services, however, were still frequently required, and in 1812 he was put in command of the New York Brigade of artillery. One of the forts built at this time for the defence of New York harbour was called Fort Stevens, in his honour, and after the laying of the foundation stone he 'gave the party a dinner at his country seat, "Mount Buonaparte"', which he had named after the hero who restored order in France.

My great-grandfather next became an East-India merchant, and carried on a large and successful trade with foreign ports. The United States War Department still entrusted him with important private missions; he was a confidential agent of both the French and English governments, and at the same time took a leading part in the municipal business of New York, and served on numerous commissions dealing with public affairs. He divided his year between his New York house in Warren Street, and Mount Buonaparte, the country place on Long Island created by the fortune he had made as a merchant; but when his hero dropped the *u* from his name and became Emperor, my scandalized great-grandfather, irrevocably committed to the Republican idea, indignantly re-named his place 'The Mount'. It stood, as its name suggests, on a terraced height in what is now the dreary waste of Astoria, and my mother could remember the stately colonnaded orangery, and the big orange-trees in tubs that were set out every summer on the upper terrace. But in her day the classical mantelpieces imported from Italy, with designs in white marble relieved against red or green, had already been torn out and replaced by black marble arches and ugly grates, and she recalled seeing the old mantelpieces stacked away in the stables. In his Bonapartist days General Stevens must have imported a good deal of Empire furniture from Paris, and one relic, a pair of fine gilt andirons crowned with Napoleonic eagles, has descended to his distant great-grand-daughter; but much was doubtless discarded when the mantelpieces went, and the stuffy day of Regency upholstery set in.

If I have dwelt too long on the career of this model citizen it is because of a secret partiality for him – for his stern high-nosed good looks, his gallantry in war, his love of luxury, his tireless commercial activities. I like above all the abounding energy, the swift adaptability and the *joie de vivre* which hurried him from one adventure to another, with war, commerce and domesticity (he had two wives and fourteen children) all carried on to the same heroic tune. But perhaps I feel nearest to him when I look at my eagle andirons, and think of the exquisite polychrome mantels that he found the time to bring all the way from Italy, to keep company with the orange-trees on his terrace.

In his delightful book on Walter Scott Mr John Buchan, excusing Scott's inability to create a lifelike woman of his own class, says that, after all, to the men of his generation, gentle-women were 'a toast' and little else. Nothing could be truer. Child-bearing was their task, fine needlework their recreation, being respected their privilege. Only in aristocratic society, and in the most sophisticated capitals of Europe, had they added to this repertory a good many private distractions. In the upper middle class 'the ladies, God bless 'em', sums it up. And so it happens that I know less than nothing of the particular virtues, gifts and modest accomplishments of the young women with pearls in their looped hair or cambric ruffs round their slim necks, who prepared the way for my generation. A few shreds of anecdote, no more than the faded flowers between the leaves of a great-grandmother's Bible, are all that remain to me.

Of my lovely great-grandmother Rhinelander (Mary Robart) I know only that she was of French descent, as her spirited profile declares, and properly jealous of her rights; for if she chanced to drive to New York in her yellow coach with its fringed hammer-cloth at the same hour when her daughter-in-law, from lower down the East River, was following the same road, the latter's carriage had to take the old lady's dust all the way, even though her horses were faster and her errand might be more urgent. I may add that once, several years after my marriage, a new coachman, who did not know my mother's carriage by sight, accidentally drove me past it on the fashionable Ocean Drive at Newport, and that I had to hasten the next morning to apologize to my mother, whose only comment was, when I explained that the coachman could not have known the offence he was committing: 'You might have told him'.

One of my great-grandmothers, Lucretia Ledyard (the second wife of General Stevens), lost her 'handsome sable cloak' one day when she was driving out General Washington in her sleigh, while on another occasion, when she was walking on the Battery in 1812, the gentleman who was with her, glancing seaward, suddenly exclaimed: 'My God, madam, there are the British!'

Meagre relics of the past; and when it comes to the next generation, that of my own grandparents, I am little better informed. My maternal grandfather Rhinelander, son of the proud dame of the yellow coach, married Mary Stevens, daughter of the General and his dusky handsome Ledyard wife. The young pair had four children, and then my grandfather died, when he was little more than thirty. He too was handsome, with frank blue eyes and a wide intelligent brow. My mother said he 'loved reading', and that particular drop of his blood must have descended to my veins, for I know of no other bookworm in the family. His young widow and her children continued to live at the country place at Hell Gate, lived there, in fact, from motives of economy, in winter as well as summer while the children were young; for my grandmother, whose property was left to the management of her husband's eldest brother, remained poor though her brother-in-law grew rich. The children, however, were carefully educated by English governesses and tutors; and to one of the latter is owing a charming study of the view across Hell Gate to Long Island, taken from my grandmother's lawn.

The little girls were taught needle-work, music, drawing and 'the languages' (their Italian teacher was Professor Foresti, a distinguished fugitive from the Austrian political prisons). In winter their 'best dresses' were low-necked and short-sleeved frocks, of pea-green merino, with gray beaver hats trimmed with tartan ribbons, white cotton stockings and heelless prunella slippers. When they walked in the snow hand-knitted woollen stockings were drawn over his frail footgear, and woollen shawls wrapped about their poor bare shoulders. They suffered, like all young ladies of their day, from chilblains and excruciating sick-headaches, yet all lived to a vigorous old age. When the eldest (my mother) 'came out', she wore a home-made gown of white tarlatan, looped up with red and white camellias from the greenhouse, and her mother's old white satin slippers; and her feet being of a different shape from grandmamma's, she suffered martyrdom, and never ceased to resent the indignity inflicted on her, and the impediment to her dancing, the more so as her younger sisters, who were prettier and probably more indulged, were given new slippers when their turn came. The girls appear to have had their horses (in that almost roadless day Americans still went everywhere in the saddle), and my mother, whose memory for the details of dress was inexhaustible, told me that she wore a beaver hat with a drooping ostrich plume, and a green veil to protect her complexion, and that from motives of modesty riding-habits were cut to trail on the ground, so that it was almost impossible to mount unassisted.

A little lower down the Sound (on the actual site of East Eighty-first Street) stood my grandfather Jones's pretty country house with classic pilasters and balustraded roof. A print in my possession shows a low-studded log-cabin adjoining it under the elms, described as the original Jones habitation; but it was more probably the slaves' quarter. In this pleasant house lived a young man of twenty, handsome, simple and kind, who was madly in love with Lucretia, the eldest of the 'poor Rhinelander' girls. George Frederic's parents thought him too young to marry; perhaps they had other ambitions for him; they bade him break off his attentions to Miss Rhinelander of Hell Gate. But George Frederic was the owner of a rowing-boat. His stern papa, perhaps on account of the proximity of the beloved, refused to give him a sailing-craft, though every youth of the day had his 'cat-boat', and the smiling expanse of the Sound was flecked with the coming and going of white wings. But George was not to be thwarted. He contrived to turn an oar into a mast; he stole down before dawn, his bed-quilt under his arm, rigged it to the oar in guise of a sail, and flying over the waters of the Sound hurried to his lady's feet across the lawn depicted in the tutor's painting. His devotion at last overcame the paternal opposition, and George and 'Lou' were married when they were respectively twenty-one and nineteen. My grandfather was rich, and must have made his sons a generous allowance; for the young couple, after an adventurous honeymoon in Cuba (of which my father kept a conscientious record, full of drives in *volantes* and visits to fashionable plantations) set up a house of their own in Gramercy Park, then just within the built-on limits of New York, and Mrs George Frederic took her place among the most elegant young married women of her day. At last the home-made tarlatans and the inherited satin shoes were avenged, and there began a long career of hospitality at home and travels abroad. My father, as a boy, had been to Europe with his father on one of the last of the great sailing passenger-ships; and he often told me of the delights of that crossing, on a yacht-like vessel with few passengers and spacious airy cabins, as compared with subsequent voyages on the cramped foul-smelling steamers that superseded the sailing ships. A year or so after the birth of my eldest brother my parents went abroad on a long tour. The new railways were beginning to transform continental travel, and after driving by *diligence* from Calais to Amiens my family journeyed thence by rail to Paris. Later they took train from Paris to Brussels, a day or two after the inauguration of this line; and my father notes in his diary: 'We were told to be at the station at one o'clock, *and by four we were actually off.*' By various means of conveyance the young couple with their infant son pursued their way through France, Belgium, Germany and Italy. They met other young New Yorkers of fashion, also on their travels, and would have had a merry time of it had not little Freddy's youthful ailments so frequently altered their plans – sometimes to a degree so disturbing that the patient young father (of twenty-three) confides to his diary how 'awful a thing it is to travel in Europe with an infant of twenty months'.

In spite of Freddy they saw many cities and countries, and on February 24, 1848, toward the hour of noon, incidentally witnessed, from the balcony of their hotel in the rue de Rivoli, the flight of Louis Philippe and Queen Marie Amélie across the Tuileries gardens. Though my mother often described this scene to mè, I suspect that the study of the Paris fashions made a more vivid impression on her than the fall of monarchies. The humiliation of the pea-green merino and the maternal slippers led to a good many extravagances; among them there is the white satin bonnet trimmed with white marabout and crystal drops in which the bride made her wedding visits, and a 'capeline' of *gorge de pigeon* taffetas with a wreath of flowers in shiny brown kid, which was one of the triumphs of her Paris shopping. She had a beautiful carriage, and her sloping shoulders and slim waist were becomingly set off by the wonderful gowns brought home from that first visit to the capital of fashion. All this happened years before I was born; but the tradition of elegance was never abandoned, and when we finally returned to live in New York (in 1872) I shared the excitement caused by the annual arrival of the 'trunk from Paris', and the enchantment of seeing one resplendent dress after another shaken out of its tissue-paper. Once, when I was a small child, my mother's younger sister, my beautiful and serious-minded Aunt Mary Newbold, asked me, with edifying interest: 'What would you like to be when you grow up?' and on my replying in all good faith, and with a dutiful air: 'The best-dressed woman in New York,' she uttered the horrified cry: 'Oh, don't say that, darling!' to which I could only rejoin in wonder: 'But, Auntie, you know Mamma *is*.'

When my grandfather died my father came into an independent fortune; but even before that my father and uncles seem to have had allowances permitting them to lead a life of leisure and amiable hospitality. The customs of the day were simple, and in my father's set the chief diversions were sea-fishing, boat-racing and wild-fowl shooting. There were no clubs as yet in New York, and my mother, whose view of life was incurably prosaic, always said that accounted for the early marriages, as the young men of that day 'had nowhere else to go'. The young married couples,

Langdons, Hones, Newbolds, Edgars, Joneses, Gallatins, etc., entertained each other a good deal, and my mother's sloping shoulders were often displayed above the elegant fringed and ruffled 'berthas' of her Parisian dinner gowns. The amusing diary of Mr Philip Hone gives a good idea of the simple but incessant exchange of hospitality between the young people who ruled New York society before the Civil War.

My readers, by this time, may be wondering what were the particular merits, private or civic, of these amiable persons. Their lives, as one looks back, certainly seem lacking in relief; but I believe their value lay in upholding two standards of importance in any community, that of education and good manners, and of scrupulous probity in business and private affairs. New York has always been a commercial community, and in my infancy the merits and defects of its citizens were those of a mercantile middle class. The first duty of such a class was to maintain a strict standard of uprightness in affairs; and the gentlemen of my father's day did maintain it, whether in the law, in banking, shipping or wholesale commercial enterprises. I well remember the horror excited by any irregularity in affairs, and the relentless social ostracism inflicted on the families of those who lapsed from professional or business integrity. In one case, where two or three men of high social standing were involved in a discreditable bank failure, their families were made to suffer to a degree that would seem merciless to our modern judgment. But perhaps the New Yorkers of that day were unconsciously trying to atone for their culpable neglect of state and national politics, from which they had long disdainfully held aloof, by upholding the sternest principles of business probity, and inflicting the severest social penalties on whoever lapsed from them. At any rate I should say that the qualities justifying the existence of our old society were social amenity and financial incorruptibility; and we have travelled far enough from both to begin to estimate their value.

The weakness of the social structure of my parents' day was a blind dread of innovation, an instinctive shrinking from responsibility. In 1824 (or thereabouts) a group of New York gentlemen who were appointed to examine various plans for the proposed laying-out of the city, and whose private sympathies were notoriously anti-Jeffersonian and undemocratic, decided against reproducing the beautiful system of squares, circles and radiating avenues which Major L'Enfant, the brilliant French engineer, had designed for Washington, because it was thought 'undemocratic' for citizens of the new republic to own building-plots which were not all of exactly the same shape, size – and *value*! This naïf document, shown to me by Robert Minturn, a descendant of a member of the original committee, and doubtless often since published, typified the prudent attitude of a society of prosperous business men who have no desire to row against the currents.

A little world so well-ordered and well-to-do does not often produce either eagles or fanatics, and both seem to have been conspicuously absent from the circle in which my forbears moved. In old-established and powerful societies originality of character is smiled at, and even encouraged to assert itself; but conformity is the bane of middle-class communities, and as far as I can recall, only two of my relations stepped out of the strait path of the usual. One was a mild and inoffensive old bachelor cousin, very small and frail, and reputed of immense wealth and morbid miserliness, who built himself a fine house in his youth, and lived in it for fifty or sixty years, in a state of negativeness and insignificance which made him proverbial even in our conforming class – and then, in his last years (so we children were told) *sat on a marble shelf, and thought he was a bust of Napoleon.*

Cousin Edmund's final illusion was not without pathos, but as a source of inspiration to my childish fancy he was a poor thing compared with George Alfred. George Alfred was another cousin, but one whom I had never seen, and could never hope to see, because years before he had – vanished. Vanished, that is, out of society, out of respectability, out of the safe daylight world of 'nice people' and reputable doings. Before naming George Alfred my mother altered her expression and lowered her voice. Thank heaven *she* was not responsible for him – he belonged to my father's side of the family! But they too had long since washed their hands of George Alfred – had ceased even to be aware of his existence. If my mother pronounced his name it was solely, I believe, out of malice, out of the child's naughty desire to evoke some nursery hobgoblin by muttering a dark incantation like *Eeena Meena Mina Mo*, and then darting away with affrighted backward looks to see if there is anything there.

My mother always darted away from George Alfred's name after pronouncing it, and it was not until I was grown up, and had acquired greater courage and persistency, that one day I drove her to the wall by suddenly asking: 'But, Mamma, *what did he do*?'

'Some woman' – my mother muttered; and no one accustomed to
the innocuous word as now used can imagine the shades of
disapproval, scorn and yet excited curiosity, that 'some' could
then connote on the lips of virtue.

George Alfred – and some woman! Who was she? From what
heights had she fallen with him, to what depths dragged him
down? For in those simple days it was always a case of 'the
woman tempted me'. To her respectable sisters her culpability
was as certain in advance as Predestination to the Calvinist. But I
was not fated to know more – thank heaven I was not! For our
shadowy Paolo and Francesca, circling together on the 'accursèd
air', somewhere outside the safe boundaries of our old New York,
gave me, I verily believe, my earliest glimpse of the poetry that
Goethe missed in the respectable world of the Hirchgraben, and
that my ancestors assuredly failed to find, or to create, between
the Battery and Union Square. The vision of poor featureless
unknown Alfred and his siren, lurking in some cranny of my
imagination, hinted at regions perilous, dark and yet lit with
mysterious fires, just outside the world of copy-book axioms, and
the old obediences that were in my blood; and the hint was useful
– for a novelist.

Chapter Two
Knee-high

I

Peopling the background of these earliest scenes there were the tall splendid father who was always so kind, and whose strong arms lifted one so high, and held one so safely; and my mother, who wore such beautiful flounced dresses, and had painted and carved fans in sandalwood boxes, and ermine scarves, and perfumed yellowish laces pinned up in blue paper, and kept in a marquetry chiffonier, and all the other dim impersonal attributes of a Mother, without, as yet, anything much more definite; and two big brothers who were mostly away (the eldest already at college); but in the foreground with Foxy there was one rich all-permeating presence: Doyley. How I pity all children who have not had a Doyley — a nurse who has always been there, who is as established as the sky and as warm as the sun, who understands everything, feels everything, can arrange everything, and combines all the powers of the Divinity with the compassion of a mortal heart like one's own! Doyley's presence was the warm cocoon in which my infancy lived safe and sheltered; the atmosphere without which I could not have breathed. It is thanks to Doyley that not one bitter memory, one uncomprehended injustice, darkened the days when the soul's flesh is so tender, and the remembrance of wrongs so acute.

I was born in New York, in my parents' house in West Twenty-third Street, and we lived there in winter, and (I suppose) at Newport in summer, during the first three years of my life. But no memories of those years survive, save those I have mentioned, and one other, a good deal dimmer, of going to stay one summer with my Aunt Elizabeth, my father's unmarried sister, who had a house at Rhinebeck-on-the-Hudson. This aunt, whom I remember as a ramrod-backed old lady compounded of steel and granite, had been threatened in her youth with the 'consumption' which had already carried off a brother and sister. Few families in that day escaped the scourge of tuberculosis, and the Protestant cemeteries of Pisa and Rome are full of the graves of wretched exiles sent to end their days by the supposedly mild shores of Arno or Tiber. My poor Aunt Margaret, my poor Uncle Joshua, both snatched in their early flower, already slept beside the Pyramid of Caius Cestius, where my grandmother was later to join them; and when Elizabeth in her turn began to pine, her parents, no doubt discouraged by the Italian experiment, decided to try curing her at home. They therefore shut her up one October in her bedroom in the New York house in Mercer Street, lit the fire, sealed up the windows, and did not let her out again till the following June, when she emerged in perfect health, to live till seventy.

My aunt's house, called Rhinecliff, afterward became a vivid picture in the gallery of my little girlhood; but among those earliest impressions only one is connected with it; that of a night when, as I was ready to affirm, there was a Wolf under my bed. This business of the Wolf was the first of other similar terrifying experiences, and since most imaginative children know these hauntings by tribal animals, I mention it only because from the moment of that adventure it became necessary, whenever I 'read' the story of Red Riding Hood (that is, looked at the pictures), to carry my little nursery stool from one room to another, in pursuit of Doyley or my mother, so that I should never again be exposed to meeting the family Totem when I sat down alone to my book.

The effect of terror produced by the house of Rhinecliff was no doubt partly due to what seemed to me its intolerable ugliness. My visual sensibility must always have been too keen for middling pleasures; my photographic memory of rooms and houses – even those seen but briefly, or at long intervals – was from my earliest years a source of inarticulate misery, for I was always vaguely frightened by ugliness. I can still remember hating everything at Rhinecliff, which, as I saw, on rediscovering it some years later, was an expensive but dour specimen of Hudson River Gothic; and from the first I was obscurely conscious of a queer resemblance between the granitic exterior of Aunt Elizabeth and her grimly comfortable home, between her battlemented caps and the turrets of Rhinecliff. But all this is merged in a blur, for by the time I was four years old I was playing in the Roman Forum instead of on the lawns of Rhinecliff.

2

The transition woke no surprise, for almost everything that constituted my world was still about me: my handsome father, my beautifully dressed mother, and the warmth and sunshine that were Doyley. The chief difference was that the things about me were now not ugly but incredibly beautiful. That old Rome of the mid-nineteenth century was still the city of romantic ruins in which Clive Newcome's 'J. J.' had depicted the Trasteverina dancing before a *locanda* to the music of a *pifferaro*. I remember, through the trailing clouds of infancy, the steps of the Piazza di Spagna thronged with Thackerayan artists' models, and heaped with early violets, daffodils and tulips; I remember long sunlit wanderings on the springy turf of great Roman villas; heavy coaches of Cardinals flashing in scarlet and gold through the twilight of narrow streets; the flowery bombardment of the Carnival procession watched with shrieks of infant ecstasy from a balcony of the Corso. But the liveliest hours were those spent with my nurse on the Monte Pincio, where I played with Marion Crawford's little half-sister, Daisy Terry, and her brother Arthur. Other children, long since dim and nameless, flit by as supernumeraries of the band; but only Daisy and her brother have remained alive to me. There we played, dodging in and out among old stone benches, racing, rolling hoops, whirling through skipping ropes, or pausing out of breath to watch the toy procession of stately barouches and glossy saddle-horses which, on every fine afternoon of winter, carried the flower of Roman beauty and nobility round and round and round the restricted meanderings of the hill-top.

Those hours were the jolliest; yet deeper impressions were gathered in walks with my mother on the daisy-strewn lawns of the Villa Doria-Pamphili, among the statues and stone-pines of the Villa Borghese, or hunting on the slopes of the Palatine for the mysterious bits of blue and green and rosy stone which cropped up through the turf as violets and anemones did in other places, and turned out to be precious fragments of porphyry, lapis lazuli, verde antico, and all the mineral flora of the Palace of the Cæsars. In those days every traveller of artistic sensibility gathered baskets-full of these marble blossoms, and had them transformed into the paper-weights, inkstands and circular 'sofa-tables' without which no gentleman's home was complete. All the glory seemed to forsake my treasures when they were forced into these lapidary combinations; but the hunt was thrilling, and it occurred to no one that these exquisite relics of ruined *opus alexandrinum*, and of Imperial vases and statues, should have been treated with more reverence. The buffaloes of Piranesi had vanished from the Forum and the Palatine, but the ruins of Imperial Rome were still a free stamping ground for the human herd.

There were other days when we drove out on the Campagna, and wandered over the short grass between the tombs of the Appian way; still others among the fountains of Frascati; and some, particularly vivid, when, in the million-tapered blaze of St Peter's, the Pope floated ethereally above a long train of ecclesiastics seen through an incense haze so golden that it seemed to pour from the blinding luminary behind the High Altar.

What clung closest in after years, when I thought of the lost Rome of my infancy? It is hard to say; perhaps simply the warm scent of the box hedges on the Pincian, and the texture of weather-worn sun-gilt stone. Those, at least, are the two impressions which, for many years after, the mightiest of names instantly conjured up for me.

3

My Roman impressions are followed by others, improbably picturesque, of a journey to Spain. It must have taken place just before or after the Roman year; I remember that the Spanish tour was still considered an arduous adventure, and to attempt it with a young child the merest folly. But my father had been reading Prescott and Washington Irving; the Alhambra was more of a novelty than the Colosseum; and as the offspring of born travellers I was expected, even in infancy, to know how to travel. I suppose I acquitted myself better than the unhappy Freddy; for from that wild early pilgrimage I brought back an incurable passion for the road. What a journey it must have been! Presumably there was already a railway from the frontier to Madrid; but I recall only the incessant jingle of *diligence* bells, the cracking of whips, the yells of gaunt muleteers hurling stones at their gaunter mules to urge them up interminable and almost unscaleable hills. It is all a jumble of excited impressions: breaking down on wind-swept sierras; arriving late and hungry at squalid *posadas*; flea-hunting, chocolate-drinking (I believe there was nothing but chocolate and olives to feed me on), being pursued wherever we went by touts, guides, deformed beggars, and all sorts of jabbering and confusing people; and, through the chaos and fatigue, a fantastic vision of the columns of Cordova, the tower of the Giralda, the pools and fountains of the Alhambra, the orange groves of Seville, and awful icy penumbra of the Escorial, and everywhere shadowy aisles undulating with incense and processions . . . Perhaps, after all, it is not a bad thing to begin one's travels at four.

4

In the course of time we exchanged the Piazza di Spagna for the Champs Elysées. It probably happened the very next winter; but life in Paris must have seemed colourless after the sunny violet-scented Italian days, for I remember far less of it than of Rome.

Two episodes, however, stand out vividly. One was the coming to dine every Sunday evening of a kindly gentleman with curly gray hair and a long moustache, an old friend and Rhode Island neighbour of the family. This was Mr Henry Bedlow, whose chief title to fame seems to have been that he lived in an old house 'up the island' called Malbone, which he had inherited from his grandfather or great-uncle, the celebrated miniature painter of that name. When Mr Bedlow dined with us I was always led in with the dessert, my red hair rolled into sausages, and the sleeves of my best frock looped up with pink coral, and was allowed to perch on his knee while he 'told me mythology'. What blessings I have since called down on the teller! Fairy stories, even Mother Goose, even Andersen's tales and the Contes de Perrault, still left me inattentive and indifferent, but the domestic dramas of the Olympians roused all my creative energy. Perhaps I scented an indefinable condescension (and often a great lack of discernment) in the stories which big people have invented about little ones; and besides, the doings of children were always intrinsically less interesting to me than those of grown-ups, and I felt more at home with the gods and goddesses of Olympus, who behaved so much like the ladies and gentlemen who came to dine, whom I saw riding and driving in the Bois de Boulogne, and about whom I was forever weaving stories of my own.

The other Parisian event concerns this story-telling. The imagining of tales (about grown-up people, 'real people', I called them – children always seemed to me incompletely realized) had gone on in me since my first conscious moments; I cannot remember the time when I did not want to 'make up' stories. But it was in Paris that I found the necessary formula. Oddly enough, I had no desire to write my stories down (even had I known how to write, and I couldn't yet form a letter); but from the first I had to have a book in my hand to 'make up' with, and from the first it had to be a certain sort of book. The page had to be closely printed, with rather heavy black type, and not much margin. Certain densely printed novels in the early Tauchnitz editions, Harrison Ainsworth's for instance, would have been my richest sources of inspiration had I not hit one day on something even better: Washington Irving's 'Alhambra'. These shaggy volumes, printed in close black characters on rough-edged yellowish pages, and bound in coarse dark-blue paper covers (probably a production of the old Galignani Press in Paris) must have been a relic of our Spanish adventure. Washington Irving was an old friend of my family's, and his collected works, in comely type and handsome binding, adorned our library shelves at home. But these would not have been of much use to me as a source of inspiration. The rude companion of our travels was the book I needed; I had only to open it for the Pierian fount to flow. There was richness and mystery in the thick black type, a hint of bursting overflowing material in the serried lines and scant margin. To this day I am bored by the sight of widely spaced type, and a little islet of text in a sailless sea of white paper.

Well – the 'Alhambra' once in hand, making up was ecstasy. At any moment the impulse might seize me; and then, if the book was in reach, I had only to walk the floor, turning the pages as I walked, to be swept off full sail on the sea of dreams. The fact that I could not read added to the completeness of the illusion, for from those mysterious blank pages I could evoke whatever my fancy chose. Parents and nurses, peeping at me through the cracks of doors (I always had to be alone to 'make up'), noticed that I often held the book upside down, but that I never failed to turn the pages, and that I turned them at about the right pace for a person reading aloud as passionately and precipitately as was my habit.

There was something almost ritualistic in the performance. The call came regularly and imperiously; and though, when it caught me at inconvenient moments, I would struggle against it conscientiously – for I was beginning to be a very conscientious little girl – the struggle was always a losing one. I had to obey the furious Muse; and there are deplorable tales of my abandoning the 'nice' playmates who had been invited to 'spend the day', and rushing to my mother with the desperate cry: 'Mamma, you must go and entertain that little girl for me. *I've got to make up*.'

My parents, distressed by my solitude (my two brothers being by this time grown up and away) were always trying to establish relations for me with 'nice' children, and I was willing enough to play in the Champs Elysées with such specimens as were produced or (more reluctantly) to meet them at little parties or dancing classes; but I did not want them to intrude on my privacy, and there was not one I would not have renounced forever rather than have my 'making up' interfered with. What I really preferred was to be alone with Washington Irving and my dream.

The peculiar purpose for which books served me probably made me indifferent to what was in them. At any rate, I can remember feeling no curiosity about it. But my father, by dint of patience, managed to drum the alphabet into me; and one day I was found sitting under a table, absorbed in a volume which I did not appear to be using for improvisation. My immobility attracted attention, and when asked what I was doing, I replied: 'Reading'. This was received with incredulity; but on being called upon to read a few lines aloud I appear to have responded to the challenge, and it was then discovered that the work over which I was poring was a play by Ludovic Halévy, called 'Fanny Lear', which was having a *succès de scandale* in Paris owing to the fact that the heroine was what ladies of my mother's day called 'one of those women'. Thereafter the books I used for 'making up' were carefully inspected before being entrusted to me; and an arduous business it must have been, for no book ever came my way without being instantly pounced on, and now that I could read I divided my time between my own improvisations and the printed inventions of others.

It was in Paris that I took my first dancing-lessons. I was no Isadora, and these beginnings would not be worth a word but for the light they throw on the manners and customs of my infancy. I used to go, with a group of little friends, children English and American, to the private *cours* of an ex-ballerina of the Grand Opera, Mademoiselle Michelet, a large stern woman with a heavy black moustache, in whom it would have been hard for the most imaginative to detect even a trace of her early calling. To us she was the severest of instructresses. The waltz and mazurka had long since been introduced into the ball-room, without even a lingering remembrance of Byron's reprobation; but they were not thought difficult enough to train the young, and we were persistently exercised in the *menuet*, the shawl dance (with a lace scarf) and the *cachucha* – of course with castanets. Mademoiselle Michelet's quarters were very small; and I can still see myself, an isolated figure in the centre of her shining *parquet*, helplessly waving my scarf or uncertainly clacking my castanets, while my fellow pupils hedged me about as rather bored spectators, and Mademoiselle Michelet's wizened little old mother, in a cap turreted with loops of purple ribbon, tinkled out the tunes at a piano squeezed into a corner of the room.

During one of our Paris winters (I think there were two or three) my dear old grandmother, my mother's mother, paid us a long visit. I call her 'old', though it is probably that at the time she was under sixty; but I had never seen her except in lace cap and lappets, a bunch of gold charms dangling from her massive watch-chain, among the folds of a rich black silk dress, and a black japanned ear-trumpet at her ear – the abstract type of an ancestress at the function was then understood.

I always recall her seated in an arm-chair, her undimmed eyes bent over some exquisitely fine needlework. I hope she sometimes went for a walk or a drive, and enjoyed a few glimpses of grown-up society; but for me she exists only as a motionless and gently smiling figure, whose one gesture was to lay aside her stitching for her ear-trumpet at my approach. When she was with us I was constantly in her room; and my way of returning her affection was to read aloud to her. I had just discovered a volume of Tennyson among my father's books, and for hours I used to shout the 'Idyls of the King', and 'The Lord of Burleigh' through the trumpet of my long-suffering ancestress. Not being more than six or seven years old I understood hardly anything of what I was reading, or rather I understood it in my own way, which was most often not the poet's; as in the line from 'The Lord of Burleigh', 'and he made a loving consort', where I read *concert* for consort, and concluded (being already addicted to rash generalizations) that a gentleman's first act after marriage was to give his spouse a concert, in gratitude for which 'a faithful wife was she'. But I enjoyed all the sonorities as much as if I had known what they meant, and perhaps even more, since my own interpretations so often enriched the text; and probably such shrill scraps as travelled through the windings of my grandmother's trumpet troubled her no more than they did me. To one whose preferred poetic reading was 'The Christian Year', the 'Idyls of the King' must have been almost as full of mystery and obscurity as Browning was to the next generation, and the rhythmic raptures tingling through me probably woke no echo in the dear old head bent to mine.

I suspect that no one else in the house could bear to be read aloud to by me, for I do not remember attempting it on any one but my grandmother; and indeed poetry did not play much part in our lives. My father knew Macaulay's 'Lays' by heart, and

> Ho, Philip, send for charity thy Mexican pistoles,

and

> Where ride Massilia's triremes
> Heavy with fair-haired slaves,

had already thrummed their march-tunes into my infant ears. The new Tennysonian rhythms also moved my father greatly; and I imagine there was a time when his rather rudimentary love of verse might have been developed had he had any one with whom to share it. But my mother's matter-of-factness must have shrivelled up any such buds of fancy; and in later years I remember his reading only Macaulay, Prescott, Washington Irving, and every book of travel he could find. Arctic explorations especially absorbed him, and I have wondered since what stifled cravings had once germinated in him, and what manner of man he was really meant to be. That he was a lonely one, haunted by something always unexpressed and unattained, I am sure.

5

I remember nothing else of my Paris life except one vision over which after-events shed a tragic glare. It was the sight, one autumn afternoon, of a beautiful lady driving down the Champs Elysées in a beautiful open carriage, a little boy in uniform beside her on a pony, and a glittering escort of officers. The carriage, of the kind called a *daumont*, was preceded by outriders, and swayed gracefully on its big C-springs to the rhythm of four high-stepping and highly-groomed horses, a postilion on one of the leaders, and two tremendous footmen perched high at the back. But all I had eyes for was the lady herself, leaning back as ladies of those days leaned in their indolently-hung carriages, flounces of *feuille-morte* taffetas billowing out about her, and on her rich auburn hair a tiny black lace bonnet with a tea-rose above one ear. I still see her serene elegance of attitude and expression, her conscious air of being, with her little boy, and the shining horses, and the flashing officers and outriders, the centre of the sumptuous spectacle. The next year she and her procession had vanished in a crimson hurricane; and the whole setting of swaying carriages and outstretched ladies, of young men caracoling on thorough-breds past stately houses glimpsed through clustering horse-chestnut foliage, has long since been rolled up in the lumber-room of discarded pageants.

We must have remained in Paris till the outbreak of the Franco-Prussian War, at which fateful moment we chanced to be at Bad Wildbad, in the Black Forest, a primitive watering-place just coming into fashion, where my mother had been sent for a cure. With a young German nursery governess who had been added to our party I took happy rambles in the pine-forests, and learned from her to make wild-flower garlands, to knit and to tat, and to practise (for the only time in my life) other Gretchenish arts. She also taught me (out of the New Testament) how to read German; and in our Bible reading I came across a phrase which has always delighted me because of the quaint contrast between its impulsive German *Gemüthlichkeit* and the majestic phraseology of our Authorized Version. When, on the Mount of Transfiguration, the disciples cry out: 'Lord, it is good for us to be here; if Thou wilt, let us make here three tabernacles', the German version causes them to say: '*So lasset uns Hütten bauen!*' The cry, which suggested to me something fresh and leafy and adventurous, like a Mayne Reid story or 'The Swiss Family Robinson', is a picturesque instance of the way in which racial character colours alien formulas.

But one morning, climbing a woodland path with my governess and some other children, I was seized by an agony of pain – and after that for many long weeks life was a confused and feverish misery. I was desperately ill with typhoid fever, and I mention the fact only because of one incredible circumstance. All the doctors of Wildbad (they were doubtless few) had already been mobilized, save one super-annuated practitioner; and he had never before seen a case of typhoid! His son, also a doctor, was with the army; and all that his father could do was to despatch bulletins to him, asking how I was to be treated. The replies, one may suppose, were long in arriving; and in the interval death came near. But at the same time a celebrated Russian physician arrived at Wildbad for a day, at the call of a princely patient. My parents persuaded him to see me, and he prescribed the new treatment: plunging the patient in baths of ice-cold water. At the suggestion my mother's courage failed her; but she wrapped me in wet sheets, and I was saved.

6

My childish world, though so well filled, lacked completeness, for my dog Foxy had not come to Europe with us. His absence left such a void that my parents finally gave me a Florentine *lupetto*, as white as Foxy, but much smaller. By that time (I think in 1870) we had exchanged Paris for Florence, and he was known as Florence Foxy. He was the joyous companion of a comparatively dull winter; for the return to Italy did not bring back the joys of Rome. Florence was much colder and less sunny; there were no children to replace the jolly Pincianites, and the Cascine Gardens are associated only with sedate walks with my elders, monotonous enough if I had not had Foxy to race with, and violets to gather.

The other high lights of those gray months were the increased enchantment of 'making up', and the fainter glow of the hours spent with a charming young lady who taught me Italian. My lessons amused me, and the new language came to me as naturally as breathing, as French and German had already. Why do so few parents know what a fortune they could bestow on their children by teaching them the modern languages in babyhood, when a playmate is the only professor needed, and the speech acquired is never afterward lost, however deep below the surface it may be embedded?

But discovering Italian, though it was to be the source of such joys, was nothing to the ecstasy of 'making up'. Learning to read, instead of distracting me from this passion, had only fed it; and during that Florentine winter it became a frenzy. Our vast and cheerless suite in the high-ceilinged *piano nobile* of an hotel overlooking the Arno was scantily furnished with threadbare carpets and heavy consoles and sofas; but the long vista of rooms, each communicating with the next through tall folding doors, was a matchless track for my sport. When the grown-ups were out, and Doyley safe with her sewing, I had the field to myself; and I still feel the rapture (greater than any I have ever known in writing) of pouring forth undisturbed the tireless torrent of my stories. The 'Faster, faster, O Circe, Goddess' of 'The Strayed Reveller' always reminds me of those youthful gallops around the racecourse of my imagination. The speed at which I travelled was so great that my mother tried in vain to take down my 'stories', and posterity will never know what it has lost! All I remember is that my tales were about what I still thought of as 'real people' (that is, grown-up people, resembling in appearance and habits my family and their friends, and caught in the same daily coil of 'things that might have happened'). My imagination was still closed to the appeal of the purely fabulous and fairy-like, and though I was already an ardent reader of poetry I felt no desire to write it. But all that was soon to be changed; for the next year we were to go home to New York, and I was to enter into the kingdom of my father's library.

Chapter Three
Little Girl

I

The depreciation of American currency at the close of the Civil War had so much reduced my father's income that, in common with many of his friends and relations, he had gone to Europe to economize, letting his town and country houses for six years to some of the profiteers of the day; but I did not learn till much later to how prosaic a cause I owed my early years in Europe. Happy misfortune, which gave me, for the rest of my life, that background of beauty and old-established order! I did not know how deeply I had felt the nobility and harmony of the great European cities till our steamer was docked at New York.

I remember once asking an old New Yorker why he never went abroad, and his answering: 'Because I can't bear to cross Murray Street.' It was indeed an unsavoury experience, and the shameless squalor of the purlieus of the New York docks in the 'seventies dismayed my childish eyes, stored with the glories of Rome and the architectural majesty of Paris. But it was summer; we were soon at Newport, under the friendly gables of Pencraig; and to a little girl long pent up in hotels and flats there was inexhaustible delight in the freedom of a staircase to run up and down, of lawns and trees, a meadow full of clover and daisies, a pony to ride, terriers to romp with, a sheltered cove to bathe in, flower-beds spicy with 'carnation, lily, rose', and a kitchen-garden crimson with strawberries and sweet as honey with Seckel pears.

The roomy and pleasant house of Pencraig was surrounded by a verandah wreathed in clematis and honeysuckle, and below it a lawn sloped to a deep daisied meadow, beyond which were a private bathing-beach and boat-landing. From the landing we used to fish for 'scuppers' and 'porgies', succulent little fish that were grilled or fried for high tea; and off the rocky point lay my father's and brothers' 'cat-boats', the graceful wide-sailed craft that flecked the bay like sea-gulls.

Adjoining our property was Edgerston, the country home of Lewis Rutherfurd, the distinguished astronomer, notable in his day for his remarkable photographs of the moon. He and his wife were lifelong friends of my parents', and in their household, besides two grown-up daughters of singular beauty, there were two little boys, the youngest of my own age. There were also two young governesses, French and German; and as I was alone, and the German governess who had been imported for me was unsympathetic and unsatisfied, she was soon sent home, and the Rutherfurd governesses (the daughters of the house being 'out,' and off their hands) took me on for French, German, and whatever else, in those ancient days, composed a little girl's curriculum. This drew the two households still closer, for though I did not study with the little boys I seem to remember that I went to Edgerston for my lessons. There was certainly a continual coming and going through the private gate between the properties; but I recalled a good deal more of our games than of my lessons.

Most vivid is my memory of the picturesque archery club meeting of which the grown daughters of the house, Margaret (afterward Mrs Henry White) and her sister Louisa were among the most brilliant performers. When the club met we children were allowed to be present, and to circulate among the grown-ups (usually all three of us astride of one patient donkey); and a pretty sight the meeting was, with parents and elders seated in a semicircle on the turf behind the lovely archeresses in floating silks or muslins, with their wide leghorn hats, and heavy veils flung back only at the moment of aiming. These veils are associated with all the summer festivities of my childhood. In that simple society there was an almost pagan worship of physical beauty, and the first question asked about any youthful newcomer on the social scene was invariably: 'Is she pretty?' or: 'Is he handsome?' – for good looks were as much prized in young men as in maidens. For the latter no grace was rated as high as 'a complexion'. It is hard to picture nowadays the shell-like transparence, the luminous red-and-white, of those young cheeks untouched by paint or powder, in which the blood came and went like the lights of an aurora. Beauty was unthinkable without 'a complexion', and to defend that treasure against sun and wind, and the arch-enemy sea air, veils as thick as curtains (some actually of woollen barège) were habitually worn. It must have been very uncomfortable for the wearers, who could hardly see or breathe; but even to my childish eyes the effect was dazzling when the curtain was drawn, and young beauty shone forth. My dear friend Howard Sturgis used to laugh at the 'heavily veiled' heroines who lingered on so late in Victorian fiction, and were supposed to preserve their incognito until they threw back their veils; but if he had known fashionable Newport in my infancy he would have seen that the novelists' formula was based on what was once a reality.

Those archery meetings greatly heightened my infantile desire to 'tell a story', and the young gods and goddesses I used to watch strolling across the Edgerston lawn were the prototypes of my first novels. The spectacle was a charming one to an imaginative child already caught in the toils of romance; no wonder I remember it better than my studies. Not that I was not eager to learn; but my long and weary illness had made my parents unduly anxious about my health, and they forbade my being taught anything that required a mental effort. Committing to memory, and preparing lessons in advance, were ruled out; it was thought that I read too much (as if a born reader could!), and that my mind must be spared all 'strain'. This was doubtless partly due to the solicitude of parents for a late-born child, partly to a natural reaction against the severities of their own early training. The sentimental theory that children must not be made to study anything that does not interest them was already in the air, and reinforced by the fear of 'fatiguing' my brain, it made my parents turn my work into play. Being deprived of the irreplaceable grounding of Greek and Latin, I never learned to concentrate except on subjects naturally interesting to me, and developed a restless curiosity which prevented my fixing my thoughts for long even on these. Of benefits I see only one. To most of my contemporaries the enforced committing to memory of famous poems must have forever robbed some of the loveliest of their bloom; but this being forbidden me, great poetry – English, French, German and Italian – came to me fresh as the morning, with the dew on it, and has never lost that early glow.

The drawbacks were far greater than this advantage. But for the wisdom of Fräulein Bahlmann, my beloved German teacher, who saw which way my fancy turned, and fed it with all the wealth of German literature, from the Minnesingers to Heine – but for this, and the leave to range in my father's library, my mind would have starved at the age when the mental muscles are most in need of feeding.

I used to say that I had been taught only two things in my childhood: the modern languages and good manners. Now that I have lived to see both these branches of culture dispensed with, I perceive that there are worse systems of education. But in justice to my parents I ought to have named a third element in my training; a reverence for the English language as spoken according to the best usage. Usage, in my childhood, was as authoritative an element in speaking English as tradition was in social conduct. And it was because our little society still lived in the reflected light of a long-established culture that my parents, who were far from intellectual, who read little and studied not at all, nevertheless spoke their mother tongue with scrupulous perfection, and insisted that their children should do the same.

This reverence for the best tradition of spoken English – an easy idiomatic English, neither pedantic nor 'literary' – was no doubt partly due to the fact that, in the old New York families of my parents' day, the children's teachers were often English. My mother and her sisters and brother had English tutors and governesses, and my own brothers were educated at home by an extremely cultivated English tutor. In my mother's family, more than one member of the generation preceding hers had been educated at Oxford or Cambridge, and one of my own brothers went to Cambridge.

Even so, however, I have never quite understood how two people so little preoccupied with letters as my father and mother had such sensitive ears for pure English. The example they set me was never forgotten; I still wince under my mother's ironic smile when I said that some visitor had stayed 'quite a while', and her dry: 'Where did you pick *that* up?' The wholesome derision of my grown-up brothers saved me from pomposity as my mother's smile guarded me against slovenliness; I still tingle with the sting of their ridicule when, excusing myself for having forgotten something I had been told to do, I said, with an assumption of grown-up dignity (*aetat* ten or eleven): 'I didn't know that it was *imperative*.'

Such elementary problems as (judging from the letters I receive from unknown readers) disturb present-day users of English in America – perplexity as to the distinction between 'should' and 'would', and the display of such half-educated pedantry as saying 'gotten' and 'you would better' – never embarrassed our speech. We spoke naturally, instinctively good English, but my parents always wanted it to be better, that is, easier, more flexible and idiomatic. This excessive respect for the language never led to priggishness, or precluded the enjoyment of racy innovations. Long words were always smiled away as pedantic, and any really expressive slang was welcomed with amusement – but used as slang, as it were between quotation marks, and not carelessly admitted into our speech. Luckily we all had a lively sense of humour, and now that my brothers were at home again the house rang with laughter. We all knew by heart 'Alice in Wonderland', 'The Hunting of the Snark', and whole pages of Lear's 'Nonsense Book', and our sensitiveness to the quality of the English we spoke doubled our enjoyment of the incredible verbal gymnastics of those immortal works. Dear to us also, though in a lesser degree, were 'Innocents Abroad', Bret Harte's parodies of novels, and, in their much later day, George Ade's 'Arty', and the first volumes of that great philosopher, Mr Dooley. I cannot remember a time when we did not, every one of us, revel in the humorous and expressive side of American slang; what my parents abhorred was not the picturesque use of new terms, if they were vivid and expressive, but the habitual slovenliness of those who picked up the slang of the year without having any idea that they were not speaking in the purest tradition. But above all abhorrent to ears piously attuned to all the inflexions and shades of meaning of our rich speech were such mean substitutes as 'back of' for behind, 'dirt' for earth (i.e., a 'dirt road'), 'any place' for anywhere, or slovenly phrases like 'a great ways', soon, alas, to be followed by the still more inexcusable 'a *barracks*', 'a *woods*', and even 'a strata', 'a phenomena', which, as I grew up, a new class of the uneducated rich were rapidly introducing.

This feeling for good English was more than reverence, and nearer: it was love. My parents' ears were wounded by an unsuitable word as those of the musical are hurt by a false note. My mother, herself so little of a reader, was exaggeratedly scrupulous about the books I read; not so much the 'grown-up' books as those written for children. I was never allowed to read the popular American children's books of my day because, as my mother said, the children spoke bad English *without the author's knowing it*. You could do what you liked with the language if you did it consciously, and for a given purpose – but if you went shuffling along, trailing it after you like a rag in the dust, tramping over it, as Henry James said, like the emigrant tramping over his kitchen oil-cloth – that was unpardonable, there deterioration and corruption lurked. I remember it was only with reluctance, and because 'all the other children read them', that my mother consented to my reading 'Little Women' and 'Little Men'; and my ears, trained to the fresh racy English of 'Alice in Wonderland,' 'The Water Babies' and 'The Princess and the Goblin', were exasperated by the laxities of the great Louisa.

Perhaps our love of good English may be partly explained by the background of books which was an essential part of the old New York household. In my grand-parents' day every gentleman had what was called 'a gentleman's library'. In my father's day, these libraries still existed, though they were often only a background; but in our case Macaulay, Prescott, Motley, Sainte-Beauve, Augustin Thierry, Victor Hugo, the Brontës, Mrs Gaskell, Ruskin, Coleridge, had been added to the French and English classics in their stately calf bindings. Were these latter ever read? Not often, I imagine; but they were there; they represented a standard; and perhaps some mysterious emanation disengaged itself from them, obscurely fighting for the protection of the languages they had illustrated.

A standard; the word perhaps gives me my clue. When I said, in my resentful youth, that I had been taught only languages and manners, I did not know how closely, in my parents' minds, the two were related. Bringing-up in those days was based on what was called 'good breeding'. One was polite, considerate of others, careful of the accepted formulas, because such were the principles of the well-bred. And probably the regard of my parents for the niceties of speech was a part of their breeding. They treated their language with the same rather ceremonious courtesy as their friends. It would have been 'bad manners' to speak 'bad' English, and 'bad manners' were the supreme offence.

This fastidiousness of speech came chiefly from my mother's side, and my father probably acquired it under her influence. His own people, though they spoke good English, had disagreeable voices. I have noticed that wherever, in old New York families, there was a strong admixture of Dutch blood, the voices were flat, the diction was careless. My mother's stock was English, without Dutch blood, and this may account for the greater sensitiveness of all her people to the finer shades of English speech. In an article on Conrad which appeared in the *Times Literary Supplement* after his death, the author said (I quote from memory): 'Conrad had worshipped the English language all his life like a lover, but he had never romped with her in the nursery'; and this it was my happy fate to do.

To the modern child my little-girl life at Pencraig would seem sadly tame and uneventful, for its chief distractions were the simple ones of swimming and riding. My mother, like most married women of her day, had long since given up exercise, my father's only active pursuits were boating and shooting, and there was no one to ride with me but the coachman – nor was our end of the island a happy place for equestrianism. I enjoyed scampering on my pony over the hard dull roads; but it was better fun to swim in our own cove, in the jolly company of brothers, cousins and young neighbours. There were always two or three 'cat-boats' moored off our point, but I never shared the passion of my father and brothers for sailing. To be a passenger was too sedentary, and I felt no desire to sail the boat myself, being too wrapt in dreams to burden my mind with so exact a science. Best of all I liked our weekly walks with Mr Rutherfurd over what we called the Rocks – the rough moorland country, at that time without road or houses, extending from the placid blue expanse of Narragansett bay to the gray rollers of the Atlantic. Every Sunday he used to collect the children of the few friends living near us, and take them, with his own, for a tramp across this rugged country to the sea.

Yet what I recall of those rambles is not so much the comradeship of the other children, or the wise and friendly talk of our guide, as my secret sensitiveness to the landscape – something in me quite incommunicable to others, that was tremblingly and inarticulately awake to every detail of wind-warped fern and wide-eyed briar rose, yet more profoundly alive to a unifying magic beneath the diversities of the visible scene – a power with which I was in deep and solitary communion whenever I was alone with nature. It was the same tremor that had stirred in me in the spring woods of Mamaroneck, when I heard the whisper of the arbutus and the starry choir of the dogwood; and it has never since been still.

2

The old New York to which I came back as a little girl meant to me chiefly my father's library. Now for the first time I had my fill of books. Out of doors, in the mean monotonous streets, without architecture, without great churches or palaces, or any visible memorials of an historic past, what could New York offer to a child whose eyes had been filled with shapes of immortal beauty and immemorial significance? One of the most depressing impressions of my childhood is my recollection of the intolerable ugliness of New York, of its untended streets and the narrow houses so lacking in external dignity, so crammed with smug and suffocating upholstery. How could I understand that people who had seen Rome and Seville, Paris and London, could come back to live contentedly between Washington Square and the Central Park? What I could not guess was that this little low-studded rectangular New York, cursed with its universal chocolate-coloured coating of the most hideous stone ever quarried, this cramped horizontal gridiron of a town without towers, porticoes, fountains or perspectives, hide-bound in its deadly uniformity of mean ugliness, would fifty years later be as much a vanished city as Atlantis or the lowest layer of Schliemann's Troy, or that the social organization which that prosaic setting had slowly secreted would have been swept to oblivion with the rest. Nothing but the Atlantis-fate of old New York, the New York which had slowly but continuously developed from the early seventeenth century to my own childhood, makes that childhood worth recalling now.

Looking back at that little world, and remembering the 'hoard of pretty maxims' with which its elders preached down every sort of initiative, I have often wondered at such lassitude in the descendants of the men who first cleared a place for themselves in the new world, and then fought for the right to be masters there. What had become of the spirit of the pioneers and the revolutionaries? Perhaps the very violence of their effort had caused it to exhaust itself in the next generation, or the too great prosperity succeeding on almost unexampled hardships had produced, if not inertia, at least indifference in all matters except business or family affairs.

Even the acquiring of wealth had ceased to interest the little society into which I was born. In the case of some of its members, such as the Astors and Goelets, great fortunes, originating in a fabulous increase of New York real estate values, had been fostered by judicious investments and prudent administration; but of feverish money-making, in Wall Street or in railway, shipping or industrial enterprises, I heard nothing in my youth. Some of my father's friends may have been bankers, others have followed one of the liberal professions, usually the law; in fact almost all the young men I knew read law for a while after leaving college, though comparatively few practised it in after years. But for the most part my father's contemporaries, and those of my brothers also, were men of leisure – a term now almost as obsolete as the state it describes. It will probably seem unbelievable to present-day readers that only one of my own near relations, and not one of my husband's, was 'in business'. The group to which we belonged was composed of families to whom a middling prosperity had come, usually by the rapid rise in value of inherited real estate, and none of whom, apparently, aspired to be more than moderately well-off. I never in my early life came in contact with the gold-fever in any form, and when I hear that nowadays business life in New York is so strenuous that men and women never meet socially before the dinner hour, I remember the delightful week-day luncheons of my early married years, where the men were as numerous as the women, and where one of the first rules of conversation was the one early instilled in me by my mother: 'Never talk about money, and think about it as little as possible.'

The child of the well-to-do, hedged in by nurses and gover-nesses, seldom knows much of its parents' activities. I have only the vaguest recollection of the way in which my father and mother spent their days. I know that my father was a director on the principal charitable boards of New York – the Blind Asylum and the Bloomingdale Insane Asylum among others; and that during Lent a ladies' 'sewing class' met at our house to work with my mother for the poor. I also recall frequent drives with my mother, when the usual afternoon round of card-leaving was followed by a walk in the Central Park, and a hunt for violets and hepaticas in the secluded dells of the Ramble. In the evenings my parents went occasionally to the theatre, but never, as far as I remember, to a concert, or any kind of musical performance, until the Opera, then only sporadic, became an established entertainment, to which one went (as in eighteenth century Italy) chiefly if not solely for the pleasure of conversing with one's friends. Their most frequent distraction was dining out or dinner giving. Sometimes the dinners were stately and ceremonious (with engraved invitations issued three weeks in advance, soups, 'thick' and 'clear', and a Roman punch half way through the *menu*), but more often they were intimate and sociable, though always the occasion of much excellent food and old wine being admirably served, and discussed with suitable gravity.

My father had inherited from his family a serious tradition of good cooking, with a cellar of vintage clarets, and of Madeira which had rounded the Cape. The 'Jones' Madeira (my father's) and the 'Newbold' (my uncle's) enjoyed a particular celebrity even in that day of noted cellars. The following generation, interested only in champagne and claret, foolishly dispersed these precious stores. My brothers sold my father's cellar soon after his death; and after my marriage, dining in a *nouveau riche* house of which the master was unfamiliar with old New York cousinships, I had pressed on me, as a treat not likely to have come the way of one of my modest condition, a glass of 'the famous Newbold Madeira'.

My mother, if left to herself, would probably not have been much interested in the pleasures of the table. My father's Dutch blood accounted for his gastronomic enthusiasm; his mother, who was a Schermerhorn, was reputed to have the best cook in New York. But to know about good cooking was a part of every young wife's equipment, and my mother's favourite cookery books (Francatelli's and Mrs Leslie's) are thickly interleaved with sheets of yellowing note paper, on which, in a script of ethereal elegance, she records the making of 'Mrs Joshua Jones's scalloped oysters with cream', 'Aunt Fanny Gallatin's fried chicken', 'William Edgar's punch', and the special recipes of our two famous negro cooks, Mary Johnson and Susan Minneman. These great artists stand out, brilliantly turbaned and ear-ringed, from a Snyders-like background of game, fish and vegetables transformed into a succession of succulent repasts by their indefatigable blue-nailed hands: Mary Johnson, a gaunt towering woman of a rich bronzy black, with huge golden hoops in her ears, and crisp African crinkles under vividly patterned kerchiefs; Susan Minneman, a small smiling mulatto, more quietly attired, but as great a cook as her predecessor.

Ah, what artists they were! How simple yet sure were their methods – the mere perfection of broiling, roasting and basting –

and what an unexampled wealth of material, vegetable and animal, their genius had to draw upon! Who will ever again taste anything in the whole range of gastronomy to equal their corned beef, their boiled turkeys with stewed celery and oyster sauce, their fried chickens, broiled red-heads, corn fritters, stewed tomatoes, rice griddle cakes, strawberry short-cake and vanilla ices? I am now enumerating only our daily fare, that from which even my tender years did not exclude me; but when my parents 'gave a dinner', and terrapin and canvas-back ducks, or (in their season) broiled Spanish mackerel, soft-shelled crabs with a mayonnaise of celery, and peach-fed Virginia hams cooked in champagne (I am no doubt confusing all the seasons in this allegoric evocation of their riches), lima-beans in cream, corn soufflés and salads of oyster-crabs, poured in varied succulence from Mary Johnson's lifted cornucopia – ah, then, the *gourmet* of that long-lost day, when cream was cream and butter butter and coffee coffee, and meat fresh every day, and game hung just for the proper number of hours, might lean back in his chair and murmur 'Fate cannot harm me' over his cup of Moka and his glass of authentic Chartreuse.

I have lingered over these details because they formed a part – a most important and honourable part – of that ancient curriculum of house-keeping which, at least in Anglo-Saxon countries, was so soon to be swept aside by the 'monstrous regiment' of the emancipated: young women taught by their elders to despise the kitchen and the linen room, and to substitute the acquiring of University degrees for the more complex art of civilized living. The movement began when I was young, and now that I am old, and have watched it and noted its results, I mourn more than ever the extinction of the household arts. Cold storage, deplorable as it is, has done far less harm to the home than the Higher Education.

And what of the guests who gathered at my father's table to enjoy the achievements of the Dark Ladies? I remember a mild blur of rosy and white-whiskered gentlemen, of ladies with bare sloping shoulders rising flower-like from voluminous skirts, peeped at from the stair-top while wraps were removed in the hall below. A great sense of leisure emanated from their kindly faces and voices. No motors waited to rush them on to ball or opera; balls were few and widely spaced, the opera just beginning; and 'Opera night' would not have been chosen for one of my mother's big dinners. There being no haste, and a prodigious amount of good food to be disposed of, the guests sat long at table; and when my mother bowed slightly to the lady facing her on my father's right, and flounces and trains floated up the red velvet stair-carpet to the white-and-gold drawing-room with tufted purple satin arm-chairs, and voluminous purple satin curtains festooned with buttercup yellow fringe, the gentlemen settled down again to claret and Madeira, sent duly westward, and followed by coffee and Havana cigars.

My parents' guests ate well, and drank good wine with discernment; but a more fastidious taste had shortened the enormous repasts and deep bumpers of colonial days, and in twenty minutes the whiskered gentlemen had joined the flounced ladies on the purple settees for another half hour of amiable chat, accompanied by the cup of tea which always rounded off the evening. How mild and leisurely it all seems in the glare of our new century! Small parochial concerns no doubt formed the staple of the talk. Art and music and literature were rather timorously avoided (unless Trollope's last novel were touched upon, or a discreet allusion made to Mr William Astor's audacious acquisition of a Bouguereau Venus), and the topics chiefly dwelt on were personal: the thoughtful discussion of food, wine, horses ('high steppers' were beginning to be much sought after), the laying out and planting of country-seats, the selection of 'specimen' copper beeches and fern-leaved maples for lawns just beginning to be shorn smooth by the new hand-mowers, and those plans of European travel which filled so large a space in the thought of old New Yorkers. From my earliest infancy I had always seen about me people who were either just arriving from 'abroad' or just embarking on a European tour. The old New Yorker was in continual contact with the land of his fathers, and it was not until I went to Boston on my marriage that I found myself in a community of wealthy and sedentary people seemingly too lacking in intellectual curiosity to have any desire to see the world.

I have always been perplexed by the incuriosity of New England with regard to the rest of the world, for New Yorkers of my day were never so happy as when they were hurrying on board the ocean liner which was to carry them to new lands. Those whose society my parents frequented did not, perhaps, profit much by the artistic and intellectual advantages of European travel, and to social opportunities they were half-resentfully indifferent. It was thought vulgar and snobbish to try to make the acquaintance, in London, Paris or Rome, of people of the class corresponding to their own. The Americans who forced their way into good society in Europe were said to be those who were shut out from it at home; and the self-respecting American on his travels frequented only the little 'colonies' of his compatriots already settled in the European capitals, and only their most irreproachable members! What these artless travellers chiefly enjoyed were scenery, ruins and historic sites; places about which some sentimental legend hung, and to which Scott, Byron, Hans Andersen, Bulwer, Washington Irving or Hawthorne gently led the timid sight-seer. Public ceremonials also, ecclesiastical or royal, were much appreciated, though of the latter only distant glimpses could be caught, since it would have been snobbish to ask, through one's Legation, for reserved seats or invitations. And as for the American women who had themselves presented at the English Court – well, one had only to see with whom they associated at home!

However, ruins, snow-mountains, lakes and water-falls – especially water-falls – were endlessly enjoyable; and in the great cities there were the shops! In them, as Henry James acutely noted in 'The Pension Beaurepas', the American woman found in-exhaustible consolation for the loneliness and inconveniences of life in foreign lands. But, lest I seem to lay undue stress on the limitations of my compatriots, it must be remembered that, even in more sophisticated societies, cultivated sight-seeing was hardly known in those days. One need only glance through the 'Travels' of the early nineteenth century to see how little, before Ruskin, the average well-educated tourist of any country was prepared to observe and enjoy. The intellectual few, at the end of the eighteenth century, had been taught by Arthur Young to travel with an eye to agriculture and geology; and Goethe, in Sicily, struck Syracuse and Girgenti from his itinerary, and took the monotonous and exhausting route across the middle of the island, in order to see with his own eyes why it had been called the granary of Rome. Meanwhile the simpler majority collected scraps of marble from the Forum, pressed maidenhair fern from the temple of Vesta at Tivoli, or daisies from the grave of Shelley, and bought edelweiss gummed on card-board from the guides of Chamonix, and copies of Guido's 'Aurora' and Caravaggio's 'Gamesters' from the Roman picture-dealers.

At that very time a handsome blue-eyed young man with a

scarred mouth was driving across the continent in his parents' travelling carriage, and looking with wondering eyes at the Giottos of the Arena Chapel and the Cimabues of Assisi; at that time a young architect, poor and unknown, was toiling through the by-ways of Castile, Galicia and Andalusia in jolting *diligences*, or over stony mule-tracks, and recording in a series of exquisite drawings the unknown wonders of Spanish architecture; and Browning was dreaming of 'The Ring and the Book' – and Shelley had long since written 'The Cenci'. But to the average well-to-do traveller Hawthorne's 'Marble Faun', Bulwer's 'Last Days of Pompeii' and Washington Irving's 'Alhambra' were still the last word on Spain and Italy.

3

I have wandered far from my father's library. Though it had the leading share in my growth I have let myself be drawn from it by one scene after another of my parents' life in New York or on their travels. But the library calls me back, and I pause on its threshold, averting my eyes from the monstrous oak mantel supported on the heads of vizored knights, and looking past them at the rows of handsome bindings and familiar names. The library probably did not contain more than seven or eight hundred volumes. My father was a younger son, and my mother had a brother to whom most of the books on her side of the family went. (I remember on my uncle's shelves an unexpurgated Hogarth, splendidly bound in eighteenth century crushed Levant, with which my little cousins and I quite innocently and unharmedly beguiled ourselves.) The library to which I had access contained therefore few inherited books; I remember chiefly, in the warm shabby calf of the period, complete editions of Swift, Sterne, Defoe, the 'Spectator', Shakespeare, Milton, the Percy Reliques – and Hannah More! Most of the other books must have been acquired by my father. Though few they were well-chosen, and the fact that their number was so limited probably helped to fix their contents in my memory. At any rate, long before the passing of years and a succession of deaths brought them back to me, I could at any moment visualize the books contained in those low oak bookcases. My mother, perplexed by the discovery that she had produced an omnivorous reader, and not knowing how to direct

my reading, had perhaps expected the governess to do it for her.
Being an indolent woman, she finally turned the difficulty by
reviving a rule of her own school-room days, and decreeing that I
should never read a novel without asking her permission. I was a
painfully conscientious child and, conforming literally to this
decree, I submitted to her every work of fiction which attracted
my fancy. In order to save further trouble she almost always
refused to let me read it – a fact hardly to be wondered at, since her
own mother had forbidden her to read any of Scott's novels,
except 'Waverley', till after she was married! At all events, of the
many prohibitions imposed on me – most of which, as I look
back, I see little reason to regret – there is none for which I am
more grateful than this, though it extended its rigours even to one
of the works of Charlotte M. Yonge! By denying me the
opportunity of wasting my time over ephemeral rubbish my
mother threw me back on the great classics, and thereby helped to
give my mind a temper which my too-easy studies could not have
produced. I was forbidden to read Whyte Melville, Rhoda
Broughton, 'The Duchess', and all the lesser novelists of the day;
but before me stretched the wide expanse of the classics, English,
French and German, and into that sea of wonders I plunged at
will. Nowadays a reader might see only the *lacunae* of the little
library in which my mind was formed; but, small as it was, it
included most of the essentials. The principal historians were
Plutarch, Macaulay, Prescott, Parkman, Froude, Carlyle,
Lamartine, Thiers; the diaries and letters included Evelyn, Pepys,
White of Selbourne, Cowper, Mme de Sévigné, Fanny Burney,
Moore, the Journals of the Misses Berry; the 'poetical works' (in
addition to several anthologies, such as Knight's 'Half Hours with
the Best Authors' and Lamb's precious selections from the
Elizabethan dramatists) were those of Homer (in Pope's and Lord
Derby's versions), Longfellow's Dante, Milton, Herbert, Pope,
Cowper, Gray, Thomson, Byron, Moore, Scott, Burns,
Wordsworth, Campbell, Coleridge, Shelley (I wonder how or
why?), Longfellow, Mrs Hemans and Mrs Browning – though not
as yet the writer described in one of the anthologies of the period
as 'the husband of Elizabeth Barrett, and himself no mean poet'.
He was to come later, as a present from my sister-in-law, and to be
one of the great Awakeners of my childhood.

Among the French poets were Corneille, Racine, Lafontaine
and Victor Hugo, though, oddly enough, of Lamartine the poet

there was not a page, nor yet of Chénier, Vigny or Musset. Among French prose classics there were, of course, Sainte-Beuve's 'Lundis', bracing fare for a young mind, Sévigné the divinely loitering, Augustin Thierry and Philarète Chasles. Art history and criticism were represented by Lacroix's big volumes, so richly and exquisitely illustrated, on art, architecture and costume in the Middle Ages, by Schliemann's 'Ilias' and 'Troja', by Gwilt's Encyclopaedia of Architecture, by Kugler, Mrs Jameson, P. G. Hamerton, and the Ruskin of 'Modern Painters' and the 'Seven Lamps', together with a volume of 'Selections' (appropriately bound in purple cloth) of all his purplest patches; to which my father, for my benefit, added 'Stones of Venice' and 'Walks in Florence' when we returned to Europe and the too-short days of our joint sight-seeing began.

In philosophy, I recall little but Victor Cousin and Coleridge ('The Friend' and 'Aids to Reflection'); among essayists, besides Addison, there were Lamb and Macaulay; in the way of travel, I remember chiefly Arctic explorations. As for fiction, after the eighteenth century classics, Miss Burney and Scott of course led the list; but, mysteriously enough, Richardson was lacking, save for an abridged version of 'Clarissa Harlowe' (and a masterly performance that abridgement was, as I remember it). No doubt Richardson, with Smollett and Fielding, fell to my uncle's share, and were too much out-of-date to be thought worth replacing. Thus, except for Scott, there was a great gap until one came to Washington Irving, that charming hybrid on whom my parents' thoughts could dwell at ease, because, in spite of the disturbing fact that he 'wrote', he was a gentleman, and a friend of the family. For my parents and their group, though they held literature in great esteem, stood in nervous dread of those who produced it. Washington Irving, Fitz-Greene Halleck and William Dana were the only representatives of the disquieting art who were deemed uncontaminated by it; though Longfellow, they admitted, if a popular poet, was nevertheless a gentleman. As for Herman Melville, a cousin of the Van Rensselaers, and qualified by birth to figure in the best society, he was doubtless excluded from it by his deplorable Bohemianism, for I never heard his name mentioned, or saw one of his books. Banished probably for the same reasons were Poe, that drunken and demoralized Baltimorean, and the brilliant wastrel Fitz James O'Brien, who was still further debased by 'writing for the newspapers'. But worse still perhaps in my parents' eyes was the case of such unhappy persons as Joseph Drake, author of 'The Culprit Fay', balanced between 'fame and infamy' as not quite of the best society, and writing not quite the best poetry. I cannot hope to render the tone in which my mother pronounced the names of such unfortunates, or, on the other hand, that of Mrs Beecher Stowe, who was so 'common' yet so successful. On the whole, my mother doubtless thought, it would be simpler if people one might be exposed to meeting would refrain from meddling with literature.

Considering the stacks of novels which she, my aunts and my grandmother annually devoured, their attitude seems singularly ungrateful; but it was probably prompted by the sort of diffidence which, thank heaven, no psycho-analyst had yet arisen to call a 'complex'. In the eyes of our provincial society authorship was still regarded as something between a black art and a form of manual labour. My father and mother and their friends were only one generation away from Sir Walter Scott, who thought it necessary to drape his literary identity in countless clumsy subterfuges, and almost contemporary with the Brontës, who shrank in agony from being suspected of successful novel-writing. But I am sure the chief element in their reluctance to encounter the literary was an awe-struck dread of the intellectual effort that might be required of them. They were genuinely modest and shy in the presence of any one who wrote or painted. To sing was still a drawing-room accomplishment, and I had two warbling cousins who had studied with the great opera singers; but authors and painters lived in a world unknown and incalculable. In addition to its mental atmosphere, its political and moral ideas might be contaminating, and there was a Kilmeny-touch about those who adventured into it and came back.

Meanwhile, though living authors were so remote, the dead were my most living companions. I was a healthy little girl who loved riding, swimming and romping; yet no children of my own age, and none even among the nearest of my grown-ups, were as close to me as the great voices that spoke to me from books. Whenever I try to recall my childhood it is in his my father's library that it comes to life. I am squatting again on the thick Turkey rug, pulling open one after another the glass doors of the low bookcases, and dragging out book after book in a secret ecstasy of communion. I say 'secret', for I cannot remember ever speaking to any one of these enraptured sessions. The child knows instinctively when it will be understood, and from the first I kept my adventures with books to myself. But perhaps it was not only the 'misunderstood' element, so common in meditative infancy, that kept me from talking of my discoveries. There was in me a secret retreat where I wished no one to intrude, or at least no one whom I had yet encountered. Words and cadences haunted it like song-birds in a magic wood, and I wanted to be able to steal away and listen when they called. When I was about fifteen or sixteen I tried to write an essay on English verse rhythms. I never got beyond the opening paragraph, but that came straight out of my secret wood. It ran: 'No one who cannot feel the enchantment of "Yet once more, O ye laurels, and once more", without knowing even the next line, or having any idea whatever of the context of the poem, has begun to understand the beauty of English poetry.' For the moment that was enough of ecstasy; but I wanted to be always free to steal away to it.

It was obvious that a little girl with such cravings, and to whom the Old Testament, the Apocalypse and the Elizabethan dramatists were open, could not long pine for Whyte Melville or even Rhoda Broughton. Ah, the long music-drunken hours on that library floor, with Isaiah and the Song of Solomon and the Book of Esther, and 'Modern Painters', and Augustin Thierry's Merovingians, and Knight's 'Half Hours', and that rich mine of music, Dana's 'Household Book of Poetry'! Presently kind friends began to endow me with a little library of my own, and I was reading 'Faust' and 'Wilhelm Meister', 'Philip Van Arteveld', 'Men and Women' and 'Dramatis Personæ' in the intervals between 'The Broken Heart' and 'The Duchess of Malfy', 'Phèdre' and 'Andromaque'. And there was one supreme day when, my mother having despairingly asked our old literary adviser, Mr North at Scribner's, 'what she could give the child for her birthday', I woke to find beside my bed Buxton Forman's great editions of Keats and Shelley! Then the gates of the realms of gold swung wide, and from that day to this I don't believe I was ever again, in my inmost self, wholly lonely or unhappy.

By the time I was seventeen, though I had not read every book in my father's library, I had looked into them all. Those I devoured first were the poets and the few literary critics, foremost of course Sainte-Beuve. Ruskin fed me with visions of the Italy for which I had never ceased to pine, and Freeman's delightful 'Subject and

Neighbour Lands of Venice', Mrs Jameson's amiable volumes, and Kugler's 'Handbook of Italian Painting', gave a firmer outline to these visions. But the books which made the strongest impression on me – doubtless because they reached a part of mind that no one had thought of arousing – were two shabby volumes unearthed among my brother's college text-books: an abridgement of Sir William Hamilton's 'History of Philosophy' and a totally forgotten work called 'Coppée's Elements of Logic'. This first introduction to the technique of thinking developed the bony structure about which my vague gelatinous musings could cling and take shape; and Darwin and Pascal, Hamilton and Coppée ranked foremost among my Awakeners.

In a day when youthful innocence was rated so high my mother may be thought to have chosen a singular way of preserving mine when she deprived me of the Victorian novel but made me free of the Old Testament and the Elizabethans. Her plan was certainly not premeditated; but had it been, she could not have shown more insight. Those great pages, those high themes, purged my imagination; and I cannot recall ever trying to puzzle out allusions which in tamer garb might have roused my curiosity. Once, at the house of a little girl friend, rummaging with her through a neglected collection of books which her parents had acquired with the property, and never since looked at, we came upon a small volume which seemed to burst into fiery bloom in our hands.

> Forth, ballad, and take roses in both arms,
>   Even till the top rose touch thee in the throat
> Where the least thornprick harms;
>   And girdled in thy golden singing-coat,
> Come thou before my lady and say this:
>   Borgia, thy gold hair's colour burns in me,
> Thy mouth makes beat my blood in feverish rhymes;
>   Therefore so many as these roses be,
>   Kiss me so many times.

But this, like all the rest, merely enriched the complex music of my strange inner world. I do not mean to defend the sheltered education against the system which expounds physiological mysteries in the nursery; I am not sure which is best. But I am sure that great literature does not excite premature curiosities in normally constituted children; and I can give a comic proof of the fact, for though 'The White Devil', 'Faust' and 'Poems and

Ballads' were among my early story-books, all I knew about adultery (against which we were warned every week in church) was that those who 'committed' it were penalized by having to pay higher fares in travelling: a conclusion arrived at by my once seeing on a ferry-boat the sign: 'Adults 50 cents; children 25 cents'!

This ferment of reading revived my story-telling fever; but now I wanted to write and not to improvise. My first attempt (at the age of eleven) was a novel, which began: ' "Oh, how do you do, Mrs Brown?" said Mrs Tompkins. "If only I had known you were going to call I should have tidied up the drawing-room".' Timorously I submitted this to my mother, and never shall I forget the sudden drop of my creative frenzy when she returned it with the icy comment: 'Drawing-rooms are always tidy.'

This was so crushing to a would-be novelist of manners that it shook me rudely out of my dream of writing fiction, and I took to poetry instead. It was not thought necessary to feed my literary ambitions with foolscap, and for lack of paper I was driven to begging for the wrappings of the parcels delivered at the house. After a while these were regarded as belonging to me, and I always kept a stack in my room. It never occurred to me to fold and cut the big brown sheets, and I used to spread them on the floor and travel over them on my hands and knees, building up long parallel columns of blank verse headed: 'Scene: A Venetian palace', or 'Dramatis Personæ' (which I never knew how to pronounce).

My dear governess, seeing my perplexity over the structure of English verse, gave me a work called 'Quackenbos's Rhetoric', which warned one not to speak of the oyster as a 'succulent bivalve', and pointed out that even Shakespeare nodded when he made Hamlet 'take arms against a sea of troubles'. Mr Quackenbos disposed of the delicate problems of English metric by squeezing them firmly into the classic categories, so that Milton was supposed to have written in 'iambic pentameters', and all superfluous syllables were got rid of (as in the eighteenth century) by elisions and apostrophes. Always respectful of the rules of the game, I tried to cabin my Muse within these bounds, and once when, in a moment of unheard-of audacity, I sent a poem to a newspaper (I think 'The World'), I wrote to the editor apologizing for the fact that my metre was 'irregular', but adding firmly that, though I was only a little girl, I wished this irregularity to be respected, as it was 'intentional'. The editor published the poem, and wrote back politely that he had no objection to irregular metres himself; and thereafter I breathed more freely. My poetic experiments, however, were destined to meet with the same discouragement as my fiction. Having vainly attempted a tragedy in five acts I turned my mind to short lyrics, which I poured out with a lamentable facility. My brother showed some of these to one of his friends, an amiable and cultivated Bostonian named Allen Thorndike Rice, who afterward became the owner and editor of the 'North American Review'. Allen Rice very kindly sent the poems to the aged Longfellow, to whom his mother's family were related; and on the bard's recommendations some of my babblings appeared in the 'Atlantic Monthly'. Happily this experiment was not repeated; and any undue pride I might have felt in it was speedily dashed by my young patron's remarking to me one day: 'You know, writing lyrics won't lead you anywhere. What you want to do is to write an epic. All the great poets have written epics. Homer . . . Milton . . . Byron. Why don't you try your hand at something like "Don Juan"?' This was a hard saying to a dreamy girl of fifteen, and I shrank back into my secret retreat, convinced that I was unfitted to be either a poet or a novelist. I did, indeed, attempt another novel, and carried this one to its close; but it was destined for the private enjoyment of a girl friend, and was never exposed to the garish light of print. It exists to this day, beautifully written out in a thick copy-book, with a title page inscribed 'Fast and Loose', and an epigraph from Owen Meredith's 'Lucile':

> Let Woman beware
> How she plays fast and loose with human despair,
> And the storm in Man's heart.

Title and epigraph were terrifyingly exemplified in the tale, but it closed on a note of mournful resignation, with the words: 'And every year when April comes the violets bloom again on Georgie's grave.'

After this I withdrew to secret communion with the Muse. I continued to cover vast expanses of wrapping paper with prose and verse, but the dream of a literary career, momentarily shadowed forth by one miraculous adventure, soon faded into unreality. How could I ever have supposed I could be an author? I had never even seen one in the flesh!

Chapter Four
Unreluctant Feet

In one of the most famous poems of my first literary protector the Maiden is supposed to arrive with reluctant feet 'where the brook and river meet'. I cannot say that my own feet were thus hampered. I was contented enough with swimming and riding, with my dogs, and my reading and dreaming, but I longed to travel and see new places, and, short of that, was by no means averse to seeing new people, and especially to being regarded as 'grown up'.

I had not long to wait, for when I was seventeen my parents decided that I spent too much time in reading, and that I was to come out a year before the accepted age. The New York mothers of that day usually gave a series of 'coming-out' entertainments for *débutante* daughters, leading off with a huge tea and an expensive ball. My mother thought this absurd. She said her daughter could meet all the people she need know without being advertised by a general entertainment; and as my family kept open house, and as the younger of my two brothers was very popular in society, it was easy enough to launch me in this informal way. I was therefore put into a low-necked bodice of pale green brocade, above a white muslin shirt ruffled with rows and rows of Valenciennes, my hair was piled up on top of my head, some friend of the family sent me a large bouquet of lilies-of-the-valley, and thus adorned I was taken by my parents to a ball at Mrs Morton's, in Fifth Avenue. Houses with ball-rooms were still few in New York: almost the only ones were those of the Astors, the Mortons, the Belmonts and my cousins the Schermerhorns. As a rule, hostesses who wished to give a dance hired the ball-room at Delmonico's restaurant; but my mother would never have consented to my making my first appearance in a public room, so to Mrs Morton's we went. To me the evening was a long cold agony of shyness. All my brother's friends asked me to dance, but I was too much frightened to accept, and cowered beside my mother in speechless misery, unable even to exchange a word with the friendly young men whom I regarded as elder brothers when they lunched and dined at our house.

This shyness, though it long troubled me in general company, soon vanished when I was with my friends. New York society was not at that time divided into water-tight compartments by differences of age. The pleasantest houses were those of a group of young married women who all through the season gave a succession of small dinners, informal Sunday lunches and after-theatre suppers. They were all friendly and welcoming to any young girl 'who could talk', and the great ambition of the *débutante* was to be invited to their houses and treated on an equal footing by them, and by the 'older men' whose attentions were thought so much more flattering than those of callow youths just out of college. This luck befell me, thanks chiefly to my brother Harry's popularity, and invitations poured in after my first sad evening. Like all agreeable societies, ours was small, and the people composing it met almost every day, and always sought each other out in any larger company. Some of the hostesses had drawing-rooms big enough for informal dances, and to be invited to these was the privilege of a half-dozen of the younger girls. A season of opera at the Old Academy of Music was now an established event of the winter, and on Mondays and Fridays we met each other there; Wednesday being, for some obscure tribal reason, the night on which boxes were sent to dull relations and visitors from out of town, while the inner circle disported itself elsewhere. Our society was, in short, a little 'set' with its private catch-words, observances and amusements, and its indifference to anything outside of its charmed circle; and no really entertaining social group has ever been anything else. The ages of the people composing it ranged from eighteen to fifty; but all were young in spirit, mostly good-looking, and full of gaiety and humour. The talk was never intellectual and seldom brilliant, but it was always easy and sometimes witty, and a charming informality had replaced the ceremonious dulness of my parents' day. I doubt if New York society was ever simpler, gayer, or more pleasantly sophisticated, than it was then.

I enjoyed myself thoroughly that winter, and still more so the following summer, when Pencraig was full of merry young people, and the new game of lawn tennis, played on our lawn by young gentlemen in tail coats and young ladies in tight whale-boned dresses, began to supersede the hitherto fashionable archery. Every room in our house was always full in summer, and I remember jolly bathing parties from the floating boat-landing at the foot of the lawn, mackerel-fishing, races in rival 'cat-boats', and an occasional excursion up the bay, or out to sea when the weather was calm enough, on one of the pretty white steam-yachts which were beginning to be the favourite toys of the rich.

On one of these yachting-parties I made an acquaintance which some unlucky chance kept me from renewing. A thin young man with intelligent eyes was brought up and introduced as Cecil Spring-Rice, then, I think, a secretary at the British Legation in Washington. Spring-Rice was already – or became soon after-ward – the friend of several of my most intimate friends, and the affectionate nickname of 'Springy' was as familiar to me as that of one of my own intimates. But, to my loss, we were never to meet again; and I record our single encounter only because his delightful talk so illuminated an otherwise dull afternoon that I have never forgotten the meeting. It also left me in possession of two nearly perfect stories – Spring-Rice was a great story-teller – one of which I never heard from any one else, while the other is usually repeated in a far less effective form. Here they are.

A young physician who was also a student of chemistry, and a dabbler in strange experiments, employed a little orphan boy as assistant. One day he ordered the boy to watch over, and stir without stopping, a certain chemical mixture which was to serve for a very delicate experiment. At the appointed time the chemist came back, and found the mixture successfully blent – but beside it lay the little boy, dead of the poisonous fumes.

The young man, who was very fond of his assistant, was horrified at his death, and in despair at having involuntarily caused it. He could not understand why the fumes should have proved fatal, and wishing to find out, in the interest of science, he performed an autopsy, and discovered that the boy's heart had been transformed into a mysterious jewel, the like of which he had never seen before. The young man had a mistress whom he adored, and full of grief, yet excited by this strange discovery, he brought her the tragic jewel, which was very beautiful, and told her how it had been produced. The lady examined it, and agreed that it was beautiful. 'But,' she added carelessly, 'you must have noticed that I wear no ornaments but earrings. If you want me to wear this jewel, you must get me another one just like it.'

The other story is that of a young man who went to spend a week-end at a big country-house where he had never been before. His train was late, and when he came down the party had already gone in to dinner. He was shown into the dining-room, and his hostess asked him to take the only remaining vacant seat. On one side of him sat a very dull and disagreeable man, on the other one of the most captivating young women he had ever met. Naturally it was to her that he devoted all his attention, and so fascinated was he that he did not even stop to wonder who she was – he simply felt that he and she must always have been friends.

They wandered delightedly from one subject to another, and toward the end of dinner the conversation touched on the supernatural. 'Do you believe in ghosts?' the young lady asked. 'No,' said he with a laugh; 'do you?' 'I am one,' she replied – and suddenly the seat she had occupied was empty. After dinner his hostess apologized for putting him next to an empty chair. 'We expected my dear friend, Mrs —; but just as you arrived we had a telegram announcing her sudden death – and there was not even time to take away her seat.'

The regular afternoon diversion at Newport was a drive. Every day all the elderly ladies, leaning back in victoria or barouche, or the new-fangled *vis-à-vis*, a four-seated carriage with a rumble for the footman, drove down the whole length of Bellevue Avenue, where the most fashionable villas then stood, and around the newly laid-out 'Ocean-Drive', which skirted for several miles the wild rocky region between Narragansett bay and the Atlantic. For this drive it was customary to dress as elegantly as for a race-meeting at Auteuil or Ascot. A brocaded or satin-striped dress, powerfully whale-boned, a small flower-trimmed bonnet tied with a large tulle bow under the chin, a dotted tulle veil and a fringed silk or velvet sunshade, sometimes with a jointed handle of elaborately carved ivory, composed what was thought a suitable toilet for this daily circuit between wilderness and waves.

If these occupations seem to us insufficient to fill a day, it must be remembered that the onerous and endless business of 'calling' took up every spare hour. I can hardly picture a lady of my mother's generation without her card-case in her hand. Calling was then a formidable affair, since many ladies had weekly 'days' from which there was no possible escape, and others cultivated an exasperating habit of being at home on the very afternoon when, according to every reasonable calculation, one might have expected them to be at Polo, or at Mrs Belmont's archery party, or abroad on their own sempiternal card-leaving. By the time I grew up the younger married women had emancipated themselves, and simply drove from house to house depositing their cards, duly turned down in the upper left-hand corner, to the indignation of stay-at-home hostesses, many of whom made their servants keep a list of the callers who 'did not ask', so that these might be struck off the next season's invitation list – a punishment borne by the young and gay with perfect equanimity, as it was only the dull hostesses who inflicted it.

In my mother's day, however, there were no palliatives to calling. The footman had to ask if Mrs So-and-so was at home, and if she was, there ensued a half hour's visit in a cool shaded drawing-room, or on a wide verandah overlooking the sea. As this had to be repeated after every lunch, dinner or ball, and even the young men were not exempt (though they usually got a mother or sister to leave their cards for them), it may be imagined how much those daughters of Danaus, the dowagers leaning back in their victorias, needed the refreshment of a 'turn' around the Ocean Drive in the intervals of their unending labour.

Still more striking than the dowagers' parade was the sight of the young ladies, married or single, who, when they were guests at a Newport villa, expected to be taken for an afternoon drive by the master of the house or one of his sons. The vehicles of the fashionable young men were either dog-carts (drawn by a pair driven tandem) or a high four-wheeled conveyance called a T-cart, which, if I am not mistaken, was drawn by one big stepper; while the older men drove handsome phaetons, with a showy pair, and an impressive groom with folded arms in the rumble.

Carriages, horses, harnesses and grooms were all of the latest and most irreproachable cut, and Bellevue Avenue was a pretty scene when the double line of glittering vehicles and showy horse-flesh paraded between green lawns and scarlet geranium-borders. The dress of the young ladies perched on the precarious height of a dog-cart or phaeton was no less elegant than that of the dowagers; and I remember, one hot summer afternoon, seeing one of the damsels who were staying at Pencraig appear for the drive arrayed in a heavy white silk dress with a broad black satin stripe, and a huge hat wreathed with crimson roses and draped with a green veil against the sun. It is only fair to add that my brother, who helped her to the giddy summit of the T-cart, and climbed to her side while a tiny groom in snowy breeches clung to the bridle of the impatient chestnut – my brother, like all the young gentlemen of his day, was arrayed in a frock-coat, a tall hat and pearl-gray trousers. What wonder that an eager-eyed little girl, watching these stately comings and goings from the verandah of Pencraig, still thought that old Mr Bedlow's Olympian gods and goddesses must have looked like her brother Harry and his lovely companion when they started off for a turn along some supernal Ocean Drive?

2

Such delights faded before what the next autumn brought. During the long eight years since our return from Europe, how often had I said to my father: 'Papa, when are we going back?' and how sadly had I not listened to his answer: 'My dear, whenever we can afford it.' Now, unhappily, his health made it necessary that he should not spend another winter in New York; but the doctors seemed to think that in a warmer climate he might live for years, and, dearly as I loved him, the impending joys of travel were much more vivid to me than any fears for his health.

To my last day I shall never forget how the prospect thrilled me. What were society and dancing and tennis compared to the rapture of seeing again all that, for eight years, my eyes had pined for? A happier pilgrim has never set foot in the November fogs of London; for what I had dimly loved as a child I was now to look on again with grown-up eyes (as I then thought them!).

My governess came with us, and I can still retravel with her every step of our first journey through the National Gallery. It was on that day, the first after our arrival in London, that I discovered my life-long friend, Franciabigio, 'Knight of Malta', with his poignant motto, *Tar ublia chi bien eima*; that day that I fitted the 'Santa Conversazione' of Bellini with the lines which Milton must have meant for it:

> There entertain him all the saints above,
> In solemn troops and sweet societies –

that day that I was first caught in the airy web of Pinturicchio's

weaving Penelope, and swept upward in the serenely circling
heavens of Botticini's Assumption. But it was not only among
pictures that I felt the stir of old associations. The streets, the
houses, the people of the countries I had lived in as a child, met me
with the faces of old friends, and every voice was music. I longed,
of course, to travel, above all to go to Italy; but on my father's
account we had to start almost immediately for the Riviera. My
parents had meant to spend the winter at Nice, but I could not
bear the thought of being pent up in a city when all the
countryside was full of roses and jasmine. I was allowed to go
with my governess to Cannes, then a small colony of villas in leafy
gardens, and there we found a quiet hotel with terraces of flowers,
where I persuaded my parents to establish themselves. My mother
was cheered by discovering in near-by villas two old friends from
Boston, the Countess de Sartiges and the Countess de Bañuelos. In
both familes there were girls a year or two older than myself; and
though my mother would not go out herself she was persuaded to
put me under the care of the Countess de Bañuelos, who took me
everywhere with her own daughters. The small and intimate
society we frequented was made up of French and English
families, mostly connected by old friendship, and some by blood.
Our amusements were simple and informal, as social pleasures
were in those days, and picnics on the shore, or among the red
rocks and pine forests of the Esterel, lawn tennis parties and small
dinners, united the same young people day after day, under the
guardianship of a pleasant group of their elders. The wooded
background of Cannes still descended almost to the shore, and my
amusements were diversified by long country walks with my
governess, and delightful rides through the cork and pine-woods
with Tonita de Bañuelos. I was received with extreme friendliness
into this little circle, which, allowing for the difference in race and
traditions, was so like the one I had left in New York: made up of
kindly and rather frivolous people, to whom my secret dreams
would have been as unintelligible as to my friends at home. I was
very happy among them, however, and twenty-five years later,
when my husband and I went to Paris to spend a winter, those
who remained of the old group welcomed me as affectionately as
though weeks and not years had intervened since our young days
in Cannes.

The following summer we spent at Homburg, then a fashionable but quiet little watering-place with gardens full of roses,

where my mother had been sent for the cure. My father's health, to my eyes at least, seemed neither to improve nor to grow worse; I became accustomed to his patient inactivity, and probably thought of him as old rather than ill. That autumn we went to Venice and Florence, and it must have been then that he gave me 'Stones of Venice' and 'Walks in Florence', and gently lent himself to my whim of following step by step Ruskin's arbitrary itineraries. But probably even this mild sight-seeing was beyond his strength, for I do not recall many walks with him; and by the time we returned to Cannes he had grown distinctly worse, and failed slowly during the winter. He died there in the early spring, suddenly stricken by paralysis; and I am still haunted by the look in his dear blue eyes, which had followed me so tenderly for nineteen years, and now tried to convey the goodbye messages he could not speak. Twice in my life I have been at the death-bed of some one I dearly loved, who has vainly tried to say a last word to me; and I doubt if life holds a subtler anguish.

My mother and I went home to Pencraig. In those days the rules of family mourning were severe, and I went out very little; but in the autumn my mother hired a house in Washington Square, and subsequently bought one in West Twenty-Fifth Street, which she altered and added to. My old friends welcomed me on our return, and there followed two gay but uneventful New York winters. I had never ceased to be a great reader, but had almost forgotten my literary dreams. I could not believe that a girl like myself could ever write anything worth reading, and my friends would certainly have agreed with me. No one in our set had any intellectual interests, though most of the men were better read than the average young American of today. Many of the group, however, were quicker and more amusing than I was, and though I was popular, and enjoyed myself in their company, I never dreamed that I was in any way their superior. Indeed, being much less pretty than many of the girls, and less quick at the up-take than the young men, I might have suffered from an inferiority complex had such ailments been known. But my powers of enjoyment have always been many-sided, and the mere fact of being alive and young and active was so exhilarating that I could seldom spare the time to listen to my inner voices. Yet when they made themselves heard again they had become irresistible.

Chapter Five
Friendships and Travels

At the end of my second winter in New York I was married; and thenceforth my thirst for travel was to be gratified. My husband, whose family came from Virginia, but whose father had married in Boston and settled there, was an intimate friend of my brother's, and had long been an annual visitor at Pencraig. He was thirteen years older than myself, but the difference in age was lessened by his natural youthfulness, his good humour and gaiety, and the fact that he shared my love of animals and out-door life, and was soon to catch my travel-fever. It was not that, either then or later, I was restless, or eager for change for its own sake. My first care was to create a home of my own; and a few months after our marriage my husband and I moved into a little cottage in the grounds of Pencraig, and rearranged it in accordance with our tastes. I was never very happy at Newport. The climate did not agree with me, and I did not care for watering-place mundanities, and always longed for the real country; but the place and the life suited my husband, and in any case we could not have afforded to buy a property of our own. So we settled down at Pencraig Cottage, and for a few years always lived there from June till February; and I was too busy with my little house and garden ever to find the time long. But every year we went abroad in February for four months of travel; and it was then that I really felt alive. Vernon Lee, John Addington Symonds and 'John Inglesant' had been added to my library of Italian travel, and 'Euphorion' and 'The Italian Renaissance' had given me joys I should be ungrateful not to record. Another book, of a totally different kind, figured among my more recent Awakeners; and that was James Fergusson's 'History of Architecture', at that time one of the most stimulating books that could fall into a young student's hands. A generation nourished on learned monographs, monumental histories, and works of reference covering every period of art from

Babylonian prehistory to the present day, would find it hard to believe how few books of the sort, especially on architecture and sculpture, were available in my youth. Fergusson's 'History of Architecture' was an amazing innovation in its day. It shed on my misty haunting sense of the beauty of old buildings the light of historical and technical precision, and cleared and extended my horizon as Hamilton's 'History of Philosophy', and my little old handbook of logic, had done in another way.

Hitherto my best beloved companions had been books, and to leave one out of this record seems like omitting the name of a human friend. But to enumerate even a fraction would turn my tale into a library catalogue, for I never stopped reading, and having new adventures in the realms of gold; and meanwhile the fate which had so long denied me any other intellectual companionship suddenly relented, and gave me a friend.

Books are alive enough to an imagination which knows how to animate them; but living companions are more living still, as I was to discover when I passed for the first time from the somewhat cramping companionship of the kindly set I had grown up in, and the cool solitude of my studies, into the warm glow of a cultivated intelligence. The man to whom I owe this was Egerton Winthrop, an old friend of my family's. He was a direct descendant of Governor Stuyvesant of New York, and John Winthrop, first Colonial Governor of Massachusetts; but he belonged to the branch of the latter family long established in New York. Having married early, and been soon left a widower, he had lived for many years in Paris; but his children were growing up, the time had come for his sons to enter Harvard, and the year of my marriage he returned to New York, where he had built himself a charming house. Besides being an ardent bibliophile he was a discriminating collector of works of art, especially of the eighteenth century, and his house was the first in New York in which an educated taste had replaced stuffy upholstery and rubbishy 'ornaments' with objects of real beauty in a simply designed setting. He delighted to receive his friends, and was one of the most popular hosts in New York. But the more I ponder over our long friendship the more I despair of portraying him; for never, I believe, have an intelligence so distinguished and a character so admirable been combined with interests for the most part so trivial. In spite of his worldly tastes he was subject, with all but his intimates, to fits of shyness which made him appear either stiff or affected; and I always said that when he came to see me nothing was safe in my small drawing-room, for if he found other visitors there he invariably stumbled across a foot-stool, or made straight for any fragile object in his path. Yet this man, so self-conscious and ill at ease with insignificant people, was the most stimulating of talkers in a congenial group. But though he was nervous and preoccupied in the company of the commonplace, and at his best only with people who shared his deeper interests, yet he attached far more importance to his merely mundane relations, and took far more trouble about the finish and perfection of his dinners than about the choice of his guests. The truth is, he was an intensely social being, and to such the New York of the day offered few intellectual resources. As in most provincial societies, the scholars, artists and men of letters shut themselves obstinately away from the people they despised as 'fashionable', and the latter did not know how to make the necessary advances to those who lived outside of their little conventions. It is only in sophisticated societies that the intellectual recognize the uses of the frivolous, and that the frivolous know how to make their houses attractive to their betters.

Though, like Egerton Winthrop, I had always lived among the worldly, I had never been much impressed by them, and he was always pleading with me to fill the part he thought I ought to play in New York, where my husband and I now had the smallest of small houses; but I suspect that he was secretly envious of an indifference to the world of fashion which he was never able to acquire. Though he was nearly twice my age, in this one respect I was his senior, and I think he knew it. But the man who was my friend was so different from the diner-out and ball-giver that I was aware of the latter's existence only when he took me to task for my disregard of society. When we were alone I saw only the lover of books and pictures, the accomplished linguist and eager reader, whose ever-youthful curiosities first taught my mind to analyze and my eyes to see. It was too late for me to acquire the mental discipline I had missed in the schoolroom, but my new friend directed and systematized my reading, and filled some of the worst gaps in my education. Through him I first came to know the great French novelists and the French historians and literary critics of the day; but his chief gift was to introduce me to the wonder-world of nineteenth century science. He it was who gave me Wallace's 'Darwin and Darwinism', and 'The Origin of

Species', and made known to me Huxley, Herbert Spencer, Romanes, Haeckel, Westermarck, and the various popular exponents of the great evolutionary movements. But it is idle to prolong the list, and hopeless to convey to a younger generation the first overwhelming sense of cosmic vastnesses which such 'magic casements' let into our little geocentric universe.

My friendship with Egerton Winthrop was perhaps the happiest I was to know, since it was the least troubled by the perturbations which mar most intimacies. From our first meeting to the last – a period of over thirty years – he was the most perfect of friends. As the years passed, and the difference in our ages made itself felt, the coming of younger friends into my life caused us to be less often together; but, though I knew he suffered from the change, it never lessened his friendly devotion, and to the day of his death we wrote often and fully to each other.

I have dwelt on our long comradeship not only because I want to record my gratitude to so dear a friend, but because, alike in his faults and his qualities, Egerton Winthrop was typical of the American gentleman of his day. The type has vanished with the conditions that produced it; but in my young days New York could show a group of men, such as my old friend Bayard Cutting, Robert Minturn, John Cadwalader, George Rives, Stephen Olin and their like, who, without having Egerton Winthrop's range of interests, combined a cultivated taste with marked social gifts. Their weakness was that, save in a few cases, they made so little use of their abilities. A few were distinguished lawyers or bankers, with busy professional careers, but too many, like Egerton Winthrop, lived in dilettantish leisure. The best class of New Yorkers had shaken off the strange apathy following on the Civil War, and begun to develop a municipal conscience, and all the men I have mentioned were active in administering the new museums, libraries and charities of New York; but the idea that gentlemen could stoop to meddle with politics had hardly begun to make its way, and none of my friends rendered the public services that a more enlightened social system would have exacted of them. In every society there is the room, and the need, for a cultivated leisure class; but from the first the spirit of our institutions has caused us to waste this class instead of using it.

In our little group Egerton Winthrop's was by far the most sensitive intelligence, and it transformed my life to find my vague enthusiasms canalized, my roving curiosities supplied with the food they needed, and a glow of participation reflected back over all my years of solitary reading. But he helped me also in other ways; for though so easily entangled in worldly trifles, he was full of wisdom in serious matters. Sternly exacting toward himself, he was humorously indulgent toward others. Throughout our friendship I found him, in difficult moments, the surest of counsellors; and even now that I am old, and he has been so many years dead, it still happens to me, when faced by a difficulty, to ask myself: 'What would Egerton have done?'

2

My husband, though a Bostonian by birth, was by blood a Virginian, and while he was greatly attached to his Boston friends, he did not care for the place, and had no desire to live there. Like most Bostonians he had travelled very little; but he soon caught my love of the road, though he too cared for travelling only as an occasional change from our quiet months at home.

After several seasons of happy wandering in Italy we both felt the longing to go farther, and one day I happened to say to our old friend James Van Alen: 'I would give everything I own to make a cruise in the Mediterranean!'

I was not prepared for his prompt reply: 'You needn't do that if you'll let me charter a yacht, and come with me.'

At first we took the suggestion as a joke; but when we found that it was made in earnest it began to fascinate our imagination. However, though we were fond of James Van Alen, and grateful for his invitation, we were not disposed to make so long a voyage as his guests, or that of any other friend. In so momentous an adventure we preferred to have our say about the itinerary, the choice of places to be seen (since, alas, it was necessary to choose), and the general arrangements for the trip. We asked Van Alen to calculate exactly how much a four months' cruise would cost, learned that to pay half of the expenses would consume our whole income for the year – and promptly decided to do so!

Loud was the outcry in our respective families. My brothers, who were my trustees under my father's will, asked, not unnaturally, what we proposed to live on for the rest of the year – and there was no answer! But the most indignant protests came from my husband's family. In Boston married couples, after a brief honeymoon abroad, were expected to divide the rest of their lives between Boston in winter and its suburbs, or the neighbouring sea-shore, in summer; and it was told of an old Mr Russell that on driving away from the church on his wedding day he remarked to his bride, perhaps rather wistfully: 'And now, my dear, there is nothing before us but Mount Auburn' (the family cemetery). For the Bostonians have never been backward in satirizing their own peculiarities.

But, of all mad schemes, our families protested, why a cruise in the Mediterranean? Who had ever before heard of such an idea? Though there were many American yacht owners with swift and beautiful craft, they cruised mainly in home waters, or if they crossed the Atlantic, did so not for sight-seeing but to try their luck in international racing. Such a voyage as we planned was almost unheard of, and in any case only a fad for the wealthy. I was more impressed than my husband by these arguments. I had been taught to treat my brothers, who were so much older than myself, with filial deference, and it seemed a sacrilege to go against their judgment and my mother's. We could not raise a loan, since my property was in trust, and my husband had only a small allowance from his father. In those days it was thought dishonourable to take financial risks one might be unable to meet; and how were we to live for the rest of the year, since neither of us could have earned a penny? But my husband said: 'Do you really want to go? And when I nodded, he rejoined: 'All right. Come along, then.' And we went.

Those four months in the Ægean were the greatest step forward in my making. I shall not enlarge here on the wonders of the cruise, or expatiate on the inexhaustible memories it left with me; but I must add, in justification of our families' astonishment at our adventure, that we met hardly any pleasure craft (and, except in the big ports, no passenger steamers), and that at Astypalæa, one of the islands we visited, the parish priest, the mayor and all the inhabitants came out on the Venetian ramparts in solemn procession to receive us, explaining that it was a great day for the island, as no steamer had ever before touched there, and many of the islanders had never seen one in the distance!

I must also say a word of our travelling companion, who not only took on himself all the trouble of chartering and provisioning our delightful little yacht, the 'Vanadis', but, although he did not altogether share my archæological ardours, bore with them with unvarying good-nature, allowing me the necessary time, between Girgenti and Sunium, to see all but the most inaccessible Greek temples, and to explore nearly every one of the then little visited Ægean islands.

James Van Alen had travelled all over the Peloponnesus in his youth, and to my imagination he was a living link with the old trackless dangerous Greece of Byron's day, for he had been invited to join the ill-fated party of Englishmen who were seized by brigands near Athens early in the 'seventies, and of whom only one (Lord Muncaster) escaped alive. Van Alen had accepted the invitation, but at the last moment an attack of malaria had prevented his going. Those perilous days were over; but at the time of our cruise their memory was still preserved in the current edition of Murray's Guide, and when one day, being driven by a gale into the gulf of Maïna (formerly one of the most dangerous regions in Greece) we consulted that invaluable work to see if the village frowning on the cliff above were worth visiting, we were rewarded by the following information: 'The Maïnotes are a brave, generous and hospitable race, but much given to acts of treachery, piracy, wreckage, robbery and murder.' The day was hot, the path was steep – and we decided to stay on the yacht.

My husband and I were so lost in enjoyment that neither of us gave a thought to the unsolved financial problem awaiting us at the end of the cruise. Only twice in my life have I been able to put all practical cares out of my mind for months, and each time it has been on a voyage in the Ægean. We reached Athens only toward the end of the cruise, and among the letters which awaited us was one telling me that a little dog we had left in America was dead, and another announcing the demise of a cousin of my father's, an old gentleman I had never seen, and hardly knew by name. This excellent man had lived all his life in one room in the old New York Hotel, and gone without a fire in winter to save money; and this enabled him to divide among his many cousins a fortune enormously increased by his privations – proving (as my sister-in-law remarked) that what we had always regarded as miserliness was only a wise economy! My share was more than enough to pay for our taste of heaven; but my husband complained that in my grief for the dog I forgot to be grateful to my cousin. It was in fact some time before I grasped my good luck, and when my gratitude woke it took, as often happens, the form of doing exactly what my benefactor would most have reproved. He had been a miser, and he nearly turned me into a spendthrift! At any rate he taught me that never again, when I had the chance to do something difficult and wonderful, must I hesitate to trust to my star – the only condition being that the risk should not be run for anything not really worth it.

Acting on this conviction we threw our families into fresh alarms by deciding, a year or two later, to charter a sailing vessel, head for the West Indies, pick up the trades for the Canaries, and thence, by way of the Azores, make for Portugal and Spain. The schooner was chosen, the charter drawn up – and what a glorious adventure it would have been! But, alas, it was not to come off, for there was cholera at the Canaries or the Azores, and we were warned that quarantine difficulties would waylay us everywhere. Our families drew a breath of relief – but we never ceased to regret our lost adventure.

Our Mediterranean cruise took place in 1888; but, owing to my not having kept a diary, I find it impossible to disentangle the chronology of our travels in Italy. We used to go there every spring, and each year we explored some new and relatively unfamiliar region, choosing in preference places which offered examples of seventeenth and eighteenth century architecture. A trifling incident had given this turn to my studies. Not long after our marriage, my husband asked his old friend Julian Story, who had a studio in Paris, to paint my portrait. I was sitting to him one day – restless, and desperately bored, for I saw the picture was going to be a failure – when my eye lit on an arm-chair, the most artlessly simple and graceful arm-chair I had ever seen. I knew a little about French eighteenth century furniture, and saw at once that this chair was different: less skilful in execution, yet freer and more individual in movement. I asked where it came from, and Story answered: 'Oh, eighteenth century Venetian. It's a pity no one knows or cares anything about eighteenth century Italian furniture or architecture. In fact everybody behaves – the historians as well as the art critics – as if Italy had ceased to exist at the end of the Renaissance.'

The words struck my imagination, for though I had read Vernon Lee's enchanting 'Eighteenth Century in Italy,' and soon afterwards was to discover Gurlitt's excellent 'Barockstil in Italien', I knew it was true in the main that, to the traveller of average reading, the eighteenth century seemed at that time to belong as exclusively to France as the Cinque Cento to Italy. The new turn thus given to my curiosity made us devote our subsequent holidays to the study of eighteenth century painting and architecture in Italy. In these pleasant explorations Egerton Winthrop was our constant companion, and among comrades of the road I have known few as responsive to beauty, as patient over disappointment and discomforts. Among many good wanderings I remember especially our drive one spring from Florence to Urbino and the Adriatic, by way of San Marino, San Leo, Loreto, Ancona, Pesaro and Rimini. Nowadays it is a quick motor-jaunt over smooth roads leading to comfortable inns, but forty years ago it was a toilsome expedition, in a heavy carriage drawn by tired horses, a journey full of the enchantments of discovery but also of fatigue and discomfort, since the well-organized travel of coaching days was over, and the inns off the direct railway routes had been almost abandoned.

I was not always patient under such discomfort. Once, in a now defunct hotel at Parma, where the conditions below stairs were so unappetizing that we persuaded the waiter to serve our dinner in Egerton's bedroom, I may have grumbled a little more than usual, for I remember his saying with gentle irony: 'My dear, no doubt your standards of cleanliness are higher than this hotel-keeper's; but I daresay the Princess of Wales [Queen Alexandra] would not consider your toilet appointments good enough for her; and the angels may think even Her Royal Highness insufficiently clean.' Another day, when my irresistible tendency to improve and organize led me, in some forlorn French hotel, to remark on the slovenly incompetence of the waiter, my old friend observed: 'If the poor man were as intelligent as he would have to be to please you, he wouldn't be a waiter in this inn, but President of the French Republic.'

Sometimes the Paul Bourgets were our companions on these wanderings. Bourget, soon after his marriage (about 1893, I think) had been commissioned by Gordon Bennett to write for the New York 'Herald' the series of articles on the United States subsequently collected in the volume called 'Outremer'. The preparation for this book sent him and his young wife to America, and a friend in Paris gave them a letter for me. Bourget had been specially instructed to do his 'fashionable watering place' article at Newport, and as soon as he and his wife arrived they came to lunch, and that day our long friendship began, a friendship as close with the brilliant and stimulating husband as with his quiet and exquisite companion. I shall never forget Minnie Bourget as I first saw her, with her little aquiline nose, her grave remote gray eyes and sensitive mouth, in the delicate oval of a small face crowned by heavy braids of brown hair. I used to call her the 'Tanagra Madonna', so curiously did that little head combine the gravity of a mediaeval Virgin with the miniature elegance of a Greek figurine. Everything about her was shy, elusive and somehow personal to herself. I have never known any one like her, and can hardly imagine any one more unlike myself; yet from our very first meeting a deep-down understanding established itself between us.

When my husband and I first joined the Bourgets for an Italian tour, Bourget had already published his 'Sensations d'Italie', and was still much interested in the art of mediaeval and Renaissance Italy; but perhaps his wife was more sensitive to the minor magic of scenes and places, the little unnoted exquisitenesses that waylaid one at every turn of the paths we followed. Minnie Bourget was a being so rare, so full of delicate and secret vibrations, yet so convinced that she had been put on earth only to be her husband's attentive shadow, that I never knew by what happy accident I penetrated what might be called her voluntary invisibility, and found myself made free of her real self. But so it was; and from our first acquaintance to the day when her last tragic illness shut her finally into the seclusion she had always sought, I never knocked at that gate in vain. We disagreed on many subjects, and she could never tolerate any discussion of a point which her convictions made sacred; but we agreed so deeply on essentials that the disagreements did not matter. I am not sure what it was that united us – perhaps poetry, perhaps pictures, and old storied scenes, and yet something deeper and more exquisite, of which the visible beauty we loved was merely a fugitive token. But I find no words delicate and imponderable enough to describe the Psyche-like tremor of those folded but never quiet wings of hers; and now that she is dead, and the wings are shut, there is a part of me which is dead also.

One enchanting journey, which I afterward sketched in a book called 'Italian Backgrounds', carried us to the hills of northern Italy. I had always maintained that in the choice of an itinerary one should be guided by the sound of names, and that in doing so I had never been disappointed. Just then I was under the spell of the phrase 'the Bergamasque Alps' (perhaps because of a recent encounter with Verlaine), and I persuaded the Bourgets to make an excursion through this mysterious region. It led us, of course, away from the railways, so we hired (for the last time, probably) an old-time travelling carriage, and my husband went ahead as *éclaireur* on his bicycle, engaging rooms and ordering dinner for the rest of the party. The excursion was full of delight, and it was only after it was over, and I returned to the study of my maps, that I found we had only skirted the magic region of 'Masques et Bergamasques', instead of travelling through it. But its magic had overflowed on us, and though we agreed to make the real trip another year, we never dared, lest it should turn out to be less perfect.

All this was soon to result in the writing of my first novel, 'The Valley of Decision', and a few years later in my 'Italian Villas and Their Gardens', and 'Italian Backgrounds'. But before reaching this stage of my literary life I must turn back and take it up at its odd and unexpected beginning.

3

Thanks to my late cousin's testamentary discernment my husband and I had been able to buy a home of our own at Newport. It was an ugly wooden house with half an acre of rock and illimitable miles of Atlantic Ocean; for, as its name, 'Land's End', denoted, it stood on the edge of Rhode Island's easternmost cliffs, and our windows looked straight across to the west coast of Ireland. I disliked the relaxing and depressing climate, and the vapid watering-place amusements in which the days were wasted; but I loved Land's End, with its windows framing the endlessly changing moods of the misty Atlantic, and the night-long sound of the surges against the cliffs.

The outside of the house was incurably ugly, but we helped it to a certain dignity by laying out a circular court with high hedges and trellis-work niches (the whole promptly done away with by our successors!); and within doors there were interesting possibilities. My husband and I talked them over with a clever young Boston architect, Ogden Codman, and we asked him to alter and decorate the house — a somewhat new departure, since the architects of that day looked down on house-decoration as a branch of dress-making, and left the field to the upholsterers, who crammed every room with curtains, lambrequins, jardinières of artificial plants, wobbly velvet-covered tables littered with silver gew-gaws, and festoons of lace on mantelpieces and dressing-tables.

Codman shared my dislike of these sumptuary excesses, and thought as I did that interior decoration should be simple and architectural; and finding that we had the same views we drifted, I hardly know how, toward the notion of putting them into a book.

We went into every detail of our argument: the idea, novel at the time though now self-evident, that the interior of a house is as much a part of its organic structure as the outside, and that its treatment ought, in the same measure, to be based on right proportion, balance of door and window spacing, and simple unconfused lines. We developed this argument logically, and I think forcibly, and then sat down to write the book – only to discover that neither of us knew how to write! This was excusable in an architect, whose business it was to build in bricks, not words, but deeply discouraging to a young woman who had in her desk a large collection of blank verse dramas and manuscript fiction. Happily I had the saving sense to know that I didn't know – that I literally could not write out in simple and precise English the ideas which seemed so clear in my mind.

The year before my marriage I had made friends with a young man named Walter Berry, the son of an old friend of my family's (and indeed a distant cousin). We had seen a great deal of each other for a few weeks, and the encounter had given me a fleeting hint of what the communion of kindred intelligence might be. But chance separated us, and we were not to meet again, but for intermittent glimpses, till he happened to come and stay with us at Land's End the very summer that Codman and I were struggling with our book. Walter Berry was born with an exceptionally sensitive literary instinct, but also with a critical sense so far outweighing his creative gift that he had early renounced the idea of writing. But though he was already a hard-working young lawyer, with a promising future at the bar, the service of letters was still his joy in his moments of leisure. I remember shyly asking him to look at my lumpy pages; and I remember his first shout of laughter (for he never flattered or pretended), and then his saying good-naturedly: 'Come, let's see what can be done', and settling down beside me to try to model the lump into a book.

In a few weeks the modelling was done, and in those weeks, as I afterward discovered, I had been taught whatever I know about the writing of clear concise English. The book was re-read by my friend, and found fit for publication; and we proceeded to seek a publisher.

Neither Codman nor I knew any of these formidable people, but my sister-in-law had her entry at Macmillan's, and she offered to submit the manuscript to them. It was promptly rejected, with the brief comment that the architect to whom they had shown it (simply to oblige my sister-in-law) had received it with cries of derision. Nobody was likely to buy an amateur work on house-decoration by two totally unknown writers, and they advised her not to continue her friendly efforts. This was a blow. To whom should we turn?

The previous year a small literary adventure of my own had introduced me to 'Scribner's Magazine'. I had suddenly taken to writing poetry again, and one day I decided to send three of my poems to three of the leading magazines of the day: 'Scribner's', 'Harper's' and the 'Century'. I can remember only one of these poems, the longest, called 'The Last Giustiniani', which I chanced to send to 'Scribner's'. I did not know how authors communicated with editors, but I copied out the verses in my fairest hand, and enclosed each in an envelope with my visiting card! A week or two elapsed, and then I received the three answers, telling me that all three poems had been accepted. We had a little house in Madison Avenue that winter (it was our first trial of New York), and as long as I live I shall never forget my sensations when I opened the first of the three letters, and learned that I was to appear in print. I can still see the narrow hall, the letter-box out of which I fished the letters, and the flight of stairs up and down which I ran, senselessly and incessantly, in the attempt to give my excitement some muscular outlet!

The letter accepting 'The Last Giustiani' was written by Edward Burlingame, editor of 'Scribner's Magazine', who became one of my most helpful guides in the world of letters. He not only accepted my verses, but (oh, rapture!) wanted to know what else I had written; and this encouraged me to go to see him, and laid the foundation of a friendship which lasted till his death. It was naturally to him that I turned after Macmillan's rejection of 'The Decoration of Houses'; but I did so with little hope, since I knew he was not connected with the publishing departments of the firm, and in any case there was little chance of the Scribners' being interested in a book of so technical a character, and one already rejected by the Macmillans. However, I took the manuscript to Mr Burlingame, he passed it on to the publishing department, where it fell into the hands of another dear friend-to-be, William Brownell – and after some hesitation it was accepted, chiefly, I suspect because Mr Burlingame and Mr Brownell liked my poetry.

The Scribners brought out a very small and tentative edition, produced with great typographical care, probably thinking that the book was more likely to succeed as a gift book among my personal friends than as a practical manual. But the first edition was sold out at once; Batsford immediately asked for the book for England; and from that day to this it has gone on from edition to edition, and still, after nearly forty years, brings in an annual tribute to its astonished authors!

Our success was not unmerited. Codman had been at great pains to cite suitable instances in support of his principles, and revolutionary as these were, we found that people of taste were only too eager to follow any guidance that would not only free them from the suffocating upholsterer, but tell them how to replace him. It became the fashion to use our volume as a touchstone of taste, and I was often taxed by my friends with not applying to the arrangement of my own rooms the rigorous rules laid down in 'The Decoration of Houses'. The popularity of the work may be judged by the fact that, a good many years later, after I had published 'The House of Mirth' and several other novels, an enthusiastic lady one day sailed up to me to say: 'I'm so glad to meet you at last, because Ogden Codman is such an old friend of mine that I've read every one of the wonderful novels he and you have written together!'

Chapter Six
Life and Letters

I

The doing of 'The Decoration of Houses' amused me very much, but can hardly be regarded as a part of my literary career. That began with the publishing, in 'Scribner's Magazine', of two or three short stories. The first was called 'Mrs Manstey's View', the second 'The Fulness of Life'. Both attracted attention, and gave me the pleasant flutter incidental to first seeing one's self in print; but they brought me no nearer to other workers in the same field. I continued to live my old life, for my husband was as fond of society as ever, and I knew of no other existence, except in our annual escapes to Italy. I had as yet no real personality of my own, and was not to acquire one till my first volume of short stories was published – and that was not until 1899. This volume, called 'The Greater Inclination', contained none of my earliest tales, all of which I had rejected as not worth reprinting. I had gone on working hard at the *nouvelle* form, and the stories making up my first volume were chosen after protracted consultation with Walter Berry, the friend who had shown me how to put 'The Decoration of Houses' into shape. From that day until his death, twenty-seven years later, through all his busy professional life, he followed each of my literary steps with the same patient interest, and I doubt if a beginner in the art ever had a sterner yet more stimulating guide.

And now the incredible had happened! Out of the Pelion and Ossa of slowly accumulating manuscripts, plays, novels and dramas, had blossomed a little volume of stories – stories which editors had wanted for their magazines, and a publisher now actually wanted for a volume! I had been astonished enough to see the stories in print, but the idea that they might in the course of time be collected in a book never occurred to me till Mr Brownell transmitted the Scribner proposal.

I had written short stories that were thought worthy of

preservation! Was it the same insignificant *I* that I had always known? Any one walking along the streets might go into any bookshop, and say: 'Please give me Edith Wharton's book', and the clerk, without bursting into incredulous laughter, would produce it, and be paid for it, and the purchaser would walk home with it and read it, and talk of it, and pass it on to other people to read! The whole business seemed too unreal to be anything but a practical joke played on me by some occult humourist; and my friends could not have been more astonished and incredulous than I was. I opened the first notices of the book with trembling hands and a suffocated heart. What I had done was actually thought important enough to be not only printed but reviewed! With a sense of mingled guilt and self-satisfaction I glanced at one article after another. They were unbelievably kind, but for the most part their praise only humbled me; and often I found it bewildering. But at length I came on a notice which suddenly stiffened my limp spine. 'When Mrs Wharton,' the condescending critic wrote, 'has learned the rudiments of her art, she will know that a short story should always begin with dialogue.'

'*Always*'? I rubbed my eyes. Here was a professional critic who seemed to think that works of art should be produced by rule of thumb, that there could be a fixed formula for the design of every short story ever written or to be written! Even I already knew that this was ridiculous. I had never consciously formulated the principles of my craft, but during my years of experimenting I had pondered on them deeply, and this egregious commentary did me the immense service of giving my ponderings an axiomatic form. Every short story, I now saw, like every other work of art, contains within itself the germ of its own particular form and dimensions, and *ab ovo* is the artist's only rule. In an instant I was free forever from the bogey of the omniscient reviewer, and though I was always interested in what was said of my books, and sometimes (though rarely) helped by the comments of the professional critics, never did they influence me against my judgment, or deflect me by a hair's-breadth from what I knew to be 'the real right' way.

In this I was much helped by Walter Berry. No critic was ever severer, but none had more respect for the artist's liberty. He taught me never to be satisfied with my own work, but never to let my inward conviction as to the rightness of anything I had done be affected by outside opinion. I remember, after writing the first chapters of 'The Valley of Decision', which I had begun in a burst of lyric rapture and didn't know how to go on with, confessing to him my difficulty and my discouragement. He looked through what I had written, handed it back, and said simply: 'Don't worry about how you're to go on. Just write down everything you feel like telling.' The advice freed me once for all from the incubus of an artificially pre-designed plan, and sent me rushing ahead with my tale, letting each incident create the next, and keeping in sight only the novelist's essential sign-post; the inner significance of the 'case' selected. Yet when the novel was done, I remember how meticulously he studied it from the point of view of language, marking down faulty syntax and false metaphors, smiling away over-emphasis and unnecessary repetitions, helping me patiently through the beginner's verbal perplexities, yet never laying hands on what he considered sacred: the *soul* of the novel, which is (or should be) the writer's own soul.

I suppose there is one friend in the life of each of us who seems not a separate person, however dear and beloved, but an expansion, an interpretation, of one's self, the very meaning of one's soul. Such a friend I found in Walter Berry, and though the chances of life then separated us, and later his successful professional career, first in Washington, afterward as one of the Judges of the International Tribunal in Cairo, for long years put frequent intervals between our meetings, yet whenever we did meet the same deep understanding drew us together. That understanding lasted as long as my friend lived; and no words can say, because such things are unsayable, how the influence of his thought, his character, his deepest personality, were interwoven with mine.

He alone not only encouraged me to write, as others had already done, but had the patience and the intelligence to teach me how. Others praised, some flattered – he alone took the trouble to analyze and criticize. The instinct to write had always been there; it was he who drew it forth, shaped it and set it free. From my first volume of short stories to 'Twilight Sleep', the novel I published just before his death, nothing in my work escaped him, no detail was too trifling to be examined and discussed, gently ridiculed or quietly praised. He never overlooked a defect, and there were times when his silence had the weight of a page of censure; yet I never remember to have been disheartened by it, for he had so deep a respect for the artist's liberty that he never sought to restrict my imagination or to check its flight. His invariable rule, though he prized above all things concision and austerity, was to encourage me to write as my own instinct impelled me; and it was only after the story or the book was done that we set out together on the 'adjective hunts' from which we often brought back such heavy bags.

Once I had found my footing and had my material in hand, his criticisms became increasingly searching. With each book he exacted a higher standard in economy of expression, in purity of language, in the avoidance of the hackneyed and the precious. Sometimes I was not able to show him a novel before publication, and in that case he confined himself to friendly generalities, often helping me to avoid, in my next book, the faults he gently hinted at. When he could follow my work in manuscript he left no detail unnoticed; but though I sometimes caught a faint smile over a situation which he did not see from my angle, or a point of view he did not share, his only care was to help me do better whatever I had set out to do.

But perhaps our long, our ever-recurring talks about the masters of fiction, helped me even more than his advice. I had never known any one so instantly and unerringly moved by all that was finest in literature. His praise of great work was like a trumpet-call. I never heard it without discovering new beauties in the work he praised; he was one of those commentators who unseal one's eyes. I remember his once saying to me, when I was very young: 'It is easy to see superficial resemblances between things. It takes a first-rate mind to perceive the differences underneath.' Nothing has ever sharpened my own critical sense as much as that.

The comrade that he was to me in my work, he was also in the enjoyment of all things beautiful, stirring and exalting. He was tireless in his appreciation of beauty – beauty of architecture, of painting, of landscape. Whatever I saw with him, in the many lands we wandered through, I saw with a keenness doubled by his, and studied afterward with an ardour with which his always kept pace. To the end, through prolonged ill-health and the bitter consciousness of failing powers, his soul still struggled out to beauty; and I remember that, summoned to him at the first attack of his fatal illness, I found him lying speechless, motionless and barely able to look up, but yet able to whisper, as he recognized me: 'Bamberg – in the hall'. After a moment's bewilderment I guessed that he must be speaking of a new book – there was not a day when they did not pour in to his admirably chosen and ever-growing library; and going out into the hall I found a newly published quarto on the sculptures of Bamberg cathedral, which he had received only the day before. I brought it to him, and as I sat beside him with the open volume he whispered one by one the names of the most beautiful statues, and signed to me to hold the book up so that he could see them.

During his arduous professional life we had met only at long intervals; but when ill-health obliged him to resign from the International Tribunal of Cairo he came to live in Paris, and after that we were more often together. During all his working years, frequently interrupted by months of serious illness, he had managed to find time to read my manuscripts and send me long letters of criticism and encouragement; but from the time when he came to Paris, where I was then living, he was able to follow my work more closely, and his reading of each chapter as it was written, and the listening to his comments as he read, gave fresh life to my writing.

Another joy was the discovering of the newest and most worth while books, and the talking them over together. He was a good linguist, and one of the most insatiable readers I have ever known; in science, history, biography, travels, archæological explorations, and the newest books on art and letters, little of real value escaped him. But best of all (when he could be induced to do it) was his reading of poetry; a reading wholly different from Henry James's, a thing apart, and unforgettable, more reticent, less emphatic, yet equally sensitive and moving.

I cannot picture what the life of the spirit would have been to me without him. He found me when my mind and soul were hungry and thirsty, and he fed them till our last hour together. It is such comradeships, made of seeing and dreaming, and thinking and laughing together, that make one feel that for those who have shared them there can be no parting.

But I must return to 'The Greater Inclination', and to my discovery of that soul of mine which the publication of my first volume called to life. At last I had groped my way through to my vocation, and thereafter I never questioned that story-telling was my job, though I doubted whether I should be able to cross the chasm which separated the *nouvelle* from the novel. Meanwhile I felt like some homeless waif who, after trying for years to take out naturalization papers, and being rejected by every country, has finally acquired a nationality. The Land of Letters was henceforth to be my country, and I gloried in my new citizenship.

I remember once saying that I was a failure in Boston (where we used to go to stay with my husband's family) because they thought I was too fashionable to be intelligent, and a failure in New York because they were afraid I was too intelligent to be fashionable. An amusing instance of this point of view happened not long after my first book had come out – at a moment, that is, when I probably seemed to my New York friends at once more formidable and less 'smart' than before I had appeared in print. I met a girl friend, herself the epitome of all 'smartness', who told me that one of New York's most fashionable hostesses had, rather apologetically, invited her to dine 'with a few people who write'. 'It will be rather Bohemian, I'm afraid,' the inviter added, 'but they say one ought to see something of those people. I hope you won't mind coming to help me out?' My young friend, who knew something of Paris and London society, was delighted at an innovation which promised to take us out of the New York rut, and so was I, for it chanced that I had been invited for the same evening. 'Oh, what fun! Who do you suppose they'll be?' I exulted, racking my brains to guess how our hostess, who was my cousin, could have made the acquaintance of the very people I was still vainly longing to know. The evening came, we assembled in the ornate drawing-room (one of those from which 'The Decoration of Houses' had not cleared a single gewgaw!) and I discovered that the Bohemians were my old friend Eliot Gregory, most popular of New York diners-out (but who had the audacity to write an occasional article in a review or daily paper), George Smalley, the New York correspondent of the London 'Times' – and myself! To emphasize our common peculiarity we were seated together, slightly below the salt, while up and down the rest of the long table the tiara-ed heads and bulging white waistcoats of the most accredited millionaires glittered between gold plate and orchids. Such was Fifth Avenue's first glimpse of Bohemia, as personified by myself and two old friends!

I have often wondered, in looking back at the slow stammering beginnings of my literary life, whether or not it is a good thing for the creative artist to grow up in an atmosphere where the arts are simply non-existent. Violent opposition might be a stimulus – but was it helpful or the reverse to have every aspiration ignored, or looked at askance? I have thought over this many times, as I have over most problems of creative art, in the fascinating but probably idle attempt to discover *how it is all done*, and exactly what happens at that 'fine point of the soul' where the creative act, like the mystic's union with the Unknowable, really seems to take place. And as I have grown older my point of view has necessarily changed, since I have seen more and more would-be creators, whether in painting, music or letters, whose way has been made smooth from the cradle, geniuses whose families were prostrate before them before they had written a line or composed a measure, and who, in middle age, still sat in ineffectual ecstasy before the blank page or the empty canvas; while, on the other hand, more and more of the baffled, the derided or the ignored have fought their way to achievement. The conclusion is that I am no believer in pampered vocations, and that Schopenhauer's *Was Einer ist* seems to me the gist of the matter. But as regards a case like my own, where a development no doubt naturally slow was certainly retarded by the indifference of every one about me, it is hard to say whether or no I was really hindered. I am inclined to think the drawbacks were outweighed by the advantages; chief among these being the fact that I escaped all premature flattery, all local celebrity, that I had to fight my way to expression through a thick fog of indifference, if not of tacit disapproval, and that when at last I met one or two kindred minds their criticisms were to me as sharp and searching as if they had been professionals in the exercise of their calling. Fortunately the fact that they were personal friends did not affect their judgment, and my craft was held in such small account in the only world I knew that I was always able to take the severest criticism without undue sensitiveness, and not unusually to profit by it. The criticism I have in mind is that given in the course of private talk, and not imparted by the reviews. I have no quarrel with the professional critics, who have often praised me beyond my merits; but the man who has to review fifty books a week, often on a great variety of subjects, can hardly deal as satisfactorily with any one of them as the friend talking over a book with a friend, and I have always found this kind of comment the most helpful.

2

The publishing of 'The Greater Inclination' broke the chains which had held me so long in a kind of torpor. For nearly twelve years I had tried to adjust myself to the life I had led since my marriage; but now I was overmastered by the longing to meet people who shared my interests. I had found two delightful friends, who had helped to educate me and to widen my interests; but one was a busy lawyer who did not live in New York, and who, as his practice grew, had less and less leisure; while the other, a man many years older than myself, and of very worldly tastes, could not understand my longing to break away from the world of fashion and be with my own spiritual kin. What I wanted above all was to get to know other writers, to be welcomed among people who lived for the things I had always secretly lived for. I knew only one novelist, Paul Bourget, one of the most stimulating and cultivated intelligences I have ever met, and perhaps the most brilliant talker I have known; but we saw each other for only two or three weeks in the year, and he too was always rebuking me for my apathy in continuing a life of wearisome frivolity, and telling me that at the formative stage of my career I ought to be with people who were thinking and creating. Egerton Winthrop was too generous not to come round also to this view, and in the end it was he who urged my husband to go to London with me for a few weeks every year, so that I might at least meet a few men of letters, and have a taste of an old society in which the various elements had been fused for generations.

These arguments prevailed, and we went to London the year that 'The Greater Inclination' appeared. Shortly after our arrival a friend gave me the address of James Bain, the well-known bookseller, and one day I dropped in at his shop to ask what interesting new books there were. In reply Mr Bain handed me my own little volume, with the remark: 'This is what everybody in London is talking about just now.' As Mr Bain had no idea who I was, his astonishment on learning my identity was as great as mine when he tried to sell me my own first-born as the book of the day! I should have enjoyed intensely following up this first glimpse of success; but my husband was bored in London, where he would have been amused only among the sporting set, while I wanted to know the writers. It is always depressing to live with the dissatisfied, and my powers of enjoyment are so varied that when I was young I did not find it hard to adapt myself to the preferences of any one I was fond of. The people about me were so indifferent to everything I really cared for that complying with the tastes of others had become a habit, and it was only some years later, when I had written several books, that I finally rebelled, and pleaded for the right to something better. Meanwhile we soon left London to take up again the Italian wanderings which we both enjoyed, and out of which, in 1904, 'The Valley of Decision' was to grow.

Before this happened, another change had come. We sold our Newport house, and built one near Lenox, in the hills of western Massachusetts, and at last I escaped from watering-place triviali-ties to the real country. If I could have made the change sooner I daresay I should never have given a thought to the literary delights of Paris or London; for life in the country is the only state which has always completely satisfied me, and I had never been allowed to gratify it, even for a few weeks at a time. Now I was to know the joys of six or seven months a year among fields and woods of my own, and the childish ecstasy of that first spring outing at Mamaroneck swept away all restlessness in the deep joy of communion with the earth. On a slope overlooking the dark waters and densely wooded shores of Laurel Lake we built a spacious and dignified house, to which we gave the name of my great-grandfather's place, the Mount. There was a big kitchen-garden with a grape pergola, a little farm, and a flower-garden outspread below the wide terrace overlooking the lake. There for over ten years I lived and gardened and wrote contentedly, and should doubtless have ended my days there had not a grave change in my husband's health made the burden of the property too heavy. But meanwhile the Mount was to give me country cares and joys, long happy rides and drives through the wooded lanes of that loveliest region, the companionship of a few dear friends, and the freedom from trivial obligations which was necessary if I was to go on with my writing. The Mount was my first real home, and though it is nearly twenty years since I last saw it (for I was too happy there ever to want to revisit it as a stranger) its blessed influence still lives in me.

The country quiet stimulated my creative zeal; and since the publication of 'The Greater Inclination' I was naturally in the first fever of authorship. A year later, in 1900, I brought out my earliest attempt at a novel – a long tale, rather – and, the year after, a second collection of short stories, under the title of

'Crucial Instances'. The long tale, which was called 'The Touchstone' – a quiet title carefully chosen for one of the quietest of my stories – had little success in America. John Lane bought the English rights, and thinking the title too colourless he renamed the book (naturally taking care not to consult me!) 'A Gift from the Grave'. This seductive but misleading label must have been exactly to the taste of the sentimental novel-reader of the day, for to my mingled wrath and amusement the book sold rapidly in England, and I have often chuckled to think how defrauded the purchasers must have felt themselves after reading the first few pages.

My short stories had attracted the attention denied to 'The Touchstone', and I think it was in reference to a tale in 'Crucial Instances' that I received what is surely one of the tersest and most vigorous letters ever penned by an amateur critic. 'Dear Madam,' my unknown correspondent wrote, 'have you never known a respectable woman? If you have, in the name of decency write about her!' It seems a long way from that comminatory cry to the point of view of the critic who, referring the other day to the republication (in an anthology of ghost stories) of one of my tales, 'The Lady's Maid's Bell', scathingly said it was hard to believe that a ghost created by so refined a writer as Mrs Wharton would do anything so gross as to ring a bell! My career began in the days when Thomas Hardy, in order to bring out 'Jude the Obscure' in a leading New York periodical, was compelled to turn the children of Jude and Sue into adopted orphans; when the most popular young people's magazine in America excluded all stories containing any reference to 'religion, love, politics, alcohol or fairies' (this is textual); the days when a well-known New York editor, offering me a large sum for the serial rights of a projected novel, stipulated only that no reference to 'an unlawful attachment' should figure in it; when Theodore Roosevelt gently rebuked me for not having caused the reigning Duke of Pianura (in 'The Valley of Decision') to make an honest woman of the humble book-seller's daughter who loved him; and when the translator of Dante, my beloved friend, Professor Charles Eliot Norton, hearing (after the appearance of 'The House of Mirth') that I was preparing another 'society' novel, wrote in alarm imploring me to remember that 'no great work of the imagination has ever been based on illicit passion'!

The poor novelists who were my contemporaries (in English-speaking countries) had to fight hard for the right to turn the wooden dolls about which they were expected to make believe into struggling suffering human beings; but we have been avenged, and more than avenged, not only by life but by the novelists, and I hope the latter will see before long that it is as hard to get dramatic interest out of a mob of irresponsible criminals as out of the Puritan marionettes who formed our stock-in-trade. Authentic human nature lies somewhere between the two, and is always there for a new great novelist to rediscover.

The amusing thing about this turn of the wheel is that we who fought the good fight are now jeered at as the prigs and prudes who barred the way to complete expression – as perhaps we should have tried to do, had we known it was to cause creative art to be abandoned for pathology! But I must return to the reigning Duke of Pianura, who about this time was more real to me than most of the people I talked and walked with in my daily life.

I have often been asked whether the writing of 'The Valley of Decision' was not preceded by months of hard study. I had never studied hard in my life, and it was far too late to learn how when I began to write 'The Valley of Decision'; but whenever I make this reply it is received with polite incredulity. The truth is that I have always found it hard to explain that gradual absorption into my pores of a myriad details – details of landscape, architecture, old furniture and eighteenth century portraits, the gossip of contemporary diarists and travellers, all vivified by repeated spring wanderings guided by Goethe and the Chevalier de Brosses, by Goldoni and Gozzi, Arthur Young, Dr Burney and Ippolito Nievo, out of which the tale grew. I did not travel and look and read with the writing of the book in mind; but my years of intimacy with the Italian eighteenth century gradually and imperceptibly fashioned the tale and compelled me to write it; and whatever its faults – and they are many – it is saturated with the atmosphere I had so long lived in.

Professor Norton, who had by this time become one of my great friends, followed the development of the tale with interest, and helped it on by one of the most graceful *gestes* ever made by a distinguished scholar to a beginner. I happened to tell him that, though I had been picking up second-hand books on eighteenth century Italy whenever I could find them (hardly any of the classics of the period being then reprinted), there were a few that I had been unable to buy, and one or two that even the public libraries could not supply. Among these were the original (French) version of Goldoni's memoirs, and the memoirs of Lorenzo da Ponte, published in Boston (of all places!) about 1824. A few weeks later there came to the Mount a box containing these unattainable treasures, and many other books, almost as rare, from the great library of travels at Shady Hill. For a whole summer these extremely valuable books, some quite irreplaceable, were left at the disposal of a young scribbler who was just starting on her first novel – and to Charles Norton it seemed perfectly natural, and almost an obligation, to hold out such help to a beginner.

The year after the publication of 'The Valley of Decision' the 'Century Magazine' asked me, to my great delight, to write the text for a series of water-colours of Italian villas by Mr Maxfield Parrish. The suggestion had originated in the unexpected popularity of 'The Decoration of Houses', and also of 'The Valley of Decision', which was now rewarding me for the long months of toil and perplexity I had undergone in writing it. I was only beginning to be known as a novelist, but on Italian seventeenth and eighteenth century architecture, about which so little had been written, I was thought to be fairly competent.

Armed with this commission I set out with my husband for Rome in the winter of 1903, and began my work in all seriousness.

3

Before telling the story of 'Italian Villas' I must speak of the friend whose kindness made its writing possible. Several years earlier, on starting on our annual pilgrimage to Italy, I had taken with me a letter from Paul Bourget to Vernon Lee (Miss Violet Paget), the author of 'Studies of the Eighteenth Century in Italy', 'Belcaro' and 'Euphorion', three of my best-loved companions of the road. Bourget warned me that, though Miss Paget was an old friend of his, he could not promise that his introduction would be of any use, as her time was so much taken up by her invalid half-brother, Eugene Lee-Hamilton, who lived with her, that she saw very few people, and those only among her intimates. It was therefore with little hope of success that I drove out from Florence to Il Palmerino, the long low villa on the hillside of San Domenico where Miss Paget has so long made her home. I left Bourget's letter, took a yearning look at the primrose-yellow house-front and the homely box-scented garden, and drove away with no expectation of ever seeing them again. But the next day Miss Paget wrote that, though her brother's illness prevented her receiving visitors, yet if I chanced to be the Edith Wharton who had written a certain sonnet (I forget its name) which had attracted his attention in 'Scribner's Magazine,' she begged me to come as soon as possible, as he wished to make my acquaintance. Luckily I *was* the author of the sonnet, and I hastened back to Il Palmerino, where I was affectionately welcomed by its mistress, and led to the darkened room where her brother lay on the mattress that seemed so likely to be a grave.

Eugene Lee-Hamilton, who was then a middle-aged man, had been one of Lord Lyons's secretaries of Embassy in Paris during the Franco-Prussian war. The long period of over-strain and over-work, followed by the privations and horrors of the siege of Paris, had brought about a bad nervous break-down, of a kind which the doctors of that day had not learned to deal with. Lee-Hamilton, his career cut short, lapsed into what seemed hopeless invalidism, and for years had lain motionless on the mattress on which I first saw him. By that time he had grown so weak that he could see only an occasional visitor, and for a very few moments. He was one of the most amusing talkers and *raconteurs* I have ever known, and a great lover of letters, and especially of poetry; but when I first met him he could neither read nor write, and was in such a state of weakness that his sister could only read a few lines to him at a time. These brief readings were usually chosen among the poets, and his literary curiosity had remained so alert that, in addition to the classics, he kept up with the new poets, even with those who had figured only in the reviews. It was in the course of these explorations that he happened on the sonnet which did me the great good turn of bringing me into contact with two of the most brilliant minds I have ever met.

His long years of suffering and helplessness had made Eugene Lee-Hamilton himself into a poet, and I have never understood why the poignant verse written during his illness, and published in a volume called 'Sonnets of the Wingless Hours', is not more widely known. I was proud to have any verse of mine praised by a poet of such quality, and I look back gratefully to the moments spent at his bedside, talking of the things of the spirit.

To lighten the gloom of the picture I must add that a few years later he rose miraculously from his mattress, learned again to walk, to write, and finally to ride a bicycle, and not long afterward came to America, where he paid us a visit to Land's End, rejoicing in his recovered vigour, and keeping us and our guests in shouts of laughter by his high spirits and inimitable stories. I have often wished that the after-death resurrection, if it comes to us, might resemble the recovery of lost youth which made Lee-Hamilton's return to life so exhilarating to all about him.

Thanks to him, my acquaintance with his sister had grown into a friendship which has never flagged, though we are so seldom together. Hitherto all my intellectual friendships had been with men, and Vernon Lee was the first highly cultivated and brilliant woman I had ever known. I stood a little in awe of her, as I always did in the presence of intellectual superiority, and liked best to sit silent and listen to a conversation which I still think almost the best of its day. I have been fortunate in knowing intimately some great talkers among men, but I have met only three woman who had the real gift. They were Vernon Lee, Matilde Serao, the Neapolitan journalist and novelist, and the French poetess, the Comtesse de Noailles. It is hard to establish any comparison between beings so unlike in race, traditions and culture – but one might suggest the difference by saying that Matilde Serao's talk was like the noonday glow of her own Mediterranean, while Vernon Lee's has the opalescent play of a northerly sky, and Madame de Noailles' resembled the most expensive fireworks.

No one welcomed 'The Valley of Decision' more warmly than Vernon Lee, and it was a great encouragement to be praised by a writer whom I so much admired, and who was so unquestioned an authority on the country and the period I had dealt with. A year or two later the editor of the *Nuova Antologia*, then the leading Italian literary review, proposed to me to bring out an Italian translation of my novel, and Vernon Lee at once offered to write the introduction. For a reason I was never able to fathom (probably owing to a change in the administration of the review), the translation never appeared; but Vernon Lee's admirable preface is in my possession, and I still hope it may serve to introduce Italian readers to my book.

These years were perhaps the happiest I was to know as regards literary hopes and achievements. My long experimenting had resulted in two or three books which brought me more encouragement than I had ever dreamed of obtaining, and were the means of my making some of the happiest friendships of my life. The reception of my books gave me the self-confidence I had so long lacked, and in the company of people who shared my tastes, and treated me as their equal, I ceased to suffer from the agonizing shyness which used to rob such encounters of all pleasure. It was in this mood that I arrived in Italy in 1903, and turned to Vernon Lee for help in preparing my new book.

Always generous to younger writers, she was doubly so to me because of my friendship with her brother, and of her interest in the task I had undertaken. At that time little had been written on Italian villa and garden architecture, and only the most famous country-seats, mostly royal or princely, had been photographed and studied. As, in 'The Decoration of Houses', Ogden Codman and I had purposely excluded palaces and royal *châteaux* from our list, and directed the attention of our readers to the study of small and simple houses, so I wished that my new book should make known the simpler and less familiar type of villa. At Frascati, for instance, I passed hurriedly over the familiar splendours of Falconieri and Mondragone in order to give more space to the lovely Muti gardens, which at that time were almost unknown; and wherever I went I followed the same plan. At first I found it difficult to get helpful information from Italians, even from those living on the spot; a 'garden' to them still meant a humpy lawn with oval beds of cannas encircling a banana-plant, and I wasted a good deal of time before learning that I must ask for '*giardini tagliati*', and not be discouraged by the usual reply: 'Oh, you mean the old-fashioned garden with clipped shrubs? Well, we believe there *is* one at the Villa So-and-so but what can you find in that to interest you?'

Vernon Lee's long familiarity with the Italian country-side, and the wide circle of her Italian friendships, made it easy for her to guide me to the right places, and put me in relation with people who could enable me to visit them. She herself took me to nearly all the villas I wished to visit near Florence, and it was thanks to her recommendation that wherever I went, from the Lakes to the Roman Campagna, I found open doors and a helpful hospitality.

Among the friendships then made I should like to record with particular gratitude that of the Countess Papafava of Padua, from whom I first heard of the fantastic Castle of Cattajo, and through whose kindness the intricately lovely gardens of Val San Zibio were opened to me; of Don Guido Cagnola of Varese, an authority on Italian villa architecture, and himself the owner of La Gazzada, the beautiful villa near Varese of which there is a painting by Canaletto in the Brera; of the Countess Rasponi, who lived in the noble villa of Font'-allerta, above Florence, and supplemented Vernon Lee in guiding me among the Florentine and Sienese villas; of the great Enrico Boito, whose powerful protection opened the doors of some little-known villas of the Brianza and the Naviglio; and lastly of Countess Rasponi's sister, my old friend the Countess Maria Pasolini of Rome and Ravenna, great lover of seventeenth and eighteenth century architecture, and an indefatigable guide in such a search as I was making. I have named them all here, because, although with the exception of the Countess Rasponi and Boito they are still alive, and I now and then have the pleasure of seeing them, I feel that I have never properly expressed my appreciation of their helpfulness. Their intelligent collaboration gave 'Italian Villas' its chief value, and I like to recall the joy I had in making the book by naming the friends who helped me.

The day of the motor was not yet, and in addition to the difficulty of discovering the type of villa I was in search of there remained the problem of how to get to it when found. I never enjoyed any work more than the preparing of that book, but neither do I remember any task so associated with physical fatigue. Most of the places I wished to visit were far from the principal railway lines, and could be reached only by a combination of slow trains and broken-down horse conveyances, and we seemed to be always either rushing through the villas in order not to miss our train, or else, the villas exhaustively inspected, kicking our heels for hours in some musty railway-station. I remember that once, after a particularly fatiguing day, we were waiting at the Pavia station to catch a crowded express back to Milan. We had taken the tea-basket, but there was no time for tea till we reached the station. There, feeling on the verge of inanition, I started to brew it, in spite of my husband's protests; but just as I filled our cups the express roared into the station, and we had to leap on board and force our way into a crowded compartment carrying the basket, the plates and the brimming cups! How we accomplished this I cannot imagine; but we did, to the astonishment and indignation of our fellow travellers.

I have said there were no motors in 1903; but as a toy of the rich they were beginning to appear, and my old friend George Meyer, then American Ambassador in Rome, was the owner of a magnificent specimen. Knowing that I wished to visit the Villa Caprarola, now familiar to every sight-seer, but then visible only to the privileged, he suggested taking me there in his car. I had never been in a motor before, and could hardly believe that we were to do the run to Caprarola and back (fifty miles each way) in an afternoon, and still have time to inspect the villa and gardens; but we did – we did with a vengeance! The car was probably the most luxurious, and certainly one of the fastest, then procurable; but that meant only a sort of high-perched phaeton without hood or screen, or any protection from the wind. My husband was put behind with the chauffeur, while I had the high seat like a coachman's box beside the Ambassador. In a thin spring dress, a sailor hat balanced on my chignon, and a two-inch tulle veil over my nose, I climbed proudly to my perch, and off we tore across the Campagna, over humps and bumps, through ditches and across gutters, wind-swept, dust-enveloped, I clinging to my sailor-hat, and George Meyer (luckily) to the wheel. We did the run in an hour, and I was able to see the villa and gardens fairly well before we tore back to Rome, in time for a big dinner to which he and we happened to be going. It was great fun doing the Witch of Atlas, and blissful not to have to worry about tired horses or inconvenient trains; but when I reached the dinner my voice was entirely gone, and I spent the next days in bed, fighting an acute laryngitis. In spite of this I swore then and there that as soon as I could make money enough I would buy a motor; and so I did – and having a delicate throat, scoured the country in the hottest weather swaddled in a stifling hood with a mica window, till some benefactor of the race invented the wind-screen and made motoring an unmixed joy.

Meanwhile my first article had appeared in the 'Century', illustrated by a number of photographs, and by one of Maxfield Parrish's brilliant idealisations of the Italian scene. Thanks to the latter, the article attracted much attention, but a note of warning soon came to me in the form of a distracted letter from the editor of the 'Century', Richard Watson Gilder, an old friend and a country neighbour in the Berkshires. It appeared that in the editorial offices of the 'Century' Mr Parrish's fairy-tale pictures were justly admired, but it was agreed that the accompanying text was too dry and technical. Would I not, Mr Gilder pleaded, introduce into the next number a few anecdotes, and a touch of human interest?

I am afraid my answer was court. I had prepared for my task conscientiously; I knew that, at least in English, there was no serious work on Italian villa and garden architecture, and I meant, as far as I was able, to fill the want. I wrote back that if the 'Century' wanted a series of sentimental and anecdotic commentaries on Mr Parrish's illustrations, I was surprised that one of the authors of 'The Decoration of Houses' should have been commissioned to write them. But I added that if, on reflection, my articles were thought unsuitable to the illustrations (as they certainly were!) I was quite willing to annul my contract. This was not accepted, and the articles continued to appear, my only punishment being that the Century Company refused (when the volume came out) to publish the plans of certain little-known but important gardens, such as those of the Villas Muti at Frascati and Gori at Siena, which I had taken great pains to procure, because, according to the publishers, the public 'did not care for plans'. I mention this because, when 'Italian Villas' became, as it soon did, a working manual for architectural students and landscape gardeners, I was often reproached for not having provided the book with plans. In a sense, of course, the editors of the 'Century' were right. My articles were quite out of keeping with the Parrish pictures, which should have been used to illustrate some fanciful tale of Lamotte-Fouqué, or Andersen's 'Improvisatore'; but I knew that, even had I had an architectural draughtsman as illustrator, the editorial scruples would not have been allayed, for what really roused them was not the lack of harmony between text and pictures but the fear their readers would be bored by the serious technical treatment of a subject associated with moonlight and nightingales. Therefore, having been given the opportunity to do a book that needed doing, I resolutely took it; and I hope the success of 'Italian Villas', which still has a steady sale, has made the publishers forgive me.

Again and again in my literary life I have encountered the same kind of editorial timidity. I think it was Edwin Godkin, then the masterly editor of the New York 'Evening Post', who said that the choice of articles published in American magazines was entirely determined by the fear of scandalizing a non-existent clergyman in the Mississippi Valley; and I made up my mind from the first that I would never sacrifice my literary conscience to this ghostly censor. Not being obliged to live solely by my pen I thought I owed it to less lucky colleagues to fight for the independence they might not always be in a position to assert. A higher standard of taste in letters can be achieved only if authors will refused to write down to the particular Mississippi Valley level of the day (for there is always a censorship of the same sort, though it is now at the other end of the moral register), and the greatest service a writer can render to letters is to follow his conscience.

In the intervals of my work on 'Italian Villas' I had published a number of short articles which I collected and brought out in 1905 in a volume called 'Italian Backgrounds'. I do not intend to burden these pages with an account of every book I have written and I speak of 'Italian Backgrounds' only because it is a convenient peg on which to hang an interesting discussion. In the 'seventies and 'eighties there had appeared a series of agreeable volumes of travel and art-criticism of the cultured dilettante type, which had found thousands of eager readers. From Pater's 'Renaissance', and Symonds' 'Sketches in Italy and Greece', to the deliciously desultory volumes of Vernon Lee, and Bourget's delicate 'Sensations d'Italie', though ranging through varying degrees of erudition, they all represented a high but unspecialized standard of culture; all were in a sense the work of amateurs, and based on the assumption that it is mainly to the cultured amateur that the creative artist must look for appreciation, and that such appreciation ought to be, and often is, worth recording.

But while the cultivated reader continued to enjoy these books, and to ask for more, the voice of the trained scholar was sounding a note of resistance. Literary 'appreciations' of works of art were being smiled away by experts trained in Bertillon-Morelli methods, and my deep contempt for picturesque books about architecture naturally made me side with those who wished to banish sentiment from the study of painting and sculpture. Then, with the publication of Berenson's first volumes on Italian painting, lovers of Italy learned that aesthetic sensibility may be combined with the sternest scientific accuracy, and I began to feel almost guilty for having read Pater and even Symonds with such zest, and ashamed of having added my own facile vibrations to the chorus. The application of scholarly standards to the judgment of works of art certainly helped to clear away the sentimental undergrowth which had sprung up in the wake of the gifted amateur; but nowadays, as was almost certain to happen, the very critics who did the necessary clearing have come to recognize that, their task once done, there remains the imponderable something, the very soul of the work contemplated, and that this something may be felt and registered by certain cultivated sensibilities, whether or not they have been disciplined by technical training. There remains a field of observation wherein the mere lover of beauty can open the eyes and sharpen the hearing of the receptive traveller, as Pater, Symonds and Vernon Lee had done to readers of my generation. The combination of gifts required is seldom found, and the volumes which guided my early wanderings were succeeded by minor dithyrambs to which I never again felt tempted to add my own pipe of ecstasy; but there is certainly room for the gifted amateur in the field of artistic impressions – if only he is sufficiently gifted.

Chapter Seven
New York and the Mount

I

We had now organized our summers at the Mount, and had acquired a small house – we used to say it was actually the smallest – in New York. I had grown very weary of our annual wanderings, and now that I had definite work to do I felt the need of a winter home where I could continue my writing, instead of having to pack up every autumn, as we had been doing for over fifteen years. Personally I should have preferred to live all the year round at the Mount, but my husband's fondness for society, and his dislike for the New England winter cold, made this impossible; and a few years later, when he found even the climate of New York too trying, we decided to spend all our winters abroad. But meanwhile I had the amusement of adorning our sixteen-foot-wide house in New York with the modest spoils of our Italian travels, and my summers being quiet I did not so much mind the social demands of the winter. Besides, life in New York, with its theatres and opera, and its new interests of all kinds, was very different from the flat frivolity of Newport; and I was happy in my work, and in the new sense of confidence in my powers.

My literary success puzzled and embarrassed my old friends far more than it impressed them, and in my own family it created a kind of constraint which increased with the years. None of my relations ever spoke to me of my books, either to praise or blame – they simply ignored them; and among the immense tribe of my New York cousins, though it included many with whom I was on terms of affectionate intimacy, the subject was avoided as though it were a kind of family disgrace, which might be condoned but could not be forgotten. Only one eccentric widowed cousin, living a life of lonely invalidism, turned to my novels for occasional distraction, and had the courage to tell me so.

At first I had felt this indifference acutely; but now I no longer cared, for my recognition as a writer had transformed my life. I had made my own friends, and my books were beginning to serve as an introduction to my fellow-writers. But it was amusing to think that, whereas in London even my modest achievements would have opened many doors, in my native New York they were felt only as a drawback and an embarrassment. The literary life of New York had changed very little since my youth. The literary men foregathered at the Century Club, and continued to turn a contemptuous shoulder on society. Our most distinguished man of letters, William Brownell, led the life of a recluse, and though he became a dear friend it was chiefly by letter that we communicated, and only on rare occasions that I could persuade him to come to our house. I have always regretted that our friendly meetings were so rare, and so seldom occurred in a more sympathetic setting than his cramped and crowded office at Scribner's. When he died in 1928 I tried to put into an article contributed to 'Scribner's Magazine' something of my deep admiration for the scholar and critic; but I found it difficult to convey the exquisite quality of the man. There was always an aloofness, an elusiveness in Brownell's manner and personality, something shy and crepuscular, as though his real self dwelt in a closely-guarded recess of contemplation from which it emerged more easily and freely in writing than in speech; and indeed his letters to me, which were long and frequent, always brought him nearer than our actual encounters. As these letters concern only, or chiefly, my own works, their interest for the general reader would obviously be less than for their recipient; but to me they were a precious link with one of the rarest intelligences I have ever known.

In writing of Brownell after his death it was inevitable that I should associate with his name that of Edward Burlingame, for many years Brownell's colleague in the house of Scribner, where he edited the magazine. I said of the two: 'I do not think I have ever forgotten one word of the counsels they gave me', and the assertion is as true today as it would have been in my youth. In Edward Burlingame also I found a devoted personal friend, as well as a literary adviser. During his editorship he raised 'Scribner's Magazine' to the highest level compatible with the tastes of the American magazine public – then apparently a higher one than now. Burlingame, who used to come and dine now and then with his wife, was far more sociably inclined than his colleague. He was a man of real cultivation, a good linguist, and genuinely interested in modern literature. It was thanks to him that Scribner had published Stevenson's best prose, and Burlingame's ambition was to keep his magazine on a level with the standard then established. He was a good-looking man whose quiet dignity of manner masked an acute sense of humour and a patient cordiality which many a young author must have had reason to bless as I did. I remember once saying to him (à propos of some young woman in straitened circumstances, whose manuscript he had reluctantly had to refuse): 'How hard it must be to say "no" in such cases!' But he answered quietly: 'Not as hard as you think, because if one isn't cruel at first one has to be so much crueller afterward.' Another of his wise answers was occasioned by my coming to him one day (in the new flush of my success) bearing with me, as it were, an armful of unwritten short stories. He listened patiently to my plans, and then said: 'If I were you I wouldn't be in such a hurry. You mustn't risk becoming *a magazine bore*.' Lastly I owe to him the neatest formulation I know of one of the first principles of every art: 'You can ask your reader to believe whatever you can induce him to believe.' These axioms have remained with me as applicable not only to literature but to life: and Burlingame abounded in such wisdom.

W. D. Howells was (partly, I believe, owing to his wife's chronic ill-health) another irreducible recluse, and though I was in a way accredited to him by my friendship with his two old friends, Charles Norton and Henry James, I seldom met him. I always regretted this, for I had a great admiration for 'A Modern Instance' and 'Silas Lapham', and should have liked to talk with their author about the art in which he stood so nearly among the first; and he himself, whenever we met, was full of a quiet friendliness. But I suppose my timidity and his social aloofness kept us apart; for though I felt that he was amicably disposed he remained inaccessible. Once, however, he did me a great kindness. I invited him to come with us to the first night (in New York) of Clyde Fitch's dramatization of 'The House of Mirth'. The play had already been tried out on the road, and in spite of Fay Davis's exquisite representation of Lily Bart I knew that (owing to my refusal to let the heroine survive) it was foredoomed to failure. Howells doubtless knew it also, and not improbably accepted my invitation for that very reason; a fact worth recording as an instance of his friendliness to young authors, and also on account of the lapidary phrase in which, as we left the theatre, he summed up the reason of the play's failure. 'Yes – what the American public always wants is a tragedy with a happy ending'.

Still another friend from the world of letters (and life-long intimate of all my husband's family), was Judge Robert Grant of Boston, who, in his rare moments of escape from the duties of the Probate Court, used to come to New York on flying visits. I have always had a great admiration for his early novel, 'Unleavened Bread', which, with W. D. Howells's 'A Modern Instance', was the forerunner of 'Main Street', of 'Babbitt', of that unjustly forgotten masterpiece 'Susan Lenox', of the best of Frank Norris, and of Dreiser's 'American Tragedy'. Howells was the first to feel the tragic potentialities of life in the drab American small town; but the incurable moral timidity which again and again checked him on the verge of a masterpiece drew him back even from the logical conclusion of 'A Modern Instance', and left Robert Grant the first in the field which he was eventually to share with Lewis and Dreiser.

But though there was little change in the attitude of the literary group, the merely fashionable were beginning to enlarge their interests. With the coming of the new millionaires the building of big houses had begun, in New York and in the country, bringing with it (though not always to those for whom the building was done) a keen interest in architecture, furniture and works of art in general. The Metropolitan Museum was waking up from its long lethargy, and the leading picture dealers from London and Paris were seizing the opportunity of educating a new clientèle, opening branch houses in New York and getting up loan exhibitions. With the coming of Edward Robinson (formerly of the Boston Museum) as Director of the Metropolitan, and the growth of the Hewitt sisters' activities in organizing their Museums of Decorative Art at the Cooper Union, the doctrines first preached by 'The Decoration of Houses' were beginning to find general expression; and in many houses there was already a new interest in letters as well as art. Men like my friends Bayard Cutting and John Cadwalader, in addition to preparing the way for the great new Public Library, and taking an active part in its creation, were forming valuable libraries of their own; others were collecting prints and pictures, and several of the younger architects were acquiring the important professional libraries which have been one of the chief elements in forming American taste in architecture, and making it the foremost influence in modern building. A few men of exceptional intelligence, such as Egerton Winthrop, Bayard Cutting, John Cadwalader, Walter Maynard, Charles McKim, Stanford White and Ogden Codman, had at last stirred the stagnant air of old New York, and in their particular circle it was full of the dust of new ideas.

This circle had happily always been mine, and I enjoyed its renovated air all the more now that I had found my own line in life; but though I liked New York well enough it was only at the Mount that I was really happy. There, every summer, I gathered about me my own group of intimates, of whom the number was slowly growing. Chief among the newcomers was a youth who, though many years my junior, at once became the closest of comrades. Walter Berry, who lived and exercised his profession, in Washington, first put me in touch with his young friend, George Cabot Lodge (always 'Bay' to his intimates). We met in Washington, where I had gone on a short visit; and from that first encounter till the day of his death Bay and I were fast friends. Bay Lodge (the eldest son of Henry Cabot Lodge, the Senator from Massachusetts) was one of the most brilliant and versatile youths I have ever known. In what direction he would eventually have developed I have never been sure; his sudden death at the age of thirty-six cut short such conjectures. He believed himself to be meant for poetry and letters; and he wrote, and published, several volumes of poetry marked by a grave rhetorical beauty. Though I admired certain lines and passages, I felt, as did most of his friends, that they showed only one side, perhaps not the most personal, of his rich and eager intelligence, and that if poetry was to be his ultimate form he must pass beyond the imitative stage into fuller self-expression. But he had a naturally scholarly mind, and might have turned in the end to history and archæology; unless indeed he was simply intended to be the most sensitive of contemplators, as he was the most varied and dazzling of talkers. In our hurried world too little value is attached to the part of the connoisseur and dilettante, and it never occurred to Bay's family that he was not meant for an active task in letters. His fate, in fact, was the reverse of mine, for he grew up in a hot-house of intensive culture, and was one of the most complete examples I have ever known of the young genius before whom an adoring family unites in smoothing the way. This kept him out of the struggle of life, and consequently out of its experiences, and to the end his intellectual precocity was combined with a boyishness of spirit at once delightful and pathetic. He had always lived in Washington, where, at the time when he was growing up, his father, Henry Adams, John Hay, and the eccentric Sturgis Bigelow of Boston, whose erudition so far exceeded his mental capacity, formed a close group of intimates. Until Theodore Roosevelt came to Washington theirs were almost the only houses where one breathed a cosmopolitan air, and where such men as Sir Cecil Spring-Rice, J.J. Jusserand and Lord Bryce felt themselves immediately at home. But Washington, even then, save for the politician and the government official, was a place to retire to, not to be young in; and Bay often complained of the lack of friends of his own age. Even more than from the narrowness of his opportunities he suffered from the slightly rarefied atmosphere of mutual admiration, and disdain of the rest of the world, that prevailed in his immediate surroundings. John Hay was by nature the most open-minded of the group, and his diplomatic years in London had enlarged his outlook; but the dominating spirits were Henry Adams and Cabot Lodge, and though they were extremely kind to me, and my pleasantest hours in Washington were spent at their houses, I always felt that the influences prevailing there kept Bay in a state of brilliant immaturity. He was at his best when he came to stay with us at the Mount, where small parties of congenial friends succeeded each other through the summer, and he was brought in contact with minds as active as his own, but more unprejudiced.

Another friend of this time was young Bayard Cutting, the son of my old friend. He was then recently married, and already menaced by the illness which cut him off a few years later. Bayard was as different as possible from his contemporary, Bay Lodge, as quiet and retiring as Bay was brilliant and exuberant; and his main interests, had he lived, would probably have been political rather than literary, though he was a great reader, and a passionate lover of letters. He was extremely intelligent and eagerly responsive to all intellectual appeals, but his rarest quality was a sort of quiet radiance which sent its beam through the dark fog of weakness and pain enveloping the years that ought to have been his happiest.

During those years, so quickly consumed by suffering, I never once heard him complain. He never ceased to struggle against his malady, trying every country and every climate in the effort to throw it off, but at the same time he took life on the normal terms of a healthy man – doing his best to get well, yet behaving, talking, and apparently thinking, as if he *were* well. In his wanderings in the pursuit of health he and his wife once spent a summer at Lenox, and during those months I learned of how fine and delicate a substance he was made. We have always needed such men sorely in American public life, and Bayard Cutting's death was a loss far beyond the immediate circle of his friends.

2

About this time we set up a motor, or perhaps I should say a series of them, for in those days it was difficult to find one which did not rapidly develop some organic defect; and selling, buying and exchanging went on continuously, though without appreciably better results. One summer, when we were all engaged on the first volumes of Mme Karénine's absorbing life of George Sand, we had a large showy car which always started off brilliantly and then broke down at the first hill, and this we christened 'Alfred de Musset', while the small but indefatigable motor which subsequently replaced 'Alfred' was naturally named 'George'. But those were the days when motor-guides still contained carefully drawn gradient-maps like fever-charts, and even 'George' sometimes balked at the state of the country roads about Lenox; I remember in particular one summer night when Henry James, Walter Berry, my husband and I sat by the roadside till near dawn while our chauffeur tried to persuade 'George' to carry us back to the Mount. The other day, in going over some old letters written to Bay Lodge by Walter Berry, I came on one dated from the Mount. 'Great fun here,' the writer exulted; 'we motor every day, and yesterday *we did sixty-five miles*' (in triumphant italics). In those epic days roads and motors were an equally unknown quantity, and one set out on a ten-mile run with more apprehension than would now attend a journey across Africa. But the range of country-lovers like myself had hitherto been so limited, and our imagination so tantalized by the mystery beyond the next blue hills, that there was inexhaustible delight in penetrating to the remoter parts of Massachusetts and New Hampshire, discovering derelict villages with Georgian churches and balustraded housefronts, exploring slumbrous mountain valleys, and coming back, weary but laden with a new harvest of beauty, after sticking fast in ruts, having to push the car up hill, to rout out the village blacksmith for repairs, and suffer the jeers of horse-drawn travellers trotting gaily past us. My two New England tales, 'Ethan Frome' and 'Summer', were the result of explorations among the villages still bedrowsed in a decaying rural existence, and sad slow-speaking people living in conditions hardly changed since their forbears held those villages against the Indians.

A frequent excursion was to Ashfield, where Charles Eliot Norton spent the summer with his daughters in his little mountain farmhouse, and where there was always a friendly welcome, and the joy of long hours of invigorating talk. What I have said of the underrated value of the connoisseur and disseminator of ideas is even more applicable to a man like Charles Eliot Norton, whose long life proved what can only be regretfully surmised in regard to a career as short as Bay Lodge's. Charles Norton of course led an active life of letters in conjunction with his teaching as Professor of Fine Arts at Harvard; but his animating influence on my generation in America was exerted through what he himself was, and what he made his pupils see and feel with him. Among those of my intimate friends who came under Norton's influence at Harvard there was none who did not regard the encounter as a turning point in his own growth. Norton was supremely gifted as an awakener, and no thoughtful mind can recall without a thrill the notes of the first voice which has called it out of its morning dream.

In his prime Charles Norton, to be really known, had to be seen in the Shady Hill library, at Cambridge, where the ripest years of his intellectual life were lived. Against the noble background of books his frail presence, the low voice, the ascetic features so full of scholarly distinction, acquired their full meaning, and his talk was at its richest and happiest. But the rusticity of the Ashfield cottage, with its rocky slopes of orchard and woodland looking out to the blue distances of his beloved New England, formed an even fitter setting to his serene old age. It was there that I was oftenest in his company, for my most intimate friends were his friends also. One such pilgrimage is delightfully recorded in a letter written from the Mount by Henry James, and others were made with Walter Berry, Gaillard Lapsley, and divers devotees and disciples; memories radiant with the beauty of the long mountain drive from Lenox to Ashfield, with sunsets watched from the summit of 'High Pasture' (where Norton always dreamed of building a house that should command the wide landscape), and the slow descent through the orchards at dusk, the lights twinkling under the eaves, a happy group gathered for high tea, and an evening of quiet talk about the fire. Charles Norton was not a great talker; he had none of the sweep and impetus of the born conversationalist; but he was one of the best guides to good conversation that I have ever known. Every word he spoke, every question he asked, was like a signal pointing to the next height, and his silences were of the kind which serve to carry on the talk.

He was too old, when I began to know him intimately, to care to travel. He often promised to come to the Mount, but I cannot remember that he ever did, though his daughter Sally was so beloved and frequent a visitor. I never failed, however, when I was in Boston, to make the pilgrimage to Shady Hill, or to go to Ashfield in summer; and in the intervals between our meetings we wrote to each other, or kept in touch through my correspondence with Sally. He never ceased to interest himself in my work, or to encourage me to go forward, although the more I developed the more, in literary matters, our points of view diverged. He was obviously disturbed by my increasing 'realism', my exclusive interest, as a novelist, in the life about me, which seemed to him so devoid of the stuff of romance; he would have been happier if I had never come any nearer to the nineteenth century than I did in 'The Valley of Decision'. But no friendly pressure, even from the critics I most esteemed, could turn me from the way I seemed meant to follow; and with a magnanimity unusual in a man of his age Charles Norton accepted this, and kept me in his heart.

In the intervals between our meetings we wrote to each other, and, though our actual hours together were not many, I had to the end the warm enveloping sense of his friendship, and the last letter he ever wrote (or dictated, for he was past writing) was addressed to me.

One of Charles Norton's great friends, Edward Robinson, came often to the Mount with his wife. Since he had given up the directorship of the Boston Museum, and been placed at the head of the Metropolitan, I had naturally more frequent opportunities of seeing him; and he was welcome not only on his own account but as a link with other Boston friends, the Nortons, Robert Grant, Barrett Wendell, and many others. Edward Robinson, tall, spare and pale, with his blond hair cut short 'en brosse', bore the physical imprint of his German University formation, and might almost have sat for the portrait of a Teutonic *Gelehrter* but for the quiet twinkle perceptible behind his eyeglasses. He had, indeed, an extremely delicate sense of humour, combined with the boyish love of pure nonsense only to be found in Anglo-Saxons. He was one of the people for whom I used to hoard up my best stories, but his own were generally better, for his professional experiences gave him many humorous sidelights on human nature, and no one could rival the dry pedantic manner in which he poked fun at pedantry. I remember particularly one story, not especially relevant to this, but which has remained with me because of its strangeness, and Robinson's dramatic way of telling it. The young Heir Apparent of a Far Eastern Empire, who was making an official tour of the United States, was taken with his suite to the Metropolitan, and shown about by Robinson and the Museum staff. For two mortal hours Robinson marched the little procession from one work of art to another, pausing before each to give the necessary explanations to the aide-de-camp (the only one of the visitors who spoke English), who transmitted them to his Imperial master. During the whole of the tour the latter's face remained as immovable as that of the Emperor Constantius entering Rome, in Gibbon's famous description. The Prince never asked a question, or glanced to right or left, and this slow and awful progress through the endless galleries was beginning to tell on Robinson's nerves when they halted before a fine piece of fifteenth century sculpture, a Pietà, or a Deposition, with a peculiarly moving figure of the dead Christ. Here His Imperial Highness opened his lips to ask, through his aide-de-camp, what the group represented, and Robinson hastened to explain: 'It is the figure of our dead God, after His enemies have crucified Him'. The Prince listened, stared, and then burst into loud and prolonged laughter. Peal after peal echoed uncannily through the startled galleries; then his features resumed their imperial rigidity and the melancholy procession moved on through new vistas of silence.

Edward Robinson's presence in New York helped to centralize the growing interest in art and architecture, and he was one of the most sympathetic among the group of friends who used to gather in my small New York drawing-room, or join in our adventurous motor trips at the Mount. If I have dwelt chiefly on the homely familiar traits of his character, the fun, the irony, the gentle malice, leaving it to others to praise his scholarship and recount his public services, it is because in trying to tell the story of my life I have found that it is these little personal characteristics (and above all others, the ironic sense of the pity and mystery of things) which have always created the closest ties between myself and my friends.

Robert Minturn, of New York, whom I had known slightly all through my girlhood, was now frequently at the Mount, or at our house in New York. He and I belonged by birth to the same 'old New York', and I hardly know what had kept us so long from becoming friends, unless perhaps the somewhat austere Minturn *milieu* (with its Boston-Abolitionist affiliations) regarded mine as incorrigibly frivolous. At any rate, as soon as I went to live in New York and began to see more of this grave young man, whose pensive dusky head was so like that of a Titian portrait, we found that we were meant to be friends – and often have I grieved that we had not discovered sooner, for Bob Minturn's was one of the affections I am proudest of having inspired. Once, as a child, I was severely rebuked for saying of a dull kindly servant, whom my father was defending because he was 'so good': 'Of course he's good – he's too stupid to be bad'. The rebuke was no doubt very salutary; yet experience has shown me that there was a grain of truth in my comment, for the intellectually eager and enquiring are seldom serenely and unquestioningly good. But Robert Minturn belonged to the happy few who have found a way of harmonizing the dissecting intellect with the accepting soul, and whose daily life reveals the inner harmony 'through chinks that grief has made'.

Bob Minturn's grief was his health; it was already menaced when our friendship began, and during his last years he was an invalid, accepting infirmity and facing death with complete serenity. One by one he had given up the activities and enjoyments of a young man's life; but he never allowed these renunciations to dull his appreciation of what remained – the love of art and letters, the love of nature, and above all, exquisitely vigilant and tender, the love of his friends. If he had kept his health he would no doubt have taken an active part in political and municipal life, for he had a lively sense of civic obligation and a natural interest in public affairs; but his activities, deprived of this outlet, had canalized themselves in an exquisite culture. He was an accomplished linguist, widely read in certain lines, a sensitive lover of words, indefatigable in the quest of their uses and meanings, handling them as a gardener does his flowers, or a collector precious jewels or porcelain, and deploring above all their barbarous misuse by our countrymen. Linguistic problems had such a fascination for him that even the letters to me which he dictated in the last months of his life, when he was too ill to write, are full of eagerly propounded etymological questions. To the last his interest in all the worth-while things kept his poor worn body aglow, and if ever a craft went down with colours flying it was that which bore the shining soul of Bob Minturn.

3

Another visitor of a very different type, but highly endowed with the sense of humour common to most of our group, was the popular playwright, Clyde Fitch. Though I had not escaped the novelist's usual temptation to write for the stage I had never taken my dramatic impulses very seriously, and after the appearance of my second novel, 'The House of Mirth', I thought no more of the theatre – indeed, as nothing in the way of drama between the extremes of Racine's 'Phèdre' and 'The Private Secretary' has ever given me much pleasure, I went to the play as seldom as possible.

Once 'The House of Mirth' had started on its prosperous career I was of course besieged with applications for leave to dramatize it; but I refused them all, convinced that (apart from the intrinsic weakness of most plays drawn from books) there was nothing in this particular book out of which to make a play. Great was my surprise, therefore, when I heard that Clyde Fitch, then at the height of his career, was eager to undertake the task, though he had never before consented to adapt any one else's material. I did not know Clyde Fitch, and had seen, I think, only one of his plays; but I had read a number of them, and though they were all disappointing, yet I thought him more gifted than was generally supposed. His sense of the theatre was keen, but that interested me less than his sense of the irony of life, his happy choice of the incidents by means of which he threw light on the human predicament. I still think the first act of one of his plays (I forget its title), in which the scene is laid in the rotunda of the Apollo Belvedere, at the Vatican, one of the most humorous exhibitions of human vacuity that I know of; and if he had written for a more sensitive and critical public, and been less tempted by easy success, he might have gone far in both mirth and pathos. As it was, he was the playwright of the hour in America, and being naturally flattered by his proposal I accepted it.

He stipulated that I should write every word of the dialogue, and as I was too much of a novice not to need continual guidance in interpreting his scenario, this led to many meetings, and to his coming several times to stay. His visits laid the foundation of a real friendship, and my husband and I both became very much attached to the plump showily dressed little man, with his olive complexion, and his beautiful Oriental eyes full of wit and understanding.

The work was longer and more difficult than he had probably foreseen. We were both fastidious, and both frank in our criticism of each other; and one day I burst out, rather despairingly: 'I can't see how you could ever have thought there was a play in this book!'

'But I never did!' he exclaimed, his beautiful eyes wide with astonishment.

'You *didn't*? But they told me you wanted so much to do it.'

He gave a sigh of understanding. 'Oh, I see! That's exactly what they told me about *you*. They said you wanted me to dramatize your novel, and had refused the rights to everybody else in the hope that I could be induced to do it.'

We sat and stared at each other, seeing that we had been tricked into collaboration by an unscrupulous intermediary. Then we both burst out laughing. 'I was so flattered—' I gasped.

'So was I!' he echoed; and we laughed again.

The play was written, the actors were bespoken, and it was too late to withdraw; but I don't think either of us had a moment's illusion as to the ultimate result. Clyde Fitch was leaving the Mount that afternoon; under my laughter he probably detected my annoyance at having been thus misrepresented to him, and the next day he sent me one of the kindest letters that one human being ever wrote to another. He told me how sorry he was to have taken up so much of my time on false pretenses (as though I had not taken up as much of his!), and begged me to believe that, whatever befell the play (and in theatrical matters, he reminded me, one could never foretell), he would always be grateful for the accident which had brought us together, since our collaboration had given him so much pleasure, and taught him so much, that the possible failure of the play mattered nothing in comparison. From an experienced playwright to an amateur no words could have been more generous; and he confirmed them by working over the staging and rehearsing as hard as if nothing had happened to disillusionize us.

In spite of his loyal efforts, and of Fay Davis's valiant and beautiful acting, the play failed; but I felt, as he did, that in the attempt I had gained a friend, and that nothing else greatly mattered.

Clyde Fitch was one of the most amusing story-tellers I ever met, and his rich treasures of observation and unfailing enjoyment of the human situation made him a delightful talker. I remember, in particular, one tale which delighted us. He had built himself a country house in Connecticut, probably, like his town house, rather over-ornate and too full of rococo Italian furniture. After a while he decided to sell it furnished, and a newly-rich western couple having asked to visit it, his secretary was delegated to receive them. They liked the house; but the husband had never heard of the *sette cento* (or perhaps of Italy) and was puzzled and put off by the furniture, and his remarks were so disparaging that his wife was obviously distressed. In one bedroom there was a delicately carved and gilded four-poster, hung with old brocade, its tester decorated with amorous allegories. This was the show room of the house, but the husband said he'd never seen a bed like that, and what the devil could anybody do with it? The scandalized secretary replied that Mr Fitch had brought it back from Venice, and considered it his best piece; and his wife, to disguise her husband's ignorance, hastily remarked: 'Why, I think it's a perfectly lovely bed! Can't you just see one of those old monks in it?'

My theatrical contacts having been so few, I had better record them all here, though the next antedates by many years the production of 'The House of Mirth'. It must have been shortly after my marriage that my husband and I encountered in Paris an old friend of his family's, Arthur Dexter, a finished specimen of the contemplator-and-appreciator type. He had always been interested in the theatre, and was intimate with several of the great actors of the Théâtre Français – in particular with Got, Coquelin the elder and Delaunay. Delaunay had, I think, already retired, but I had an exquisite recollection of his last performances in the Musset comedies (in which I think he succeeded Bressant), and in the last plays of his modern repertory. My father, who was very fond of the theatre, often took me to the Français when I was a girl of eighteen (the year before his death), and I then saw, in the last faint light of their setting, the great stars of the old group: Madeleine Brohan, Delaunay, Got, with their juniors, Reichemberg, Baretta, Worms and Coquelin.

When, therefore, Arthur Dexter asked me if I would like to go to one of Delaunay's dramatic classes at the Conservatoire, I could hardly believe my luck. It was not easy to obtain permission to assist at any of these classes, and to be admitted to Delaunay's was particularly difficult; but being much attached to Dexter he had consented to make an exception in my favour. I don't believe he often did so; that day, at any rate, no one was present in the dreary *salle* but the young students, men and girls, and the mothers (seemingly authentic) of the latter – for in those days even budding actresses were chaperoned when they went to their classes! They all looked so surprised at our intrusion that shyness overcame me; but I forgot this as soon as one of the pupils mounted to the stage, and Delaunay sat down facing it. It was all so long ago that I recall but few details; but at the moment I had the sense of assisting at something masterly. Delaunay was very small, very withered, very old and rheumatic, and the golden voice was cracked; but the old fire still burned in him. One episode interested me particularly. A young man had prepared a scene (from Corneille's 'Menteur', I think) in which his dropping his handkerchief formed an important episode. For some time the would-be comedian failed to drop the handkerchief to Delaunay's satisfaction: the gesture was not charged with all the signficance the master thought it should contain. Delaunay explained his point carefully, gave his reasons, took the stage himself to enact the dropping of the handkerchief, and finally clenched his exposition by saying: 'We know that this was the way in which it has always been dropped since the play was first acted' – giving the names of the actors by whom the tradition had been handed down unbroken since the seventeenth century.

Still more interesting was the great love scene from 'Phèdre', in which the unhappy Queen declares (shades of the Mississippi Valley clergyman!) her unholy passion for her stepson. The young girl who played Phaedra was beautiful, and had a good voice; but the famous apostrophe which should have poured from her like lava – '*Oui, Prince, je brûle, je languis pour Thésée*', and all the rest of it – failed to become incandescent on the actress's inexperienced lips. Patiently, repeatedly, Delaunay tried to ignite her with the sacred flame, but it was like striking a succession of damp matches; she remained blankly lovely and uncomprehending. At last he took the stage again, pushed her quietly aside, and saying in a sad but unreproachful voice: '*Que voulez-vous, Mademoiselle? Vous êtes trop jeune pour comprendre l'inceste*', proceeded to transform himself into the guilty Queen avowing her desperate desire to its loved and hated object. I saw Sarah Bernhardt afterward in 'Phèdre' – and she could not woo and cajole, and taunt and curse and rave, like the old Delaunay.

My other experiences of the stage were few and fleeting. I was once asked – though how it came about I no longer remember – to make a play out of 'Manon Lescaut' for that delightful actress, Marie Tempest. It must have happened very long ago, for I have forgotten who the intermediary was, or how Miss Tempest happened to think of me. There is no doubt that I did the play, however, for the manuscript still exists; and I remember, as the chief result, a very pleasant little supper after the theatre, at Miss Tempest's house near Regent's Park, for the purpose of talking the matter over. Soon afterward her manager notified me that she had decided to renounce 'costume plays' for modern comedy, a resolve I could not but applaud; and that was the end of that.

Oddly different was the end of my last theatrical venture, which, like the others, was thrust on me and not solicited. A good many years after 'Manon' – at the time when we were living in New York – Mrs Patrick Campbell asked me to translate for her Sudermann's new play, 'Es lebe das Leben', of which she had acquired the rights. I admired Mrs Campbell's acting greatly, but after reading the play I felt obliged to tell her that I did not see how a tragedy based on the German 'point of honour' in duelling, a convention which had so long since vanished from our customs, could be intelligible or interesting to English or American audiences. However she insisted, and the translation was made and delivered. I told her that the German title ('Long Live Life', in its most bitterly ironic sense) was virtually untranslatable; but some one persuaded her that it meant 'The Joy of Living'! I protested vehemently, not wishing the dramatic critics to accuse me of such a flagrant error; but I was overruled, the play was brought out under that comic title, and in spite of Mrs Campbell's brilliant acting, it promptly failed – not without the critics having seized the occasion to remark that, if the accuracy of the rest of Mrs Wharton's translation was on a par with that of the title, etc., etc. . . .

But the odd conclusion was that, the Scribners having, to my surprise, proposed to publish my translation, that work, with its absurd title (which they said it was then too late to change), and its unintelligible discussion on the technical why-and-why-not of duelling, has gone on selling steadily in America ever since (a matter of over twenty-five years); indeed it figured as usual, on a modest scale, in my last royalty returns a few months ago. I have often, but always vainly, asked for a credible explanation of this phenomenon, which I am sure is as unintelligible to my publishers as to me – though they are too polite to tell me so.

In spite of the ill-success of this experiment I enjoyed my brief association with Mrs Campbell; and in fact my experience of the stage has left me none but kindly memories of the theatre-folk with whom I had to do, though in each case the doing rendered them so little service.

Chapter Eight

Henry James

I

What is one's personality, detached from that of the friends with whom fate happens to have linked one? I cannot think of myself apart from the influence of the two or three greatest friendships of my life, and any account of my own growth must be that of their stimulating and enlightening influence. From a childhood and youth of complete intellectual isolation – so complete that it accustomed me never to be lonely except in company – I passed, in my early thirties, into an atmosphere of the rarest understanding, the richest and most varied mental comradeship. Some of my friends were men exceptionally distinguished in their own walk of life, without being public figures; others were already celebrated when I first knew them, and of these I shall find it difficult to give an adequate account because of my unhappy lack of verbal memory. Once I had emerged from my long inner solitude my opportunities, though limited in extent (for I have always been fundamentally un-'social'), were of a quality so rare that it ought to illuminate all my pages. I have lived in intimate friendship with two or three great intelligences; but I am not a Boswell myself, and have never had a Boswell of my own, both of which facts I deplore, since in the former case I might have set down the dazzling talk I spent such enchanted hours in absorbing, and in the latter have handed it on to my recording satellite. As it is, having a tendency to pass, when in high company, into a state of exhilaration that precludes anything as precise as taking notes, I enjoy the commerce with great minds as a painter enchanted by the glories of an Alpine meadow rather than as a botanist cataloguing its specimens.

Once, happening to sit next to M. Bergson at a dinner, I confided to him my distress and perplexity over the odd holes in my memory. How was it, I asked, that I could remember, with exasperating accuracy, the most useless and insignificant things, such as the address of every one I knew, and the author of the libretto of every opera I had ever heard since the age of eighteen – while, when it came to poetry, my chiefest passion and my greatest joy, my verbal memory failed me completely, and I heard only the inner cadence, and could hardly ever fill it out with the right words?

I had the impression, before I ended, that my problem did not greatly interest my eminent neighbour; and his reply was distinctly disappointing. '*Mais c'est précisément parce que vous êtes éblouie*' ('It's just because you are dazzled'), he answered quietly, turning to examine the dish which was being handed to him, and making no effort to pursue the subject. It was only afterward that I saw he had really said all there was to say: that the gift of precision in ecstasy (the best definition I can find for the highest poetry) is probably almost as rare in the appreciator as in the creator, and that my years of intellectual solitude had made me so super-sensitive to the joys of great talk that precise recording was impossible to me. Good talk seems, instead, to pass into my mind with a gradual nutritive force sometimes felt only long afterward; it permeates me as a power, an influence, it encloses my universe in a dome of many-coloured glass from which I can detach but few fragments while it builds itself up about me. The reader may here object that I have taken more than a page to say that I have a bad memory; but to say only that would not quite cover the case, since the talk I hear is not forgotten, but stored in some depth from which it still returns in its essential implications, though so seldom in its verbal shape.

Since I have already spoken of Henry James's visits to the Mount, it is perhaps best to put his name first on the list of the friends who composed my closest group during the years I spent there, and those that followed. In fact, however, my first meeting with Henry James happened many years earlier, probably in the late 'eighties; though it is at the Mount that he first comes into the foreground of the picture.

For a long time there seemed small hope of his ever figuring there, for when we first met I was still struck dumb in the presence of greatness, and I had never doubted that Henry James was great, though how great I could not guess till I came to know the man as well as I did his books. The encounter took place at the house of Edward Boit, the brilliant water-colour painter whose talent Sargent so much admired. Boit and his wife, both Bostonians, and old friends of my husband's, had lived for many years in Paris, and it was there that one day they asked us to dine with Henry James. I could hardly believe that such a privilege could befall me, and I could think of only one way of deserving it – to put on my newest Doucet dress, and try to took my prettiest! I was probably not more than twenty-five, those were the principles in which I had been brought up, and it would never have occurred to me that I had anything but my youth, and my pretty frock, to commend me to the man whose shoe-strings I thought myself unworthy to unloose. I can see the dress still – and it *was* pretty; a tea-rose pink, embroidered with iridescent beads. But, alas, it neither gave me the courage to speak, nor attracted the attention of the great man. The evening was a failure, and I went home humbled and discouraged.

A year or two later, in Venice (probably in 1889 or 1890), the same opportunity came my way. Another friend of my husband's, Ralph Curtis of Boston, had the happy thought of inviting us to meet Henry James, who was, I think, staying either with Curtis at the Palazzo Barbaro, or with Robert Browning's old friend, Mrs Arthur Bronson. Again fortune held out her hand – and again mine slipped out of it. Once more I thought: How can I make myself pretty enough for him to notice me? Well – this time I had a new hat; *a beautiful new hat!* I was almost sure it was becoming, and I felt that if he would only tell me so I might as last pluck up courage to blurt out my admiration for 'Daisy Miller' and 'The Portrait of a Lady'. But he noticed neither the hat nor its wearer – and the second of our meetings fell as flat as the first. When I spoke to him of them years afterward he owned that he could not even remember having seen me on either occasion! And as for the date of the meeting which finally drew us together, without hesitations or preliminaries, we could neither of us recall when or where that happened. All we knew was that suddenly it was as if we had always been friends, and were to go on being (as he wrote to me in February 1910) 'more and more never apart'.

The explanation, of course, was that in the interval I had found myself, and was no longer afraid to talk to Henry James of the things we both cared about; while he, always so helpful and hospitable to younger writers, at once used his magic faculty of drawing out his interlocutor's inmost self. Perhaps it was our common sense of fun that first brought about our understanding. The real marriage of true minds is for any two people to possess a sense of humour or irony pitched in exactly the same key, so that their joint glances at any subject cross like interarching searchlights. I have had good friends between whom and myself that bond was lacking, but they were never really intimate friends; and in that sense Henry James was perhaps the most intimate friend I ever had, though in many ways we were so different.

The Henry James of the early meetings was the bearded Penseroso of Sargent's delicate drawing, soberly fastidious in dress and manner, cut on the approved pattern of the *homme du monde* of the 'eighties; whereas by the time we got to know each other well the compact upright figure had expanded to a rolling and voluminous outline, and the elegance of dress given way to the dictates of comfort, while a clean shave had revealed in all its sculptural beauty the noble Roman mask and the big dramatic mouth. The change typified something deep beneath the surface. In the interval two things had happened: Henry James had taken the measure of the fashionable society which in youth had subjugated his imagination, as it had Balzac's, and was later to subjugate Proust's and had fled from it to live in the country, carrying with him all the loot his adventure could yield; and in his new solitude he had come to grips with his genius. Exquisite as the early novels are – and in point of perfection probably none can touch 'The Portrait of a Lady' – yet measured by what was to come Henry James, when he wrote them, had but skimmed the surface of life and of his art. Even the man who wrote, in 'The Portrait of a Lady', the chapter in which Isabel broods over her fate at night by the fire, was far from the man in whom was already ripening that greater night-piece, the picture of Maggie looking in from the terrace at Fawns at the four bridge-players, and renouncing her vengeance as 'nothing nearer to experience than a wild eastern caravan, looming into view with crude colours in the sun, fierce pipes in the air, high spears against the sky . . . but turning off short before it reached her and plunging into other defiles'.

But though he had found his genius and broken away from the social routine, he never emancipated himself in small matters from the conformities. Though he now affected to humour the lumbering frame whose physical ease must be considered first, he remained spasmodically fastidious about his dress, and about other trifling social observances, and once when he was motoring with us in France in 1907, and suddenly made up his mind (at

Poitiers, of all places!) that he must then and there buy a new hat, almost insuperable difficulties attended its selection. It was not until he had announced his despair of ever making the hatter understand 'that what he wanted was a hat like everybody else's', and I had rather impatiently suggested his asking for a head-covering '*pour l'homme moyen sensuel*', that the joke broke through his indecisions, and to a rich accompaniment of chuckles the hat was bought.

Still more particular about his figure than his dress, he resented any suggestion that his silhouette had lost firmness and acquired volume; and once, when my friend Jacques-Emile Blanche was doing the fine seated profile portrait which is the only one that renders him *as he really was*, he privately implored me to suggest to Blanche 'not to lay such stress on the resemblance to Daniel Lambert'.

The truth is that he belonged irrevocably to the old America out of which I also came, and of which − almost − it might paradoxically be said that to follow up its last traces one had to come to Europe; as I discovered when my French and English friends told me, on reading 'The Age of Innocence', that they had no idea New York life in the 'seventies had been so like that of the English cathedral town, or the French '*ville de province*', of the same date. As for the nonsense talked by critics of a later generation, who never knew James, much less the world he grew up in, about his having thwarted his genius by living in Europe, and having understood his mistake too late, as a witness of his long sojourns in America in 1904, 1905 and 1910, and of the reactions they produced (expressed in all the letters written at the time), I can affirm that he was never really happy or at home there. He came several times for long visits to the Mount, and during his first visit to America, in 1904−5, he also stayed with us for some time in New York; and responsive as he always was, interested, curious, and heroically hospitable to new ideas, new aspects, new people, the nostalgia of which he speaks so poignantly in one of his letters to Sir Edmund Gosse (written from the Mount) was never for a moment stilled. Henry James was essentially a novelist of manners, and the manners he was qualified by nature and situation to observe were those of the little vanishing group of people among whom he had grown up, or their more picturesque prototypes in older societies. For better or worse he had to seek that food where he could find it, for it was the only food his imagination could fully assimilate. He was acutely conscious of this limitation, and often bewailed to me his total inability to use the 'material', financial and industrial, of modern American life. Wall Street, and everything connected with the big business world, remained an impenetrable mystery to him, and knowing this he felt he could never have dealt fully in fiction with the 'American scene', and always frankly acknowledged it. The attempt to portray the retired financier in Mr Verver, and to relate either him or his native 'American City' to any sort of concrete reality, is perhaps proof enough of the difficulties James would have found in trying to depict the American money-maker in action.

On his first visit, however, he was still in fairly good health, and in excellent spirits, exhilarated (at first) by the novelty of the adventure, the success of his revolt against his own sedentary habit (he called me 'the pendulum-woman' because I crossed the Atlantic every year!), and, above all, captivated by the new experience of motoring. It was the summer when we were experimenting with 'Alfred de Musset' and 'George'; in spite of many frustrations there were beautiful tours successfully carried out 'in the Whartons' commodious new motor, which has fairly converted me to the sense of all the thing may do for one and one may get from it', and this mode of locomotion seemed to him, as it had to me, an immense enlargement of life.

2

It is particularly regrettable in the case of Henry James that no one among his intimates had a recording mind, or rather that those who had did not apply it to noting down his conversation, for I have never known a case in which an author's talk and his books so enlarged and supplemented each other. Talent is often like an ornamental excrescence; but the quality loosely called genius usually irradiates the whole character. 'If he but so much as cut his nails,' was Goethe's homely phrase of Schiller, 'one saw at once that he was a greater man than any of them.' This irradiation, so abundantly basked in by the friends of Henry James, was hidden from those who knew him slightly by a peculiarity due to merely physical causes. His slow way of speech, sometimes mistaken for affectation – or, more quaintly, for an artless form of Anglomania! – was really the partial victory over a stammer which in his boyhood had been thought incurable. The elaborate politeness and the involved phraseology that made off-hand intercourse with him so difficult to casual acquaintances probably sprang from the same defect. To have too much time in which to weigh each word before uttering it could not but lead, in the case of the alertest and most sensitive of minds, to self-consciousness and self-criticism; and this fact explains the hesitating manner that often passed for a mannerism. Once, in New York, when I arranged a meeting between him and the great Mr Dooley, whose comments on the world's ways he greatly enjoyed, I perceived, as I watched them after dinner, that Peter Dunne was floundering helplessly in the heavy seas of James's parentheses; and the next time we met, after speaking of his delight in having at last seen James, he added mournfully: 'What a pity it takes him so long to say anything! Everything he said was so splendid – but I felt like telling him all the time: "Just 'pit it right up into Popper's hand".'

To James's intimates, however, these elaborate hesitancies, far from being an obstacle, were like a cobweb bridge flung from his mind to theirs, an invisible passage over which one knew that silver-footed ironies, veiled jokes, tiptoe malices, were stealing to explode a huge laugh at one's feet. This moment of suspense, in which there was time to watch the forces of malice and merriment assembling over the mobile landscape of his face, was perhaps the rarest of all in the unique experience of a talk with Henry James.

His letters, delightful as they are, give but hints and fragments of his talk; the talk that, to his closest friends, when his health and the surrounding conditions were favourable, poured out in a series of images so vivid and appreciations so penetrating, the whole so sunned over by irony, sympathy and wide-flashing fun, that those who heard him at his best will probably agree in saying of him what he once said to me of M. Paul Bourget: 'He was the first, easily, of all the talkers I ever encountered.'

Of all qualities most impossible to preserve in his letters, because so impossible to explain with whatever fulness of footnotes, was the quality of fun – often of sheer abstract 'fooling' – that was the delicious surprise of his talk. His letter to Walter Berry 'on the gift of a dressing-bag' is almost the only instance of this genial play that is intelligible to the general reader. From many of the letters to his most intimate group it was necessary to excise long passages of chaff, and recurring references to old heaped-up pyramidal jokes, huge cairns of hoarded nonsense. Henry James's memory for a joke was prodigious; when he got hold of a good one, he not only preserved it piously, but raised upon it an intricate superstructure of kindred nonsense, into which every addition offered by a friend was skilfully incorporated. Into his nonsense-world, as four-dimensional as that of the Looking Glass, or the Land where the Jumblies live, the reader could hardly have groped his way without a preparatory course in each correspondent's private history and casual experience. The merest hint was usually enough to fire the train; and, as in the writing of his tales a tiny mustard-seed of allusion spread into a many-branched 'subject', so his best nonsense flowered out of unremembered trifles.

I recall a bubbling over of this nonsense on one of our happy motor-trips among the hills of Western Massachusetts. We had motored so much together in Europe that allusions to Roman ruins and Gothic cathedrals furnished a great part of the jests with which his mind played over what he has called 'the thin empty lonely American beauty'; and one day, when his eye caught the fine peak rising alone in the vale between Deerfield and Springfield, with a wooden barrack of a 'summer hotel' on its highest ledge, I told him that the hill was Mount Tom, and the building 'the famous Carthusian monastery'. 'Yes, where the monks make Moxie,' he flashed back, referring to a temperance drink that was blighting the landscape that summer from a thousand hoardings.

Sometimes his chaff was not untinged with malice. I remember a painful moment, during one of his visits, when my husband imprudently blurted out an allusion to 'Edith's new story – you've seen it in the last "Scribner"?' My heart sank; I knew it always embarrassed James to be called on, in the author's presence, for an 'appreciation'. He was himself so engrossed in questions of technique and construction – and so increasingly detached from the short-story form as a medium – that very few 'fictions' (as he called them) but his own were of interest to him, except indeed Mr Wells's, for which he once avowed to me an incurable liking, 'because everything he writes is so alive and kicking'. At any rate I always tried to keep my own work out of his way, and once accused him of ferreting out and reading it just to annoy me – to which charge his sole response was a guilty chuckle. In the present instance, as usual, he instantly replied: 'Oh, yes, my dear Edward,

I've read the little work – of course I've read it.' A gentle pause, which I knew boded no good; then he softly continued: 'Admirable, admirable; a masterly little achievement.' He turned to me, full of a terrifying benevolence. 'Of course so accomplished a mistress of the art would not, without deliberate intention, have given the tale so curiously conventional a treatment. Though indeed, in the given case, no treatment *but* the conventional was possible; which might conceivably, my dear lady, on further consideration, have led you to reject your subject as – er – in itself a totally unsuitable one.'

I will not deny that he may have added a silent twinkle to the shout of laughter with which – on that dear wide sunny terrace of the Mount – his fellow-guests greeted my 'dressing-down'. Yet it would be a mistake to imagine that he had deliberately started out to destroy my wretched tale. He had begun, I am sure, with the sincere intention of praising it; but no sooner had he opened his lips than he was overmastered by the need to speak the truth, and the whole truth, about anything connected with the art which was sacred to him. Simplicity of heart was combined in him with a brain that Mr Percy Lubbock has justly called robust, and his tender regard for his friends' feelings was equalled only by the faithfulness with which, on literary questions, he gave them his view of their case when they asked for it – and sometimes when they did not. On all subjects but that of letters his sincerity was tempered by an almost exaggerated tenderness; but when *le métier* was in question no gentler emotion prevailed.

Another day – somewhat later in our friendship, since this time the work under his scalpel was 'The Custom of the Country' – after prolonged and really generous praise of my book, he suddenly and irrepressibly burst forth: 'But of course you know – as how should you, with your infernal keenness of perception, *not* know? – that in doing your tale you had under your hand a magnificent subject, which ought to have been your main theme, and that you used it as a mere incident and then passed it by?'

He meant by this that for him the chief interest of the book, and its most original theme, was that of a crude young woman such as Undine Spragg entering, all unprepared and unperceiving, into the mysterious labyrinth of family life in the old French aristocracy. I saw his point, and recognized that the contact between the Undine Spraggs and the French families they marry into was, as the French themselves would say, an 'actuality' of immense interest to the novelist of manners, and one which as yet had been little dealt with; but I argued that in 'The Custom of the Country' I was chronicling the career of a particular young woman, and that to whatever hemisphere her fortunes carried her, my task was to record her ravages and pass on to her next phase. This, however, was no argument to James; he had long since lost all interest in the chronicle-novel, and cared only for the elaborate working out on all sides of a central situation, so that he could merely answer, by implication if not openly: 'Then, my dear child, you chose the wrong kind of subject.'

Once when he was staying with us in Paris I had a still more amusing experience of this irresistible tendency to speak the truth. He had chanced to nose out the fact that, responding to an S.O.S. from the *Revue des Deux Mondes*, for a given number of which a promised translation of one of my tales had not been ready, I had offered to replace it by writing a story myself – in French! I knew what James would feel about such an experiment, and there was nothing I did not do to conceal the horrid secret from him; but he had found it out before arriving, and when in my presence some idiot challenged him with: 'Well, Mr James, don't you think it's remarkable that Mrs Wharton should have written a story in French for the *Revue*?' the twinkle which began in the corner of his eyes and trickled slowly down to his twitching lips showed that his answer was ready. 'Remarkable – most remarkable! An altogether astonishing feat.' He swung around on me slowly. 'I do congratuate you, my dear, on the way in which you've picked up every old worn-out literary phrase that's been lying about the streets of Paris for the last twenty years, and managed to pack them all into those few pages.' To this withering comment, in talking over the story afterwards with one of my friends, he added more seriously, and with singular good sense: 'A very creditable episode in her career. *But she must never do it again.*'

He knew I enjoyed our literary rough-and-tumbles, and no doubt for that reason scrupled the less to hit straight from the shoulder; but with others, though he tried to be more merciful, what he really thought was no less manifest. My own experience has taught me that nothing is more difficult than to talk indifferently or insincerely on the subject of one's craft. The writer, without much effort, can reel off polite humbug about pictures, the painter about books; but to fib about the art one practises is incredibly painful, and James's overscrupulous conscience, and passionate reverence for letters, while always inclining him to mercy, made deception doubly impossible.

I think it was James who first made me understand that genius is not an indivisible element, but one variously apportioned, so that the popular system of dividing humanity into geniuses and non-geniuses is a singularly inadequate way of estimating human complexity. In connection with this, I once brought him a phrase culled in a literary review. 'Mr— has *almost a streak* of genius'. James, always an eager collector of verbal oddities, fell on the phrase with rapture, and earnest requests to every one to define the exact extent of 'almost a streak' caused him amusement for months afterward. I mention this because so few people seem to have known in Henry James the ever-bubbling fountain of fun which was the delight of his intimates.

One of our joys, when the talk touched on any great example of prose or verse, was to get the book from the shelf, and ask one of the company to read the passage aloud. There were some admirable readers in the group, in whose gift I had long delighted; but I had never heard Henry James read aloud – or known that he enjoyed doing so – till one night some one alluded to Emily Brontë's poems, and I said I had never read 'Remembrance'. Immediately he took the volume from my hand, and, his eyes filling, and some far-away emotion deepening his rich and flexible voice, he began:

> Cold in the earth, and the deep snow piled above thee,
> Far, far removed, cold in the dreary grave,
> Have I forgot, my only Love, to love thee,
> Severed at last by Time's all-severing wave?

I had never before heard poetry read as he read it; and I never have since. He chanted it, and he was not afraid to chant it, as many good readers are, who, though they instinctively feel that the genius of the English poetical idiom requires it to be spoken *as poetry*, are yet afraid of yielding to their instinct because the present-day fashion is to chatter high verse as though it were colloquial prose. James, on the contrary, far from shirking the rhythmic emphasis, gave it full expression. His stammer ceased as by magic as soon as he began to read, and his ear, so sensitive to the convolutions of an intricate prose style, never allowed him to falter over the most complex prosody, but swept him forward on great rollers of sound till the full weight of his voice fell on the last cadence.

James's reading was a thing apart, an emanation of his inmost self, unaffected by fashion or elocutionary artifice. He read from his soul, and no one who never heard him read poetry knows what that soul was. Another day some one spoke of Whitman, and it was a joy to me to discover that James thought him, as I did, the greatest of American poets. 'Leaves of Grass' was put into his hands, and all that evening we sat rapt while he wandered from 'The Song of Myself' to 'When lilacs last in the door-yard bloomed' (when he read 'Lovely and soothing Death' his voice filled the hushed room like an organ adagio), and thence let himself be lured on to the mysterious music of 'Out of the Cradle', reading, or rather crooning it in a mood of subdued ecstasy till the fivefold invocation to Death tolled out like the knocks in the opening bars of the Fifth Symphony.

James's admiration of Whitman, his immediate response to that mighty appeal, was a new proof of the way in which, above a certain level, the most divergent intelligences walk together like gods. We talked long that night of 'Leaves of Grass', tossing back and forth to each other treasure after treasure; but finally James, in one of his sudden humorous drops from the heights, flung up his hands and cried out with the old stammer and twinkle: 'Oh, yes, a great genius; undoubtedly a very great genius! Only one cannot help deploring his too-extensive acquaintance with the foreign languages.'

3

I believe James enjoyed those days at the Mount as much as he did (or could) anything connected with the American scene; and the proof of it is the length of his visits and their frequency. But on one occasion his stay with us coincided with a protracted heat-wave; a wave of such unusual intensity that even the nights, usually cool and airy at the Mount, were as stifling as the days. My own dislike of heat filled me with sympathy for James, whose sufferings were acute and uncontrollable. Like many men of genius he had a singular inability for dealing with the most ordinary daily incidents, such as giving an order to a servant, deciding what to wear, taking a railway ticket, or getting from one place to another; and I have often smiled to think how far nearer the truth than he could possibly have known was the author of that cataclysmic sketch in the famous 'If—' series: 'If Henry James had written Bradshaw.'

During a heat-wave this curious inadaptability to conditions or situations became positively tragic. His bodily surface, already broad, seemed to expand to meet it, and his imagination to become a part of his body, so that the one dripped words of distress as the other did moisture. Always uneasy about his health, he became visibly anxious in hot weather, and this anxiety added so much to his sufferings that his state was pitiful. Electric fans, iced drinks and cold baths seemed to give no relief; and finally we discovered that the only panacea was incessant motoring. Luckily by that time we had a car which would really go, and go we did, daily, incessantly, over miles and miles of lustrous landscape lying motionless under the still glaze of heat. While we were moving he was refreshed and happy, his spirits rose, the twinkle returned to lips and eyes; and we never halted except for tea on a high hillside, or for a 'cooling drink' at a village apothecary's – on one of which occasions he instructed one of us to bring him 'something less innocent than Apollinaris', and was enchanted when this was interpreted as meaning an 'orange phosphate', a most sophisticated beverage for that day.

On another afternoon we had encamped for tea on a mossy ledge in the shade of great trees, and as he seemed less uneasy than usual somebody pulled out an anthology, and I asked one of the party to read aloud Swinburne's 'Triumph of Time', which I knew to be a favourite of James's; but after a stanza or two I saw the twinkle of beatitude fade, and an agonized hand was lifted up. 'Perhaps, in view of the abnormal state of the weather, our young friend would have done better to choose a poem of less inordinate length –' and immediately we were all bundled back into the car and started off again on the incessant quest for air.

James was to leave for England in about a fortnight; but his suffering distressed me so much that, the day after this expedition, feeling sure that there was nothing to detain him in America if he chose to go, I asked a friend who was staying in the house to propose my telephoning for a passage on a Boston steamer which was sailing within two days. My ambassador executed the commission, and hurried back with the report that the mere hint of such a plan had thrown James into a state of helpless perturbation. To change his sailing date at two days' notice – to get from the Mount to Boston (four hours by train) in *two days* –

how could I lightly suggest anything so impracticable? And what about his heavy luggage, which was at his brother William's in New Hampshire? And his wash, which had been sent to the laundry only the afternoon before? Between the electric fan clutched in his hand, and the pile of sucked oranges at his elbow, he cowered there, a mountain of misery, repeating in a sort of low despairing chant: 'Good God, what a woman – what a woman! Her imagination boggles at nothing! She does not even scruple to project me in a naked flight across the Atlantic . . .' The heat collapse had been as nothing to the depths into which my rash proposal plunged him, and it took several hours to quiet him down and persuade him that, if he preferred enduring the weather to flying from it, we were only too glad to keep him at the Mount.

A similar perturbation could be produced (I later learned, to my cost) by asking him to explain any phrase in his books that did not seem quite clear, or any situation of which the motive was not adequately developed; and still more disastrous was the effect of letting him know that any of his writings had been parodied. I had always regarded the fact of being parodied as one of the surest evidences of fame, and once, when he was staying with us in New York, I brought him with glee a deliciously droll article on his novels by poor Frank Colby, the author of 'Imaginary Obligations'. The effect was disastrous. I shall never forget the misery, the mortification even, which tried to conceal itself behind an air of offended dignity. His ever-bubbling sense of fun failed him completely on such occasions; as it did also (I was afterward to find) when one questioned him, in a way that even remotely implied criticism, on any point in the novels. It was in England, I think – when he and I, and a party of intimate friends, were staying together at Howard Sturgis's – that I brought him, in all innocence, a passage from one of his books which, after repeated readings, I still found unintelligible. He took the book from me, read over the passage to himself, and handed it back with a lame attempt at a joke; but I saw – we all saw – that even this slight, and quite involuntary, criticism, had wounded his morbidly delicate sensibility.

Once again – and again unintentionally – I was guilty of a similar blunder. I was naturally much interested in James's technical theories and experiments, though I thought, and still think, that he tended to sacrifice to them that spontaneity which is the life of fiction. Everything, in the latest novels, had to be fitted into a predestined design, and design, in his strict geometrical sense, is to me one of the least important things in fiction. Therefore, though I greatly admired some of the principles he had formulated, such as that of always letting the tale, as it unfolded, be seen through the mind most capable of reaching to its periphery, I thought it was paying too dear even for such a principle to subordinate to it the irregular and irrelevant movements of life. And one result of the application of his theories puzzled and troubled me. His latest novels, for all their profound moral beauty, seemed to me more and more lacking in atmosphere, more and more severed from that thick nourishing human air in which we all live and move. The characters in 'The Wings of the Dove' and 'The Golden Bowl' seem isolated in a Crookes tube for our inspection: his stage was cleared like that of the Théâtre Français in the good old days when no chair or table was introduced that was not *relevant to the action* (a good rule for the stage, but an unnecessary embarrassment to fiction). Preoccupied by this, I one day said to him: 'What was your idea in suspending the four principal characters in 'The Golden Bowl' in the void? What sort of life did they lead when they were not watching each other, and fencing with each other? Why have you stripped them of all the *human fringes* we necessarily trail after us through life?'

He looked at me in surprise, and I saw at once that the surprise was painful, and wished I had not spoken. I had assumed that his system was a deliberate one, carefully thought out, and had been genuinely anxious to hear his reason. But after a pause of reflection he answered in a disturbed voice: 'My dear – I didn't know I had!' and I saw that my question, instead of starting one of our absorbing literary discussions, had only turned his startled attention on a pecularity of which he had been completely unconscious.

This sensitiveness to criticism or comment of any sort had nothing to do with vanity; it was caused by the great artist's deep consciousness of his powers, combined with a bitter, a life-long disappointment at his lack of popular recognition. I am not sure that Henry James had not secretly dreamed of being a 'best seller' in the days when that odd form of literary fame was at its height; at any rate he certainly suffered all his life – and more and more as time went on – from the lack of recognition among the very readers who had most warmly welcomed his early novels. He could not understand why the success achieved by 'Daisy Miller' and 'The Portrait of a Lady' should be denied to the great novels of his maturity: and the sense of protracted failure made him miserably alive to the least hint of criticism, even from those who most completely understood, and sympathized with, his later experiments in technique and style.

4

Those long days at the Mount, in the deep summer glow or the crisp glitter of autumn, the walks in the woods, motor-flights over hill and dale, evening talks on the moonlit terrace and readings around the library fire, come back with a mocking radiance as I write – and with them the figures of our other most beloved guests, Walter Berry, Bay Lodge, and three dear friends from England, Gaillard Lapsley, Robert Norton and John Hugh Smith.

Still others, friendly and delightful also, came and went; but these, with Henry James, if not by the actual frequency of their visits, yet from some secret quality of participation, had formed from the first the nucleus of what I have called the inner group. In this group an almost immediate sympathy had established itself between the various members, so that our common stock of allusions, cross-references, pleasantries was always increasing, and new waves of interest in the same book or picture, or any sort of dramatic event in life or letters, would simultaneously flood through our minds.

I think I may safely say that Henry James was never so good as with this little party at the Mount, or when some of its members were reunited, as often happened in after years, under Howard Sturgis's welcoming roof at Windsor. The mere fact that we had in common so many topics, and such innumerable allusions, made James's talk on such occasions easier and wider-ranging than I ever heard it elsewhere; and the free and rapid give-and-take of ideas animated his mind, which so easily drooped in dull company.

In one respect Henry James stood alone among the great talkers I have known, for while he was inexhaustible in repartee, and never had the least tendency to monopolize the talk, yet it was really in monologue that he was most himself. I remember in particular one summer evening, when we sat late on the terrace at the Mount, with the lake shining palely through dark trees, and one of us suddenly said to him (in response to some chance allusion to his Albany relations): 'And now tell us about the Emmets – tell us all about them.'

The Emmet and Temple families composed, as we knew, the main element of his vast and labyrinthine cousinship – 'the Emmetry', as he called it – and for a moment he stood there brooding in the darkness, murmuring over to himself: 'Ah, my dear, the Emmets – ah, the Emmets!' Then he began, forgetting us, forgetting the place, forgetting everything but the vision of his lost youth that the question had evoked, the long train of ghosts flung with his enchanter's wand across the wide stage of the summer night. Ghostlike indeed at first, wavering and distinct, they glimmered at us through a series of disconnected ejaculations, epithets, allusions, parenthetic rectifications and restatements, till not only our brains but the clear night itself seemed filled with a palpable fog; and then, suddenly, by some miracle of shifted lights and accumulated strokes, there they stood before us as they lived, drawn with a million filament-like lines, yet sharp as an Ingres, dense as a Rembrandt; or, to call upon his own art for an analogy, minute and massive as the people of Balzac.

I often saw the trick repeated; saw figures obscure or famous summoned to the white square of his magic-lantern, flickering and wavering there, and slowly solidifying under the turn of his lens; but never perhaps anything so ample, so sustained, as that summoning to life of dead-and-gone Emmets and Temples, old lovelinesses, old follies, old failures, all long laid away and forgotten under old crumbling grave-stones. I wonder if it may not have been that very night, the place and his reawakened associations aiding, that they first came to him and constrained him to make them live for us again in the pages of 'A Small Boy' and 'A Son and Brother'?

5

In New York James was a different being. He hated the place, as his letters abundantly testify; its aimless ugliness, its noisy irrelevance, wore on his nerves; but he was amused by the social scene, and eager to leave nothing of it unobserved. During his visits, therefore, we invited many people to the house, and he dined out frequently, and went to the play – for he was still intensely interested in the theatre. But this mundane James, his attention scattered, his long and complex periods breaking against a dull wall of incomprehension, and dispersing themselves in nervous politenesses, was a totally different being from our leisurely companion at the Mount. I always enjoyed having him under my roof, wherever that good fortune befell me; but my hurried preoccupied New York guest seemed a mere fragment of the great 'Henry' of our country hours.

New York in those days, though more cosmopolitan than in my youth, was still a small place, with so limited a range of intellectual interests and allusions that dinner-table talk was a good deal like the 'local items' column in a country newspaper; and I remember depressing evenings when the hosts, contributing orchids and gold plate, remained totally unconscious of the royal gifts their guest had brought them in exchange.

James knew that his treasures were largely unmarketable in Fifth Avenue, but it perplexed and saddened him that they should, as a rule, be equally so in the world of letters, which he was naturally even more eager to explore. I remember one occasion when a dinner was especially arranged to make known to him a brilliant essayist whose books he greatly enjoyed. Unhappily the essayist's opaque countenance revealed nothing of the keenness within, and he on his part, though appreciative of James's genius, was obviously put off by his laborious hesitations. Their comments on the meeting were, on the essayist's side, a joke about James's stammer, and on James's the melancholy exclamation: 'What a mug!'

I suspect that he was much happier, and more at his ease, in Boston than in New York. At Cambridge, in the houses of his brother, William James, and of Charles Eliot Norton, and their kindred circles, he had the best of Boston; and in Boston itself, where the sense of the past has always been so much stronger than in New York, he found all sorts of old affinities and relations, and early Beacon Hill traditions, to act as life-belts in the vast ocean of strangeness. He had always clung to his cousinage, and to any one who represented old friendly associations, whether in Albany, New York or Boston, and I remember his once saying: 'You see, my dear, they're so much easier to talk to, because I can always ask them questions about uncles and aunts, and other cousins.' He had brought this question-asking system to a high state of perfection, and practised it not only on relations and old friends, but on transatlantic pilgrims to Lamb House, whom he would literally silence by a friendly volley of interrogations as to what train they had taken to come down, and whether they had seen all the cathedral towns yet, and what plays they had done; so that they went away aglow with the great man's cordiality, 'and, you see, my dear, they hadn't time to talk to me about my books' – the calamity at all costs to be averted.

Chapter Nine
The Secret Garden

This wielding of the unreal trowel.
Walter Scott's Diary (December 26, 1825)

I

I have hesitated for some time before beginning this chapter, since any attempt to analyze work of one's own doing seems to imply that one regards it as likely to be of lasting interest, and I wish at once to repudiate such an assumption. Every artist works, like the Gobelins weavers, on the wrong side of the tapestry, and if now and then he comes around to the right side, and catches what seems a happy glow of colour, or a firm sweep of design, he must instantly retreat again, if encouraged yet still uncertain; and once the work is done, and he hopes to contemplate it dispassionately, the result of his toil too often presses on his tired eyes with the nightmare weight of a cinema 'close-up'.

Nevertheless, no picture of myself would be more than a profile if it failed to give some account of the teeming visions which, ever since my small-childhood, and even at the busiest and most agitated periods of my outward life, have incessantly peopled my inner world. I shall therefore try to describe, as simply as I can, what seems to have gone to the making of my books; and there is the more reason for doing so because so few writers seem to have watched themselves while they wrote, or if they did, to have set down their observations. Not a few painters have painted themselves at their easels, but I can think of nothing corresponding to these self-confessions in the world of letters, or at any rate of fiction, except the prefaces of Henry James. These, however, are mainly analyses of the way in which he focussed a given subject, and of the technical procedure employed, his angle of vision once determined. Even that deeply moving fragment, the appeal to his Genius, the knowledge of which we owe to Percy Lubock, in an invocation to the goddess and not an objective notation of her descent into his soul. What I mean to try for is the observation of that strange moment when the vaguely adumbrated characters whose adventures one is preparing to

record are suddenly *there*, themselves, in the flesh, in possession of
one, and in command of one's voice and hand. It is there that the
central mystery lies, and perhaps it is as impossible to fix in words
as that other mystery of what happens in the brain at the precise
moment when one falls over the edge of consciousness into sleep.

My impression is that, among English and American novelists,
few are greatly interested in these deeper processes of their art;
their conscious investigation of method seldom seem to go deeper
than syntax, and it is immeasurably deeper that the vital interest
begins. Therefore I shall try to depict the growth and unfolding of
the plants in my secret garden, from the seed to the shrub-top – for
I have no intention of magnifying my vegetation into trees!

When I began to talk with novelists about the art of fiction I was
amazed at the frequently repeated phrase: 'I've been hunting
about for months for a good subject'. Hunting about for a subject!
Good heavens! I remember once, when an old friend of the pen
made this rather wistful complaint, carelessly rejoining: 'Subjects? But they swarm about me like mosquitoes! I'm sick of them;
they stifle me. I wish I could get rid of them!' And only years
afterward, when I had learned more from both life and letters, did
I understand how presumptuous such an answer must have
sounded. The truth is that I have never attached much importance
to subject, partly because every incident, every situation, presents
itself to me in the light of story-telling material, and partly from
the conviction that the possibilities of a given subject are –
whatever a given imagination can make of them. But by the time I
had written three or four novels I had learned to keep silence on
this point.

The analysis of the story-telling process may be divided into
two parts: that which concerns the technique of fiction (in the
widest sense), and that which tries to look into what, for want of a
simpler term, one must call by the old bardic name of inspiration.
On the subject of technique I have found only two novelists
explicitly and deeply interested: Henry James and Paul Bourget. I
have talked long and frequently with both, and profitably also, I
hope, though on certain points we always disagreed. I have also,
to the best of my ability, analyzed this process, as I understood it,
in my book 'The Writing of Fiction'; and therefore I shall deal
here not with any general theory of technique but simply with the
question of how some of my own novels happened to me, how
each little volcanic island shot up from the unknown depths, or

each coral-atoll slowly built itself. But first I will try to capture the elusive moment of the arrival of the characters.

In the birth of fiction, it is sometimes the situation, the 'case', which first presents itself, and sometimes the characters who appear, asking to be fitted into a situation. It is hard to say what conditions are likely to give the priority to one or the other, and I doubt if fiction can be usefully divided into novels of situation and of character, since a novel, if worth anything at all, is always both, in inextricable combination. In my own case a situation some-times occurs to me first, and sometimes a single figure suddenly walks into my mind. If the situation takes the lead, I leave it lying about, as it were, in a quiet place, and wait till the characters creep stealthily up and wriggle themselves into it. All I seem to have done is to say, at the outset: 'This thing happened – but to whom?' Then I wait, holding my breath, and one by one the people appear and take possession of the case. When it happens in the other way, I may be strolling about casually in my mind, and suddenly a character will start up, coming seemingly from nowhere. Again, but more breathlessly, I watch; and presently the character draws nearer, and seems to become aware of me, and to feel the shy but desperate need to unfold his or her tale. I cannot say in which way a subject is most likely to present itself – though perhaps in short stories the situation, in novels one of the characters, generally appears first.

But this is not the most interesting point of the adventure. Compared with what follows it is not interesting at all, though it has, in my case, one odd feature I have not heard of elsewhere – that is, that my characters always appear with their names. Sometimes these names seem to me affected, sometimes almost ridiculous; but I am obliged to own that they are never funda-mentally unsuitable. And the proof that they are not, that they really belong to the people, is the difficulty I have in trying to substitute other names. For many years the attempt always ended fatally; any character I unchristened instantly died on my hands, as if it were some kind of sensitive crustacean, and the name it brought with it were its shell. Only gradually, and in very few cases, have I gained enough mastery over my creatures to be able to effect the change; and even now, when I do, I have to resort to hypodermics and oxygen, and not always successfully.

These names are hardly ever what I call 'real names', that is, the current patronymics one would find in an address-book or a telephone directory; and it is their excessive oddness which often makes me try to change them. When in a book by some one else I meet people called by current names I always say to myself: 'Ah, those names were tied on afterward'; and I often find that the characters thus labelled are less living than the others. Yet there seems to be no general rule, for in the case of certain famous novelists whose characters have out-of-the-way names, many are tied on too. Balzac had to hunt the streets of Paris for names on shop-signs; and Thackeray and Trollope bent their genius to the invention of the most laboured and dreary pleasantries in the pointless attempt to characterize their people in advance. Yet Captain Deuceace and the Rev. Mr Quiverful are alive enough, and I can only suppose that this odd fact of the prenamed characters is a peculiarity of my own mental make-up. But I often wonder how the novelist whose people arrive without names manages to establish relations with them!

A still more spectral element in my creative life is the sudden appearance of names without characters. Several times, in this way, a name to which I can attach no known association of ideas has forced itself upon me in a furtive shadowy way, not succeeding in making its bearer visible, yet hanging about obstinately for years in the background of my thoughts. The Princess Estradina was such a name. I knew nothing of its origin, and still less of the invisible character to whom it presumably belonged. Who was she, what were her nationality, her history, her claims on my attention? She must have been there, lurking and haunting me, for years before she walked into 'The Custom of the Country', in high-coloured flesh and blood, cool, dominant and thoroughly at home. Another such character haunts me today. Her name is still odder: Laura Testvalley. How I should like to change that name! But it has been attached for some time now to a strongly outlined material form, the form of a character figuring largely in an adventure I know all about, and have long wanted to relate. Several times I have tried to give Miss Testvalley another name, since the one she bears, should it appear ever in print, will be even more troublesome to my readers than to me. But she is strong-willed, and even obstinate, and turns sulky and unmanageable whenever I hint at the advantages of a change; and I foresee that she will eventually force her way into my tale burdened with her impossible patronymic.

But this is a mere parenthesis; what I want to try to capture is an impression of the elusive moment when these people who haunt my brain actually begin to speak within me with their own voices. The situating of my tale, and its descriptive and narrative portions, I am conscious of conducting, though often unaware of how the story first came to me, pleading to be told; but as soon as the dialogue begins, I become merely a recording instrument, and my hand never hesitates because my mind has not to choose, but only to set down what these stupid or intelligent, lethargic or passionate, people say to each other in a language, and with arguments, that appear to be all their own. It is because of this that I attach such importance to dialogue, and yet regard it as an effect to be sparingly used. By dialogue I do not mean the pages of 'Yes' and 'No', of platitudes and repetitions, of which most actual talk is composed, and which any writer with a photographic mind and a good memory can set down by the yard (and does, in most modern fiction). The vital dialogue is that exchanged by characters whom their creator has really vitalized, and his instinct will be to record only the significant passages of their talk, in high relief against the narrative, and not uselessly embedded in it.

These moments of high tension, when the creature lives and its creator listens to it, have nothing in common with the 'walking away with the subject', the 'settling it in their own way', with which some novelists so oddly charge their characters. It is always a necessity to me that the note of inevitableness should be sounded at the very opening of my tale, and that my characters should go forward to their ineluctable doom like the 'murdered man' in 'The Pot of Basil'. From the first I know exactly what is going to happen to every one of them; their fate is settled beyond rescue, and I have but to watch the record. When I read that great novelists like Dickens and Trollope 'killed off' a character, or changed the conclusion of a tale, in response to the request or the criticism of a reader, I am dumbfounded. What then was their own relation to their subject? But to show how mysterious and incalculable the whole business is, one has only to remember that Trollope 'went home and killed' Mrs Proudie because he had overheard some fool at his club complaining that she had lived long enough; and yet that the death scene thus arbitrarily brought about is one of the greatest pages he ever wrote, and places him momentarily on a level with Balzac and Tolstoy!

But these people of mine, whose ultimate destiny I know so well, walk to it by ways unrevealed to me beforehand. Not only their speech, but what I might call their subsidiary action, seems to be their very own, and I am sometimes startled at the dramatic effect of a word or gesture which would never have occurred to me if I had been pondering over an abstract 'situation', as yet uninhabited by its 'characters'.

I do not think I can get any nearer than this to the sources of my story-telling; I can only say that the process, though it takes place in some secret region on the sheer edge of consciousness, is always illuminated by the full light of my critical attention. What happens there is as real and as tangible as my encounters with my friends and neighbours, often more so, though on an entirely different plane. It produces in me a great emotional excitement, quite unrelated to the joy or sorrow caused by real happenings, but as intense, and with as great an appearance of reality; and my two lives, divided between these equally real yet totally unrelated worlds, have gone on thus, side by side, equally absorbing, but wholly isolated from each other, ever since in my infancy I 'read stories' aloud to myself out of Washington Irving's 'Alhambra', which I generally held upside down.

2

After 'The Valley of Decision', and my book on Italian villas, the idea of attempting a novel of contemporary life in New York began to fascinate me. Still, I hesitated. 'The Valley of Decision' was not, in my sense of the term, a novel at all, but only a romantic chronicle, unrolling its episodes like the frescoed legends on the palace-walls which formed its background; my idea of a novel was something very different, something far more compact and centripetal, and I doubted whether I should ever have enough constructive power to achieve anything beyond isolated character studies, or the stringing together of picturesque episodes. But my mind was full of my new subject, and whatever else I was about, I went on, in Tyndall's brooding phrase, trying to 'look into it till it became luminous'.

Fate had planted me in New York, and my instinct as a storyteller counselled me to use the material nearest to hand, and most familiarly my own. Novelists of my generation must have noticed, in recent years, as one of the unforeseen results of 'crowd-mentality' and standardizing, that the modern critic requires every novelist to treat the same kind of subject, and relegates to insignificance the author who declines to conform. At present the demand is that only the man with the dinner pail shall be deemed worthy of attention, and fiction is classed according to its degree of conformity to this rule.

There could be no greater critical ineptitude than to judge a novel according to *what it ought to have been about*. The bigger the imagination, the more powerful the intellectual equipment, the more different subjects will come within the novelist's reach; and Balzac spread his net over nearly every class and situation in the French social system. As a matter of fact, there are but two essential rules: one, that the novelist should deal only with what is within his reach, literally or figuratively (in most cases the two are synonymous), and the other that the value of a subject depends almost wholly on what the author sees in it, and how deeply he is able to see *into* it. Almost – but not quite; for there are certain subjects too shallow to yield anything to the most searching gaze. I had always felt this, and now my problem was how to make use of a subject – fashionable New York – which, of all others, seemed most completely to fall within the condemned category. There it was before me, in all its flatness and futility, asking to be dealt with as the theme most available to my hand, since I had been steeped in it from infancy, and should not have to get it up out of note-books and encyclopaedias – and yet!

The problem was how to extract from such a subject the typical human significance which is the story-tellers's reason for telling one story rather than another. In what aspect could a society of irresponsible pleasure-seekers be said to have, on the 'old woe of the world', any deeper bearing than the people composing such a society could guess? The answer was that a frivolous society can acquire dramatic significance only through what its frivolity destroys. Its tragic implications lies in its power of debasing people and ideals. The answer, in short, was my heroine, Lily Bart.

Once I had understood that, the tale rushed on toward its climax. I already had definite ideas as to how any given subject should be viewed, and from what angle approached; my trouble was that the story kept drawing into its web so many subordinate themes that to show their organic connection with the main issue, yet keep them from crowding to the front, was a heavy task for a beginner. The novel was already promised to 'Scribner's

Magazine', but no date had been fixed for its delivery, and between my critical dissatisfaction with the work, and the distractions of a busy and hospitable life, full of friends and travel, reading and gardening, I had let the months drift by without really tackling my subject. And then, one day, Mr Burlingame came to my rescue by asking me to come to his. A novel which was to have preceded mine in the magazine could not be ready in time, and I was asked to replace it. The first chapters of my tale would have to appear almost at once, and it must be completed within four or five months! I have always been a slow worker, and was then a very inexperienced one, and I was to be put to the severest test to which a novelist can be subjected: my novel was to be exposed to public comment before I had worked it out to its climax. What that climax was to be I had known before I began. My last page is always latent in my first; but the intervening windings of the way become clear only as I write, and now I was asked to gallop over them before I had even traced them out! I had expected to devote another year or eighteen months to the task, instead of which I was asked to be ready within six months; and nothing short of 'the hand of God' must be suffered to interrupt my labours, since my first chapters would already be in print!

I hesitated for a day, and then accepted, and buckled down to my job; and of all the friendly turns that Mr Burlingame ever did me, his exacting this effort was undoubtedly the most helpful. Not only did it give me what I most lacked – self-confidence – but it bent me to the discipline of the daily task, that inscrutable 'inspiration of the writing table' which Baudelaire, most untrammelled and nerve-racked of geniuses, proclaimed as insistently as Trollope. When the first chapters appeared I had written hardly fifty thousand words; but I kept at it, and finished and delivered my novel on time.

It was good to be turned from a drifting amateur into a professional; but that was nothing compared to the effect on my imagination of systematic daily effort. I was really like Saul the son of Kish, who went out to find an ass, and came back with a kingdom: the kingdom of mastery over my tools. When the book was done I remember saying to myself: 'I don't yet know how to write a novel; *but I know how to find out how to*.'

I went on steadily trying to 'find out how to'; but I wrote two or three novels without feeling that I had made much progress. It was not until I wrote 'Ethan Frome' that I suddenly felt the artisan's full control of his implements. When 'Ethan Frome' first appeared I was severely criticized by the reviewers for what was considered the clumsy structure of the tale. I had pondered long on this structure, had felt its peculiar difficulties, and possible awkwardness, but could think of no alternative which would serve as well in the given case; and though I am far from thinking 'Ethan Frome' my best novel, and am bored and even exasperated when I am told that it is, I am sure that its structure is not its weak point.

From that day until now I have always felt that I had my material fairly well in hand, though so often, alas, I am conscious that the strange beings who have commissioned me to tell their story are not satisfied with the portraits I have drawn of them. I think it was Sargent who said that, when a portrait was submitted to the sitter's family, the comment of the latter was always: 'There's something wrong about the mouth'. It is the same with my sitters; though they are free to talk and even to behave, in their own way, the image of them reflected in my pages is often, I fear, wavering, or at least blurred. 'There is something wrong about the mouth' – and the great masters of portraiture, Balzac, Tolstoy, Thackeray, Trollope, have neglected to tell us by what means they not only 'caught the likeness', but carried it on, in all its flesh-and-blood actuality and changefulness, to the very last page.

3

All novelists who describe (whether from without or within) what is called 'society life', are pursued by the exasperating accusation of putting flesh-and-blood people into their books. Any one gifted with the least creative faculty knows the absurdity of such a charge. 'Real people' transported into a work of the imagination would instantly cease to be real; only those born of the creator's brain can give the least illusion of reality. But it is hopeless to persuade the unimaginative – who make up the bulk of novel-readers – that to introduce actual people into a novel would be exactly like gumming their snapshots into the vibrating human throng of a Guardi picture. If one did, they would be the only dead and unreal objects in a scene quivering with life. The low order, in fiction, of the genuine *roman à clef* (which is never written by a born novelist) naturally makes any serious writer of fiction indignant at being suspected of such methods. Nothing can be more trying to the creative writer than to have a clumsy finger point at one of the beings born in that mysterious other-world of invention, with the playful accusation: 'Of course we all recognize your aunt Eliza!', or to be told (and this has more than once happened to me): 'We all thought your heroine must be meant for Mrs X, *because their hair is exactly the same colour.*'

Of what, then, are the mysterious creatures compounded who come to life sometimes) under the novelist's pen? Well, it would be insincere to deny that there are bits of Aunt Eliza in this one, of Mrs X in that – though in the case of Mrs X it is hardly likely that the psychological novelist would use the colour of her hair as a mark of identity, and more than probable that the bits of Mrs X which have actually served him are embedded in some character where the reader alive only to outward signs would never think of seeking them. The process is in fact inexplicable enough to the author, and doubly so to his readers. No 'character' can be made out of nothing, still less can it be successfully pieced together out of heterogeneous scraps of the 'real', like dismembered statues of which the fragments have been hopelessly mixed up by the restorer. The process is more like that by which sham Tanagra statuettes used formerly, I have been told, to be manufactured for the unsuspecting. The experts having discovered that ancient terra-cotta acquires, though long burial, a peculiar flavour, were in the habit of assuring themselves of the genuineness of the piece by *tasting it*; and the forgers, discovering this, ground fragments of old Tanagras into powder, ran the powder into one of the old moulds, and fearlessly presented the result as an antique. Experience, observation, the looks and ways and words of 'real people', all melted and fused in the white heat of the creative fires – such is the mingled stuff which the novelist pours into the firm mould of his narrative. And yet even this does not wholly solve the problem; it is only a step or two nearer the truth than the exasperating attributions of the simple-minded . . .

These attributions are exasperating, no doubt; but they are less so because of the accidental annoyance that may result in a given case than because they bring home to the creator, each time with a fresh shock, the lack of imaginative response to his effort. It is discouraging to know that the books into the making of which so much of one's soul has entered will be snatched at by readers curious only to discover which of the heroes and heroines of the 'society column' are to be found in it. But I made up my mind long ago that it is foolish and illogical to resent so puerile a form of criticism. If one has sought the publicity of print, and sold one's wares in the open market, one has sold to the purchasers the right to think what they choose about one's books; and the novelist's best safeguard is to put out of his mind the quality of the praise or blame bestowed on him by reviewers and readers, and to write only for that dispassionate and ironic critic who dwells within the breast.

Chapter Ten
London, 'Qu'Acre' and 'Lamb'

I

I must go back a long way to recover the threads leading to my earliest acquaintance with London society. My husband and I took our first dip into it just after the appearance of 'The Greater Inclination'; but a dip so brief that I brought back from it hardly more than a list of names. It was then, probably, that I first met Lady Jeune, afterward Lady St Helier, whose friendly interest put me in relation with her large and ever-varying throng of guests. The tastes and interests of Lady St Helier, one of the best-known London hostesses of her day, could hardly have been more remote from my own. She was a born 'entertainer' according to the traditional London idea, which regarded (and perhaps still regards) the act of fighting one's way through a struggling crowd of celebrities as the finest expression of social intercourse. I have always hated 'general society', and Lady St Helier could conceive of no society that was not general. She took a frank and indefatigable interest in celebrities, and was determined to have them all at her house, whereas I was shy, or indifferent, and without any desire to meet any of them, at any rate on such wholesale occasions, except one or two of my own craft. Yet Lady Jeune and I at once became fast friends, and my affection and admiration for her grew with the growth of our friendship. For many years I stayed with her whenever I went to London, gladly undergoing the inevitable series of big lunches and dinners for the sake of the real pleasure I had in being with her. Others have done justice to her tireless and intelligent activities on the London County Council, and in every good cause, political, municipal or philanthropic, which appealed to her wide sympathies. What I wish to record is that this woman, who figured to hundreds merely as the most indefatigable and imperturbable of hostesses, a sort of automatic entertaining machine, had a vigorous personality of her own, and the most generous and independent character. Psychologically, the professional hostess and celebrity-seeker will always remain an enigma to me; but I have known intimately three who were famous in their day, and though nothing could be more divergent than their tastes and mine, yet I was drawn to all three by the same large and generous character, the same capacity for strong individual friendships.

Lady St Helier was perfectly aware of her own foible for hospitability on a large scale, and I remember her being amused and touched by an incident which happened just before one of my visits to her. One of her two married daughters shared her interest in the literary and artistic figures of the day, and as this daughter lived in the country she depended on her mother for her glimpses of the passing show. One day she wrote begging Lady St Helier to invite to dinner, at a date when she, the daughter, was to be in London, a young writer whose first book had caused a passing flutter. Lady St Helier, delighted at the pretext, wrote to the young man, who was a total stranger to her, telling him of her daughter's admiration, and her own, for his book, and begging him to dine with her the following week. The novelist replied that he could not accept her invitation; he hated dining out, and moreover owned no evening clothes; but he added that he was desperately hard up, and as Lady St Helier had liked his book he hoped she would not mind lending him five pounds. His would-be hostess was disappointed at his refusing her invitation, but delighted with his frankness; and I am certain she sent him the five pounds – and not as a loan.

She would, I am sure, have been equally amused if she had ever heard (as I daresay she did) the story of the cannibal chief who, on the point of consigning a captive explorer to the pot, snatched him back to safety with the exclamation: 'But I think I've met you at Lady St Helier's!'

Among the friends I made at that friendly table I remember chiefly Sir George Trevelyan, the historian, Lord Haldane and Lord Goschen – the two latter, I imagine, interested by the accident of my familiarity with German literature. I saw at Lady St Helier's a long line of men famous in letters and public affairs, but our meetings were seldom renewed, for my visits to London were so crowded and hurried, owing to my husband's unwilling-ness to remain in England for more than a few days at a time, that the encounters were at best but passing glimpses. Thomas Hardy, however, I met several times, and though he was as remote and uncommunicative as our most unsocial American men of letters, his silence seemed due to an unconquerable shyness rather than to the great man's disdain for humbler neighbours. I sometimes sat next to him at luncheon at Lady St Helier's, and I found it comparatively easy to carry on a mild chat on literary matters. I remember once asking him if it were really true that the editor of the American magazine which had the privilege of publishing 'Jude the Obscure' had insisted on his transforming the illegitimate children of Jude and Sue into adopted orphans. He smiled, and said yes, it was a fact; but he added philosophically that he was not much surprised, as the editor of the Scottish magazine which had published his first short story had objected to his making his hero and heroine go for a walk on a Sunday, and obliged him to transfer the stroll to a week-day! He seemed to take little interest in the literary movements of the day, or in fact in any critical discussion of his craft, and I felt that he was completely enclosed in his own creative dream, through which I imagine few voices or influences ever reached him.

One of the things that most struck me when I began to go into general society in England was this indifference of the kind and friendly people whom I met to any but their individual occupations or hobbies. At that time – over thirty years ago – an interest in general ideas, and indeed in any topic whatever outside of the political and social preoccupations of the England of the day, was almost non-existent, except in a small group with which I was not thrown until later. There were, of course brilliant exceptions, and many of the most cultivated and widely ranging intelligences I have known have been among the Englishmen of that generation. But in general, in the big politico-worldly society in which men of all sorts, sportsmen, soldiers, lawyers, scholars and statesmen, were mingled with the merely frivolous, I found the greater number rather narrowly confined to their own particular topics, and general conversation as rigorously excluded as general ideas.

I remember, at one big dinner in this portion of the London world, hearing some one name Lord Basil Blackwood as we entered the dining-room, and turning eagerly to my neighbour (a famous polo-player, I think) with the question: 'Oh, *can* you tell me if that is the wonderful Basil Blackwood who did the pictures for "The Bad Child's Book of Beasts"? 'My neighbour gave me a glance of undisguised dismay, and hastily replied: 'Oh, please don't ask me that sort of question! I'm not in the least literary.'

His hostess, in sending him in with me, had probably whispered to the unhappy man: '*She writes*', and he was determined to make his position clear from the outset.

On another evening I had as neighbour, at another big dinner in the same set, a friendly young army officer, evidently much engrossed in his profession, who at once disarmed me by confessing that he didn't know how to talk anything but 'shop'. As I foresaw at least ten courses (I think the dinner was at Lord Rothschild's) I was somewhat disconcerted; but the encounter must have taken place not long after the Boer War, and having just read Conan Doyle's vivid narrative of that campaign I plunged at once into the subject, and thus kept more or less afloat for the first half hour. But what in the world were we to talk of next – ? My neighbour knew I was an American, and I thought his manifest interest in military history might have led him to hear of the American Revolution. I therefore asked him if he had read Sir George Trevelyan's lately published history of that event. He had never heard of the book or of the author, and to rouse his interest I said I had been told that Lord Wolseley regarded Sir George's account of the battle of Bunker Hill as the finest description of a military engagement written in our day.

'Ah,' said my neighbour, with awakening interest – 'the author's a soldier himself, then, I suppose?'

'No, he's not; which makes it all the more remarkable,' I replied (though at the moment I was not sure that it did!).

My reply plunged the young officer into perplexity; then his face lit up. 'Ah – I see; he was out there as military correspondent, was he?'

2

Now and then, of course, there were rich compensations for such evenings. I always said that London dinners reminded me of Clärchen's song; they could be so '*freudvoll*' or so '*leidvoll*' – though '*gedankenvoll*' they seldom were. But in the course of my London visits I gradually made friends with various intelligent people of the world whose interests were much nearer my own. Most of them figured among the 'Souls', who prided themselves on a title which had been ironically conferred, or among a kindred set of fashionable cosmopolitans, always ready to welcome new ideas, though they could seldom spare the time to understand them. The latter group, though not affiliated to the 'Souls', yet for the most part had the same interests and amusements, and I passed some pleasant hours with both.

One night at a dinner in this *milieu* – I think at Lady Ripon's – I found myself next to a man of about thirty-five or forty, whose name I had not caught. We fell into conversation, and within five minutes I was being whirled away on such a quick current of talk as I had not dipped into for many a day. My neighbour moved with dazing agility from topic to topic, tossing them to and fro like glittering glass balls, always making me share in the game, yet directing it with a practised hand. We soon discovered a common love of letters, and I think it was our main theme that evening. At all events, what I chiefly remember is our having matched, so to speak, the most famous kisses in literature, and my producing as my crowning effect, and to my neighbour's great admiration, the kiss on the stairs in 'The Spoils of Poynton' (which I have always thought one of the most moving love-scenes in fiction), while he quoted in exchange the last desperate embrace of Troilus:

> Injurious Time now with a robber's haste
> Crams his rich thievery up, he knows not how;
> As many farewells as be stars in heaven . . .
> He fumbles up into a loose adieu,
> And scants us with a single famished kiss
> Distasted with the salt of broken tears.

Only at the end of the evening did I learn that I had sat next to Harry Cust, one of the most eager and radio-active intelligences in London, unhappily too favoured by fortune to have been forced to canalize his gifts, but a captivating talker and delightful companion in the small circle of his intimates. We struck up a prompt friendship, and thereafter I seldom missed seeing him when I was in London, and keep the memory of delightful lunches and dinners at his picturesque house, looking out over a quiet rose-garden, a stone's throw from the roar of Knightsbridge.

Among these fashionable cosmopolitans (of whom Lady Ripon was one of the most accomplished) I found again an old friend and contemporary, the beautiful Lady Essex, who had been Adèle Grant of New York. She lived at that time at Bourdon House, Mayfair, the charming little brick manor of a famous heiress who, in the seventeenth century, brought her immense estates to the

Dukes of Westminster; one of the last, I suppose, of the old country houses to survive till our day in that intensely urban quarter. There, in the friendly setting of old pictures and old furniture of which her friends keep so happy a memory, I met a number of well-known people, among whom I remember especially Claude Phillips, the witty and agreeable director of the Wallace collection, Sir Edmund Gosse, who always showed me great kindness, Mr H. G. Wells, most stirring and responsive of talkers, the silent William Archer, dramatic critic and translator of Ibsen, and Max Beerbohm the matchless. It was not my good luck to meet the latter often, though he was still living in London, and far from being the recluse he has since (like myself) become. But when we did sit next to each other at lunch or dinner, it was like suddenly growing wings! I don't, alas, after all these years, remember many of our topics of conversation, or of his lapidary comments; but one of the latter still delights me. We were discussing the works of a well-known novelist whose talk was full of irony and humour, but whose fiction was heavy, and over-burdened with unnecessary detail. I remarked that a woman friend of his, who was aware of the defect, had once said to me: 'I believe X's insistence on detail is caused by his having to look at everything too closely, owing to his being so short-sighted.'

Max looked at me gravely. 'Ah, really? She thinks it's because he's so short-sighted? I should have said it was because he was so long-winded!'

The Essexes at that time were in the habit of entertaining big week-end parties at Cassiobury, Lord Essex's place near St Albans, and one Sunday at the end of a brilliant London season, when my husband and I motored down there to lunch, we found, scattered on the lawn under the great cedars, the very flower and pinnacle of the London world: Mr Balfour, Lady Desborough, Lady Poynder (now Lady Islington), Lady Wemyss (then Lady Elcho), and John Sargent, Henry James, and many others of that shining galaxy — but one and all so exhausted by the social labours of the last weeks, so talked out with each other and with all the world, that beyond benevolent smiles they had little to give; and I remarked that evening to my husband that meeting them in such circumstances was like seeing their garments hung up in a row, with nobody inside.

To Adèle Essex, always a devoted friend and responsive companion, and to Lady Ripon, whose sense of fun and quick enthusiasm always delighted me, I owed on the whole the pleasantest hours of my London visits; though I should be ungrateful not to add to their names those of Sir George Trevelyan, who kept up till his death a friendly interest in my books, of Mrs Wilfrid Meynell, Mrs Humphry Ward and my shrewd and independent old friend, Mrs Alfred Austin. Mrs Meynell, whose poems I admired far more than her delicate but too self-conscious essays, became interested in me, I think, through her liking for 'The Valley of Decision', and always showed me great kindness when I was in London. On one occasion, knowing my admiration for the poetry of Francis Thompson, she carried her kindness so far as to invite me to lunch with that elusive being (having previously extracted from him a promise that he would really come). But, alas, though Mr Meynell, for greater security, called at Thompson's lodgings to fetch him, the poor poet was in an opium dream from which he was not to be roused; and I never met him.

The first time I lunched at Mrs Meynell's I was struck by the solemnity with which this tall thin sweet-voiced woman, with melancholy eyes and rather catafalque-like garb, was treated by her husband and children. Mr Meynell, small and brisk, bustled in ahead of her, as though preceding a sovereign; and all through the luncheon Mrs Meynell's utterances, murmured with soft deliberation, were received in an attentive silence punctuated by: 'My wife was saying the other day,' 'My wife always thinks' – as though each syllable from those lips were final.

I, who had been accustomed at home to dissemble my literary pursuits (as though, to borrow Dr Johnson's phrase about portrait painting, they were 'indelicate in a female'), was astonished at the prestige surrounding Mrs Meynell in her own family; and at the Humphry Wards' I found the same affectionate deference toward the household celebrity.

I was often a guest of the Wards, in London or at their peaceful country-house near Tring. There were many ties of old friendship, English and American, between us, and Mrs Ward was unfailingly kind in her estimation of my work, and always eager to make me known to interesting people. Indeed, whenever I have been in England I have found there kindness, hospitality, and a disposition to put me at once on a footing of old friendship. I should be sorry to leave out the names of any to whom I am thus indebted, and at least must add those of Sir Ian and Lady

Hamilton, still my friends and my kind hosts on my frequent visits to England, of those dear friends of my childhood, now both dead, Henry and Margaret White (he was then first secretary of our Embassy in London), of Lord and Lady Charles Beresford, Sir Edmund Gosse, Lord and Lady Burghclere, and my husband's hospitable cousin, Mrs Adair. Of country life I saw next to nothing, for we were never in England in the autumn and winter, and at the season when we *were* there my husband's dates were so unalterable that we once missed a week-end at Mentmore with Lord Rosebery because it was considered impossible that we should postpone our sailing for a few days. I have always regretted this, as well as my having been unable to accept two or three invitations to Lord Rosebery's house in London; for as a girl of seventeen I had met him when he came to America after his marriage, and I had a vivid memory of the light and air he let into the stuffy atmosphere of a Newport season. Unhappily I never saw him again.

Much as I enjoyed these London glimpses they are now no more than a golden blur. So many years have gone by, and that old world of my youth has been so convulsed and shattered, that as I look back, and try to recapture the details of particular scenes and talks, they dissolve into the distance. But in any case I was not made to extract more than a passing amusement from such fugitive dips into a foreign society. My idea of society was (and still is) the daily companionship of the same five or six friends, and its pleasure is based on continuity, whereas the hospitable people who opened their doors to me in London, though of course they all had their own intimate circles, were as much exhilarated by the yearly stream of new faces as a successful shot by the size of his bag. Most of my intimate friendships in England were made later, and in circumstances more favourable (to me, at any rate) than the rush and confusion of a London season. Some of the dearest of them I owe to Howard Sturgis, and to him, and to Queen's Acre, his house at Windsor, I turn for the setting of my next scene.

3

A long low drawing-room; white-panelled walls hung with water-colours of varying merit; curtains and furniture of faded slippery chintz; French windows opening on a crazy wooden verandah, through which, on one side, one caught a glimpse of a weedy lawn and a shrubbery edged with an unsuccessful herbaceous border, on the other, of a not too successful rose garden, with a dancing faun poised above an incongruously 'arty' blue-tiled pool. Within, profound chintz arm-chairs drawn up about a hearth on which a fire always smouldered; a big table piled with popular novels and picture-magazines; and near the table a lounge on which lay outstretched, his legs covered by a thick shawl, his hands occupied with knitting-needles or embroidery silks, a sturdily-built handsome man with brilliantly white wavy hair, a girlishly clear complexion, a black moustache, and tender mocking eyes under the bold arch of his black brows.

Such was Howard Sturgis, perfect host, matchless friend, drollest, kindest and strangest of men, as he appeared to the startled eyes of newcomers on their first introduction to Queen's Acre.

It was not there, but at a dinner at Newport, that I first met him, a few years after my marriage. I did not even know who he was; but if ever there was a case of friendship at first sight it was struck up between us then and there. Like me he was a great lover of good talk, and shared my inability to enjoy it except in a small and intimate circle. Continuity in friendship he valued also as much as I did, and from that day until his death, many years later, he and I shared the same small group of intimates.

Howard Sturgis was the youngest son of Mr Russell Sturgis, of the old Boston family of that name, who for many years had been at the head of an important American banking-house in London. Mr Sturgis, as became an international banker, was rich, popular and hospitable, kept up a large household, and entertained a great deal in London and at Givens Grove, his country place near Leatherhead. Howard, I think, was born in England, and had probably never been to America till he came out on a visit to his Boston relations, the year I met him at Newport. His mother, Mr Sturgis's third wife, was also a Bostonian, and his cousinage was as large as mine in New York, and far more assiduously cultivated. Howard's closest associations, however, were English, for he had been sent to Eton and thence to Cambridge. At Eton he had been a pupil of Mr Ainger's, a privilege never forgotten by an Etonian fortunate enough to have enjoyed it; and Mr Ainger, whom I often met at Queen's Acre, had remained one of his most devoted friends. Another friend of his youth was the eccentric and tragic William Cory Johnson, an Eton master of a different stamp, and an exquisite poet in a minor strain; and it is to Howard that I owe my precious first edition of 'Ionica', royally clothed in crimson morocco.

Mr Russell Sturgis died when Howard was still a youth, and after his father's death, and the marriages of his brothers and his sister, he found himself alone at home with his mother. Mrs Sturgis, whom I never knew, is said to have been a very beautiful woman. She was as luxurious in her tastes as her husband, but, I imagine, without his gift of easy hospitality. She continued to keep up handsome establishments at Givens and in London; but she and her son, who was her devoted slave, were frequently absent from England, and when at home kept more and more to themselves; and her death left him, a middle-aged man, as lost and helpless as a child.

When I first knew him this sad phase was past; the London house had been sold, Givens had gone to Howard's eldest half-brother, and Howard was happily settled in a roomy friendly house on the edge of Windsor Park, where he had gathered about him a company of devoted friends, some of whom were soon to become mine. He detested pomp and circumstance as much as his parents had valued it, and his life was already organized on the simple easy lines from which it never afterward departed. Some of his mother's old servants remained with him, and when he went to Windsor he took with him Hall, the majestic butler. Hall had been with the family for many years, and was devoted to Howard; but after a few months at Queen's Acre he announced his intention of leaving. Howard, much distressed, said he supposed Hall did not care to remain in so small an establishment; but Hall replied sadly: 'Oh, no, sir, it's not that; it's only that I can't bear never to 'ear you ring a bell, and 'ave you always putting your 'ead out of the door and 'ollering 'all [Hall] down the passage.'

Howard felt the justice of the rebuke, but also the impossibility of living up to the old butler's standards. Always impatient of conventional observances, he could never ring a bell when ' 'ollering' brought the necessary response; so Hall departed, and was replaced by a small thin worried man, more in scale with the reduced household whose burdens (and they were not light) he was to bear till death relieved him, soon after the loss of his beloved master. This excellent man, whose name was Robinson, but who had been baptized by Henry James 'the little saint and angel', was dear to all visitors to Queen's Acre, as were the admirable cook, Mrs Lees (shall I ever again eat the like of her braised tongue?), and the sturdy old Scottish housemaid, Christina.

There was also, I believe, an old family coachman in the stable behind the shrubbery; but he and his 'old family' horses, and the still older and more decayed family brougham, had reached a decrepitude so advanced that they hardly ever emerged from the stable-yard, and guests at Queen's Acre depended chiefly on station flies, or, in motoring days, on their own cars. Howard, though his means permitted every comfort, would never introduce electric light into the house, much less the telephone and central heating; and his reluctance to repair, to repaint or in any way renovate his dear old house, must have been part of the deep-seated 'complex' which made him unwilling to take any decision on whatever subject; for he was the most generous of men, and as careless of money as he was indifferent to all material comforts except good food.

I have sometimes thought that Howard's old servants represented not inaptly the odd duality of his nature: Robinson his long-suffering sweetness and unselfishness, and the devoted but dour Christina the streak of asperity which sometimes came to the surface. Once when I was staying at Queen's Acre I was at work on a novel, and writing in bed in the early morning, as my reprehensible habit is, with my inkstand balanced on a writing board. An inadvertent movement caused me to upset the ink, and instantly it poured over my sumptuously monogrammed sheet – doubtless a survival from Mrs Sturgis's stores of fine linen. Inkstands and tea-cups are never as full as when one upsets them, and seeing that the disaster was beyond the help of blotting-paper, I hastily rang for Christina. At the sight she threw up her hands in horror, and was seizing the sheet to fly with it to the tub, when I said: 'Just a moment, Christina. I want you first to take the sheet to Mr Sturgis, with this note from me.'

Christina's jaw fell, and her look said: 'Is there no limit to the craziness of these Americans?'

'Did ye say I was to tek a note, mem, to Mr Sturgis?'

'*With* the sheet.'

'Not the sheet, mem? There's no reason for Mr Sturgis to be told about the accident, mem—' in the conciliatory tone of one who remembers that it is safer to humour lunatics than to oppose them.

'Yes, please, Christina; note *and* sheet.'

Reluctantly Christina departed on this insane mission. In the note I had written: 'Dearest Howard, the book has been going slowly of late; but the stimulating air of Queen's Acre has had its usual effect, and as you will see this morning's chapter has come with a rush.'

A jubilant message of congratulation was brought back, with a clean sheet, by Christina. When the sheet was in place she lingered, perplexity on her face; then, determined to protect her master's interests, though suspecting that he would be horrified by her means of doing so, she broke out in her fiercest Scots: 'I dinna suppose ye mean to replace it, mem? But if ye *did*, they coom from Marshall's.'

The sheet was promptly duplicated by Marshall and Snelgrove, and when it arrived Christina's heart was softened, and thereafter we were the best of friends.

At Queen's Acre some of the happiest hours of my life were passed, some of my dearest friendships formed or consolidated, and my own old friends welcomed because they were mine. For Howard Sturgis was not only one of the most amusing and lovable of companions, but untiring in hospitality to the friends of his friends. Indolent and unambitious though he was, his social gifts were irresistible, and his drawing-room – where he spent most of this hours, not from ill-health but through inertia – was always full of visitors. There one found all that was most intelligent and agreeable in the world of Eton, as well as a chosen few from London, and mingled with them a continual and somewhat incongruous stream of cousins from Boston and New York – for Howard cherished with sentimental fervour the ties of consanguinity. There were also other cousins, long established in England and old habitués of Queen's Acre; chief among them the three daughters of Motley, the historian, Lily Lady Harcourt, Mrs Sheridan, the kindly hostess of Frampton Court, and Mrs Mildmay; besides a succession of amiable nieces and nephews, children of Howard's brothers and sister. But among the transients the chief current was fed by Bostonians and New Yorkers of the old school, whom Howard welcomed with effusion, undismayed by the difficulty of harmonizing them at short notice with the small intimate group who were *de fondation* about his fireside.

This inner group I see now, gathered around him as the lamps are brought in at the end of a foggy autumn afternoon. In one of the arm-chairs by the fire is sunk the long-limbed frame of the young Percy Lubbock, still carrying in his mind the delightful books he has since given us, and perhaps as yet hardly aware that he was ever to put them on paper; in another sits Gaillard Lapsley, down for the week-end from his tutorial duties at Cambridge, while John Hugh-Smith faces Percy across the fireside, and Robert Norton and I share the corners of the wide chintz sofa behind the tea-table; and dominating the hearth, and all of us, Henry James stands, or heavily pads about the room, listening, muttering, groaning disapproval, or chuckling assent to the paradoxes of the other tea-drinkers. And then, when tea is over, and the tray has disappeared, he stops his prowling to lean against the mantelpiece and plunge into reminiscences of the Paris or London of his youth, or into some slowly elaborated literary disquisition, perhaps on the art of fiction or the theatre, on Balzac, on Tolstoy, or, better still, on one of his own contemporaries. I remember, especially, one afternoon when the question: 'And Meredith—?' suddenly freed a 'full-length' of that master which, I imagine, still hangs in the mental picture-galleries of all who heard him.

It began, mildly enough, with a discussion of Meredith's importance as a novelist, in which I think Howard was his principal champion. James, deep-sunk in an armchair and in silence, sat listening, and weighing our views, till he suddenly pounced on my avowal that, much as I admired some of the novels, I had never been able to find out what any of them, except 'The Egoist' and 'Harry Richmond', were about. I tried to temper this by adding that in many passages, and especially the descriptive ones, the author's style rose to a height of poetic imagery which – but here James broke in with the cry that I had put my finger on the central weakness of Meredith's art, its unconscious insincerity. Words – words – poetic imagery, metaphors, epigrams, descriptive passages! How much did any of them weigh in the baggage of the authentic novelist? (By this time he was on his feet, swaying agitatedly to and fro before the fire.) Meredith, he continued, was a sentimental rhetorician, whose natural indolence or congenital insufficiency, or both, made him, in life as in his art, shirk every climax, dodge around it, and veil its absence in a fog of eloquence. Of course, he pursued, neither I nor any other reader could make out what Meredith's tales were about; and not only what they were about, but even in what country and what

century they were situated, all these prosaic details being hopelessly befogged by the famous poetic imagery. He himself, James
said, when he read Meredith, was always at a loss to know where
he was, or what causes had led to which events, or even to
discover by what form of conveyance the elusive characters he
was struggling to identify moved from one point of the globe to
another (except, Howard interpolated, that the heroines always
did so on horseback); till as last the practical exigencies of the
subject forced the author to provide some specific means of
transport, and suddenly, through the fog of his verbiage, the
reader caught the far-off tinkle of a bell that (here there was a
dramatic pause of suspense) – that turned out to be that of a mere
vulgar hansom-cab: 'Into which,' James concluded with his
wicked twinkle, 'I always manage to leap before the hero, and
drive straight out of the story.'

Such *boutades* implied no lack of appreciation of Meredith the
poet, still less of regard for the man. James liked and admired
Meredith, and esteemed him greatly for the courage and dignity
with which he endured the trial of his long illness; but, when the
sacred question of the craft was touched upon, all personal
sympathies seemed irrelevant, and our friend pronounced his
judgments without regard to them.

4

In Howard Sturgis's case, even more than in that of James, the
lack of a Boswell is to be deplored, for in his talk there was the
same odd blending of the whimsical and the shrewd, of scepticism
and emotion, as in his character, and the chosen friends who
frequented Qu'acre (as its intimates called it) were always at their
best in his company. But he has now been dead for over twelve
years, and since voices more qualified to speak are still silent, I
cannot part from his dear shade without trying to call it back for a
moment.

Everything in Howard Sturgis's life was contradictory, perplex-
ing, and in a sense incomplete. He had begun by writing two
charming, if slightly over-sentimental tales, 'Tim' and 'All That
Was Possible', both of which had been greatly admired by a small
circle of appreciative readers, while the latter had won him a
wider public. Thereafter he was silent for a number of years, and

then, about 1906, he published a long novel called 'Belchamber', which to my mind stands very nearly in the first rank. But 'Belchamber' had no success with the public, and less than his other books with most of his friends. Henry James (never to be trusted about the value of any 'fiction' which was not built according to his own rigid plan) pointed out with some truth that Howard had failed to utilize what should have been his central effect, and privately pronounced the book old-fashioned and feebly Thackerayan; while the reviewers dismissed it as too 'painful' and 'unnecessarily disagreeable', meaning thereby that it 'faced the facts' at a time when English fiction had not begun to practise that now too common exercise. The book was in truth a striking study of fashionable London in the 'nineties, lifted above the level of anecdote by a touch of tragedy, and rising in certain scenes to the quiet power of great fiction. But it was born out of its due time, and sank almost at once into an abscurity from which I am persuaded it will some day emerge, with that entirely different but equally neglected masterpiece, Graham Phillip's 'Susan Lenox'.

Howard, after the failure of 'Belchamber', apparently lost all interest in writing. He was unduly distressed by Henry James's criticism, and it was in vain that I pointed out how foolish it was to be discouraged by the opinion of a novelist who could no longer judge impartially any novel but built according to his own theories. Howard, by the way, was to see those theories suddenly demolished when, a good many years later, I sent James a copy of *Du Côté de chez Swann* on its first appearance, and all his principles and prejudices went down like straws in the free wind of Proust's genius; but that was long afterward, and meanwhile, Howard's native indolence and geniune humility aiding, he accepted James's verdict and relapsed into knitting and embroidery.

For the joy of his friends this was hardly to be regretted, since it left him free to give them his whole time. Intellectually he combined a kind of sentimental socialism with a hard lucidity of judgment, emotionally he was at once tender and malicious, indulgent and penetrating, and one felt that he saw through one to the marrow at the very moment when, in all sincerity, he was smothering one under exaggerated praise. There was nothing perfidious or calculated in these sudden changes; his affection for his friends co-existed with a pitiless discernment of their weaknesses, but his heart always poured balm on what his tongue could not refrain from lashing.

Howard's days, once he had abandoned literature, were methodically divided into brief moments of exercise and long hours of immobility. Every morning at the same hour he took a short toddle in Windsor Park with the sad little dog Misery and her rickety out-of-wedlock son, who was the cause of her being so named; Howard's Puritan blood having compelled him to put this brand on his frail pet. He walked very slowly and potteringly and I have known few more chilly forms of exercise, on a cold damp day, than a 'constitutional' with him and James, the latter stopping short every few yards to elaborate a point or propound a problem, while, just as one had got James moving again, Howard was sure to dive into the bushes in pursuit of Misery or her illegitimate offspring.

The walk ended, and an excellent luncheon enjoyed, Howard returned to his lounge and his embroidery, seldom leaving the drawing-room again till it was time to dress for dinner, and gently deriding the vain activities of those who did. I remember, in particular, one occasion when he had invited down for the day my friend Jacques-Emile Blanche and his wife, who were staying in London. It was a lovely summer day, and my impression is that the charms of the Thames valley were unknown to our French guests. At any rate, it was suggested that I should take them, after luncheon, to see the beautiful old alms-houses at Bray, and when this brief excursion was over, and I had driven them back to the railway station, I returned to King's Road to find Howard in his usual place on the lounge. The afternoon was still young, and as I entered the room I cried out: 'Come along, Howard! Put on your bonnet and shawl, and let's walk down to Eton!'

Cries of dismay and incredulity from Howard. 'Walk down to Eton with you? *Now* – at this hour of the day? But you went for a walk this morning; and you've been motoring all over the place all the afternoon with the Blanches; and now you're actually suggesting that I should walk all the way to Eton with you before dinner?'

So horrified was he at my mad proposal that it rankled in him for the rest of the evening, and every now and then, as we sat in the drawing-room after dinner, he would appeal plaintively to his other guests: 'Did you ever hear of such a thing? After motoring all over the place all the afternoon with the Blanches, she actually came back and said to me: "Put on your bonnet and shawl, and let's walk down to Eton!" '

In my day Howard's social relations with Eton were limited, at least as far as his guests were concerned, to taking us to call now and then on Mrs Cornish or Mr Ainger. But on one occasion we were bidden there for a public ceremony, and one I would not willingly have missed: the inauguration by King Edward VII of the beautiful hall which had been recently built in commemoration of the Etonians who fell in the Boer War. I had never seen King Edward before, and my recollection of the simple and dignified ceremony is naturally centred in his stout but stately figure. I remember being at first slightly shocked by the thick guttural intonation so reminiscent of his Hanoverian descent, and then captivated by the simplicity of his manner and the genuine emotion which his words expressed. Between the King's disquietingly Teutonic presence, and his audience of so deeply English subjects, the mourning relatives of the dead, one felt at once the current of understanding, the sharing of private grief and national pride, which gives such symbolic value to inherited rule.

As far as I can remember I was taken only once to see Mrs Cornish, and on this occasion, as so often happened, my incorrigible shyness turned the meeting into a damp-match affair. Mrs Cornish, wife of the distinguished Vice-Provost of Eton, was one of the most striking figures of that highly specialized world; wherever Eton was mentioned people always said: 'You don't know Mrs Cornish? Oh, but you *must* know her!'

Mrs Cornish had once been thrown with the Bourgets, of whom she kept an admiring recollection, and when she heard that I was an intimate friend of theirs she instructed Howard to bring me to tea at the Vice-Provost's Lodge. The only day on which I was free was one on which she happened to have invited a party of Eton boys, and she excused herself for this; but I thought their rosy faces and shining collars well suited to the serene and studious beauty of The Cloisters, with its long low-studded drawing-room, and the flowers and turf of the garden seen through mullioned windows. Mrs Cornish was eager to hear all I could tell her of the Bourgets, but in spite of my desire to enjoy (and be enjoyed), the silent pink audience communicated its shyness to me. At any rate, no other topic of interest occurred to me or to my hostess when we had used up the theme of our serviceable friends; and after a while Mrs Cornish, visibly aware of my distress, and herself affected by it, caught at the Bourgets again, like a man overboard swimming back to the spar he has abandoned. One of the Eton boys, a dark good-looking lad, who had been introduced to us as Prince Ruspoli, suddenly fixed her attention, and she swept around on him with her great dominant air.

'And you, Carlo Ruspoli – have you ever read the novels of Paul Bourget?' she abruptly challenged him. All the boys turned pinker at the startling enquiry, and the young prince pinkest.

'I – n-no – I'm afraid I haven't,' he stammered, disconcerted.

Mrs Cornish's inquiring gaze darkened to disapproval. 'What, you've not read them? Not any of them? Then you should, Carlo Ruspoli; you should read *all of them* immediately,' she surprisingly commanded – for a counsel from Mrs Cornish was always a command. An inarticulate murmur and a deeper blush were the only response; and thereafter the conversation so excitingly begun trailed off again into commonplaces – or I fear it must have, no doubt through my fault, for I remember of it nothing else of moment.

5

Not infrequently, on my annual visit to Qu'acre, I 'took off' from Lamb House, where I also went annually for a visit to Henry James. The motor run between Rye and Windsor being an easy one, I was often accompanied by Henry James, who generally arranged to have his visit to Qu'acre coincide with mine. James, who was a frequent companion on our English motor-trips, was firmly convinced that, because he lived in England, and our chauffeur (an American) did not, it was necessary that the latter should be guided by him through the intricacies of the English country-side. Sign-posts were rare in England in those days, and for many years afterward, and a truly British reserve seemed to make the local authorities reluctant to communicate with the invading stranger. Indeed, considerable difficulty existed as to the formulating of advice and instructions, and I remember in one village the agitated warning: 'Motorists! Beware of the children!' – while in general there was a marked absence of indications as to the whereabouts of the next village.

It chanced, however, that Charles Cook, our faithful and skilful driver, was a born path-finder, while James's sense of direction was non-existent, or rather actively but always erroneously alert; and the consequences of his intervention were always bewildering, and sometimes extremely fatiguing. The first time that my husband and I went to Lamb House by motor (coming from France) James, who had travelled to Folkestone by train to meet us, insisted on seating himself next to Cook, on the plea that the roads across Romney marsh formed such a tangle that only an old inhabitant could guide us to Rye. The suggestion resulted in our turning around and around in our tracks till long after dark, though Rye, conspicuous on its conical hill, was just ahead of us, and Cook could easily have landed us there in time for tea.

Another year we had been motoring in the west country, and on the way back were to spend a night at Malvern. As we approached (at the close of a dark rainy afternoon) I saw James growing restless, and was not surprised to hear him say: 'My dear, I once spent a summer at Malvern, and know it very well; and as it is rather difficult to find the way to the hotel, it might be well if Edward were to change places with me, and let me sit beside Cook.' My husband of course acceded (though with doubt in his heart), and James having taken his place, we awaited the result. Malvern, if I am not mistaken, is encircled by a sort of upper boulevard, of the kind called in Italy a *strada di circonvallazione*, and for an hour we circled about above the outspread city, while James vainly tried to remember which particular street led down most directly to our hotel. At each corner (literally) he stopped the motor, and we heard a muttering, first confident and then anguished. 'This – this, my dear Cook, yes . . . this certainly is the right corner. But no; stay! A moment longer, please – in this light it's so difficult . . . appearances are so misleading . . . It may be . . . yes! I think it *is* the next turn . . . "a little farther lend thy guiding hand" . . . that is, drive on; but slowly, please, my dear Cook; *very* slowly!' And at the next corner the same agitated monologue would be repeated; till at length Cook, the mildest of men, interrupted gently: 'I guess any turn'll get us down into the town, Mr James, and after that I can ask—' and late, hungry and exhausted we arrived at length at our destination, James still convinced that the next turn would have been the right one, if only we had been more patient.

The most absurd of these episodes occurred on another rainy evening, when James and I chanced to arrive at Windsor long after dark. We must have been driven by a strange chauffeur – perhaps Cook was on a holiday; at any rate, having fallen into the lazy habit of trusting to him to know the way, I found myself at a loss to direct his substitute to the King's Road. While I was hesitating, and peering out into the darkness, James spied an ancient doddering man who had stopped in the rain to gaze at us. 'Wait a moment, my dear – I'll ask him where we are'; and leaning out he signalled to the spectator.

'My good man, if you'll be good enough to come here, please; a little nearer – so,' and as the old man came up: 'My friend, to put it to you in two words, this lady and I have just arrived here from *Slough*; that is to say, to be more strictly accurate, we have recently *passed through* Slough on our way here, having actually motored to Windsor from Rye, which was our point of departure; and the darkness having overtaken us, we should be much obliged if you would tell us where we now are in relation, say, to the High Street, which, as you of course know, leads to the Castle, after leaving on the left hand the turn down to the railway station.'

I was not surprised to have this extraordinary appeal met by silence, and a dazed expression on the old wrinkled face at the window; nor to have James go on: 'In short' (his invariable prelude to a fresh series of explanatory ramifications), 'in short, my good man, what I want to put to you in a word is this: supposing we have already (as I have reason to think we have) driven past the turn down to the railway station (which, in that case, by the way, would probably not have been on our left hand, but on our right), where are we now in relation to . . .'

'Oh, please,' I interrupted, feeling myself utterly unable to sit through another parenthesis, 'do ask him where the King's Road is.'

'Ah—? The King's Road? Just so! Quite right! Can you, as a matter of fact, my good man, tell us where, in relation to our present position, the King's Road exactly *is*?'

'Ye're in it,' said the aged face at the window.

6

It would be hard to imagine a greater contrast than between the hospitality of Queen's Acre and that of Lamb House. In the former a cheerful lavishness prevailed, and a cook enamoured of her art set a variety of inviting dishes before a table-full of guests, generally reinforced by transients from London or the country. At Lamb House an anxious frugality was combined with the wish that the usually solitary guest (there were never, at most, more than two at a time) should not suffer too greatly from the contrast between his or her supposed habits of luxury, and the privations imposed by the host's conviction that he was on the brink of ruin. If any one in a pecuniary difficulty appealed to James for help, he gave it without counting; but in his daily life he was haunted by the spectre of impoverishment, and the dreary pudding or pie of which a quarter or half had been consumed at dinner reappeared on the table the next day with its ravages unrepaired.

We used to laugh at Howard Sturgis because, when any new subject was touched on in our talks, he always interrupted us to cry out: 'Now please remember that I've read nothing, and know nothing, and am not in the least quick or clever or cultivated'; and one day, when I prefaced a remark with 'Of course, to people as intelligent as we all are,' he broke in with a sort of passionate terror: 'Oh, how can you say such things about us, Edith?' – as though my remark had been a challenge to the Furies.

The same scruples weighed on Henry James; but in his case the pride that apes humility concerned itself (oddly enough) with material things. He lived in terror of being thought rich, worldly or luxurious, and was forever contrasting his visitors' supposed opulence and self-indulgence with his own hermit-like asceticism, and apologizing for his poor food while he trembled lest it should be thought too good. I have often since wondered if he did not find our visits more of a burden than a pleasure, and if the hospitality he so conscientiously offered and we so carelessly enjoyed did not give him more sleepless nights than happy days.

I hope not; for some of my richest hours were spent under his roof. From the moment when I turned the corner of the grass-grown street mounting steeply between squat brick houses and caught sight, at its upper end, of the wide Palladian window of the garden-room, a sense of joyous liberation bore me on. There *he* stood on the doorstep, the white-panelled hall with its old prints and crowded book-cases forming a background to his heavy loosely-clothed figure. Arms outstretched, lips and eyes twinkling, he came down to the car, uttering cries of mock amazement and mock humility at the undeserved honour of my visit. The arrival at Lamb House was an almost ritual performance, from those first ejaculations to the large hug and the two solemn kisses executed in the middle of the hall rug. Then, arm in arm, through the oak-panelled morning-room we wandered out onto the thin worn turf of the garden, with its ancient mulberry tree, its unkempt flower-borders, the gables of Watchbell Street peeping like village gossips over the creeper-clad walls, and the scent of roses spiced with a strong smell of the sea. Up and down the lawn we strolled with many pauses, exchanging news, answering each other's questions, delivering messages from the other members of the group, inspecting the strawberries and lettuces in the tiny kitchen-garden, and the chrysanthemums 'coming along' in pots in the greenhouse; till at length the parlour-maid appeared with a tea-tray, and I was led up the rickety outside steps to the garden-room, that stately and unexpected appendage to the unadorned cube of the house.

In summer the garden-room, with its high ceiling, its triple window commanding the grass-grown declivity of West Street, and its other window looking along another ancient street to the Gothic mass of the parish church, was the centre of life at Lamb House. Here, in the morning, James dictated to his secretary, striding incessantly up and down the room, and in the afternoon and evening, when the weather was too cool for the garden, sat with outstretched legs in his deep armchair before the hearth, laughing and talking with his guests.

On the whole, he was very happy at Rye, and in spite of the house-keeping cares which he took so hard the change was all to the good for a man who could never resist invitations, yet was wearied and irritated by the incessant strain of social life in London. At Rye, in summer at least, he had as many guests as his nerves could endure, and his sociable relations with his neighbours – among whom were, at one time, his beloved friends, Sir George and Lady Prothero – must have prevented his feeling lonely. He was very proud of his old house, the best of its sober and stately sort in the town, and he who thought himself so detached from material things tasted the simple joys of proprietorship when, with a deprecating air, he showed his fine Georgian panelling and his ancient brick walls to admiring visitors.

Like Howard Sturgis he was waited upon by two or three faithful servants. Foremost among them was the valet and factotum, Burgess, always spoken of by his employer as 'poor little Burgess'. Burgess's broad squat figure and phlegmatic countenance are a familiar memory to all who frequented Lamb House, and James's friends gratefully recall his devotion to his master during the last unhappy years of nervous break-down and illness. He had been preceded by a man-servant whom I did not know, but of whom James spoke with regard as an excellent fellow. 'The only trouble was that, when I gave him an order, he had to go through three successive mental processes before he could understand what I was saying. First he had to register the fact that he was being spoken to, then to assimilate the meaning of the order given to him, and lastly to think out what practical consequences might be expected to follow if he obeyed it.'

Perhaps these mental gymnastics were excusable in the circumstances; but Burgess apparently soon learned to dispense with them, and without any outward appearance of having understood what his master was saying, carried out his instructions with stolid exactitude. Stolidity was his most marked characteristic. He seldom gave any sign of comprehension when spoken to, and I remember once saying to my Alsatian maid, who was always as quick as a flash at the uptake: 'Do you know, I think Burgess must be very stupid. When I speak to him I'm never even sure that he's heard what I've said.'

My maid looked at me gravely. 'Oh, no, Madam: Burgess is remarkably intelligent. *He always understands what Mr James says.*' And that argument was certainly conclusive.

At Lamb House my host and I usually kept to ourselves until luncheon. Our working hours were the same, and it was only now and then that we went out before one o'clock to take a look at the green peas in the kitchen-garden, or to stroll down the High Street to the Post Office. But as soon as luncheon was despatched (amid unnecessary apologies for its meagreness, and sarcastic allusions to my own supposed culinary extravagances) the real business of the day began. Henry James, an indifferent walker, and incurably sedentary in his habits, had a passion for motoring. He denied himself (I believe quite needlessly) the pleasure and relaxation which a car of his own might have given him, but took advantage, to the last drop of petrol, of the travelling capacity of any visitor's car. When, a few years after his death, I stayed at Lamb House with the friend who was then its tenant, I got to know for the first time the rosy old town and its sea-blown neighbourhood. In Henry James's day I was never given the chance, for as soon as luncheon was over we were always whirled miles away, throwing out over the country-side what he called our 'great loops' of exploration. Sometimes we went off for two or three days. I remember one beautiful pilgrimage to Winchester, Gloucester and beyond; another long day carried us to the ancient house of Brede, to lunch with the Morton Frewens, another to spend a day near Ashford with the Alfred Austins, in their pleasant old house full of books and flowers. Usually, however, to avoid an interruption to the morning's work, we lunched at Lamb House, and starting out immediately afterward pushed our explorations of down and weald and seashore to the last limit of the summer twilight.

James was as jubilant as a child. Everything pleased him – the easy locomotion (which often cradled him into a brief nap), the bosky softness of the landscape, the discovery of towns and villages hitherto beyond his range, the magic of ancient names, quaint or impressive, crabbed or melodious. These he would murmur over and over to himself in a low chant, finally creating characters to fit them, and sometimes whole families, with their domestic complications and matrimonial alliances, such as the Dymmes of Dymchurch, one of whom married a Sparkle, and was the mother of little Scintilla Dymme-Sparkle, subject of much mirth and many anecdotes. Except during his naps, nothing escaped him, and I suppose no one ever felt more imaginatively, or with deeper poetic emotion, the beauty of sea and sky, the serenities of the landscape, the sober charm of villages, manor-houses and humble churches, and all the implications of that much-storied corner of England.

One perfect afternoon we spent at Bodiam – my first visit there. It was still the old spell-bound ruin, unrestored, guarded by great trees, and by a network of lanes which baffled the invading charabancs. Tranquil white clouds hung above it in a windless sky, and the silence and solitude were complete as we sat looking across at the crumbling towers, and at their reflection in a moat starred with water-lilies, and danced over by great blue dragon-flies. For a long time no one spoke; then James turned to me and said solemnly: 'Summer afternoon – summer afternoon; to me those have always been the two most beautiful words in the English language.' They were the essence of that hushed scene, those ancient walls; and I never hear them spoken without seeing the towers of Bodiam mirrored in their enchanted moat.

Another day was memorable in another way. We were motoring from Rye to Windsor, to stay, as usual, with Howard Sturgis, and suddenly James said: 'The day is so beautiful that I should like to make a little *détour*, and show you Box Hill.' I was delighted at the prospect of seeing a new bit of English scenery, and perhaps catching a glimpse of George Meredith's cottage on its leafy hillside. But James's next words chilled my ardour: 'I want you to know Meredith,' he added.

'Oh, no, no!' I protested. I knew enough, by this time, of my inability to profit by such encounters. I was always benumbed by them, and unable to find the right look or the right word, while inwardly I bubbled with fervour, and the longing to express it. I remember once being taken to see Miss Jekyll's famous garden at Great Warley. On that long-desired day I had a hundred questions to ask, a thousand things to learn. I went with a party of fashionable and indifferent people, all totally ignorant of gardens and gardening; I put one timid question to Miss Jekyll, who answered curtly, and turned her back on me to point out a hybrid iris to an eminent statesman who knew neither what a hybrid nor an iris was; and for the rest of the visit she gave me no chance of exchanging a word with her.

To see Meredith and talk with him was a more important affair. In spite of all reservations, my admiration for certain parts of his work was very great. I delighted in his poetry, and treasured two of his novels – 'The Egoist' and 'Harry Richmond' – and I should have enjoyed telling him just what it was that I most admired in them. But I foresaw the impossibility of doing so at a first meeting which would probably also be the last. I told James this, and added that the great man's deafness was in itself an insurmount-able obstacle, since I cannot make myself heard even by the moderately deaf. James pleaded with me, but I was firm. For months he had been announcing his visit to Meredith, but had always been deterred by the difficulty of getting from Rye to Box Hill without going up to London; and I should really be doing him a great service by allowing him to call there on the way to Windsor. To this, of course, I was obliged to consent; but I stipulated that I should be allowed to wait in the car, and though he tried to convince me that 'just to have taken a look at the great man' would be an interesting memory, he knew I hated that kind of human sight-seeing, and did not insist. So we deflected our course to take in Box Hill, and the car climbed the steep ascent to the garden-gate where James was to get out. As he did so he turned to me and said: 'Come, my dear! I can't leave you sitting here alone. I should have you on my mind all the time; and supposing somebody were to come out of the house and find you?'

There was nothing for it but to comply; and somewhat sulkily I followed him up the narrow path, between clumps of sweet-william and Scotch pinks. It was a tiny garden patch, and a few steps brought us to the door of a low-studded cottage in a gap of the hanging woods. It was useless to notify Meredith in advance when one went to see him; he had long since been immobilized by illness, and was always there, and always, apparently, delighted to receive his old friends. The maid who announced us at once returned to say that we were to come in, and we were shown into a very small-ceilinged room, so small and so low that it seemed crowded though there were only four people in it. The four were the great man himself, white of head and beard, and statuesquely throned in a Bath chair; his daughter, the handsome Mrs Henry Sturgis (wife of Howard's eldest brother), another man who seemed to me larger than life, perhaps on account of the exiguity of the room, and who turned out to be Mr Morley Roberts – and lastly a trained nurse, calmly eating her supper at a table only a foot or two from her patient's chair.

It was the nurse's presence – and the way she went on steadily eating and drinking – that I found most disconcerting. The house was very small indeed; but was it really so small that there was not a corner of it in which she could have been fed, instead of consuming her evening repast under our eyes and noses? I have always wondered, and never found the answer.

Meanwhile I was being led up and explained by James and Mrs Sturgis – a laborious business, and agonizing to me, as the room rang and rang again with my unintelligible name. But finally the syllables reached their destination; and then, as they say in detective novels, the unexpected happened. The invalid stretched out a beautiful strong hand – everything about him was strong and beautiful – and lifting up a book which lay open at his elbow, held it out with a smile. I read the title, and the blood rushed over me like fire. It was my own 'Motor Flight through France', then lately published; and he had not known I was to be brought to see him, and he had actually been reading my book when I came in!

At once, in his rich organ tones, he began to say the kindest, most appreciative things; to ask questions, to want particulars –

but, alas, my unresonant voice found no crack in the wall of his deafness. I longed to tell him that Henry James had been our companion on most of the travels described in my modest work; and James, joining in, tried to explain, to say kind things also; but it was all useless, and Meredith, accustomed to steering a way through these first difficult moments, had presently taken easy hold of the conversation, never again letting it go till we left.

The beauty, the richness, the flexibility of his voice held me captive, and it is that which I remember, not what he said; except that he was all amenity, all kindliness, as if the voice were poured in a healing tide over the misery of my shyness. But the object of the visit was, of course, to give him a chance of talking with James, and presently I drew back and chatted with Mrs Sturgis and Morley Roberts, while the great bright tide of monologue swept on over my friend. After all, it had been worth coming for; but the really interesting thing about the visit was James's presence, and the chance of watching from my corner the nobly confronted profiles of the two old friends: Meredith's so classically distinguished, from the spring of the wavy hair to the line of the straight nose, and the modelling of cheek and throat, but all like a slightly idealized bas-relief 'after' a greater original; and James's heavy Roman head, so realistically and vigorously his own, not a bas-relief but a bust, wrought in the round by harsher but more powerful hands. As they sat there, James benignly listening, Meredith eloquently discoursing, and their old deep regard for each other burning steadily through the surface eloquence and the surface attentiveness, I felt I was in great company, and was glad.

'Well, my dear,' James said to me, as we went out into the dusk, 'wasn't I right?' Yes, he had been right, and I had to own it.

7

Henry James, after buying Lamb House, had given up his flat in London; but in the autumn and winter he often went up to town for a short visit, staying at his club (the Athenaeum) and 'doing' as many lunches and dinners as he could crowd in, besides anything new at the theatres – for his interest in matters theatrical had not waned. Now that he had given up London he returned to it on these occasions with the zest of a truant school-boy. Everything he did exhilarated him, every one he saw amused him, everything he ate agreed with him – and when it was over he would go back, feeling guilty but rejuvenated, to a long stretch of work, and a diet of herbs and cold pudding.

When I was in London he generally joined me there for a day or two, especially if any theatrical event were impending; and I remember going one evening with him to see Mr Knoblock's Arabian Nights' fantasy, 'Kismet', then an innovation in stage-setting and lighting. We were enchanted with this lovely evocation of the bazaars, to which all London was thronging; it was the first time we had either of us seen what was in some sort a dematerialized pantomime, freed of its too realistic trappings – a first bud in the coming springtide of the Russian ballet. Another evening we went to 'Androcles and the Lion', and I think James laughed as much as I did at that enormous fooling, though doubtless with more self-restraint. In reality he was a much better theatre-goer than I, for the material limitations of the stage, and its violent foreshortenings, which always contract my vision, and cut rudely into my dream, seemed to stimulate his imagination, however much he found to criticize in a given play or its acting.

Sometimes, too, our little knot of friends would contrive to be in London at the same time, and I recall one happy evening when Howard Sturgis, Walter Berry, Percy Lubbock and Gaillard Lapsley were dining with me at my hotel. We had hoped that James would join us; but he was already booked for a fashionable dinner from which it was useless to try to detach him. Hardly had we sat down when, to our astonishment, in he walked, resplendent in white waistcoat and white tie, and rubbing his hands as though he nursed between his palms the smile striking up into his face. He had made a mistake in his date; had presented himself at the great house, and been told the dinner was not till the next evening; so here he was, and did we still want him, and was there room for him at the table – oh, he could squeeze into the least little corner, if we'd only let him! And let him we did; and how he enjoyed his dinner, and his glass of champagne (he who, at Rye, thought he could digest nothing heavier than a squeeze of orange juice!), and what a good evening of talk and laughter we had! As I write I yearn back to those lost hours, all the while aware that those who read of them must take their gaiety, their

jokes and laughter, on faith, yet unable to detach my memory
from them, and loath not to give others a glimpse of that jolliest
of comrades, the laughing, chaffing, jubilant yet malicious James,
who was so different from the grave personage known to less
intimate eyes.

Chapter Eleven
Paris

I

A year or two after the publication of 'The House of Mirth' my husband and I decided to exchange our little house in New York for a flat in Paris. My husband suffered increasingly from the harsh winds and sudden changes of temperature of the New York winter, and latterly we spent the cold months in rather aimless drifting on the French and the Italian Rivieras. Alassio, San Remo, Bordighera, Menton, Monte Carlo, Cannes; we knew them all to satiety, and in none could I hope to find the kind of human communion I cared for. In none, that is, but Hyères, where we had begun to go nearly every year since the Paul Bourgets had acquired there a little peach-coloured villa above the peach-orchards of Costebelle. But even the companionship of these friends could not fill the emptiness of life in a Riviera hotel. A house and garden of my own, anywhere on the coast between Marseilles and Fréjus, would have made me happy; since that could not be, my preference was for a flat in Paris, where I could see people who shared my tastes, and whence it was easy to go south for sunshine when the weather grew too damp for my husband. On this, therefore, we decided in 1907, thereafter spending our winters in Paris, and going back to the Mount every summer. For two years we occupied an apartment sublet to us by American friends, in a stately Louis XIV *hôtel* of the rue de Varenne; then we hired a flat in a modern house in the same street, and there I remained till 1920, so that my thirteen years of Paris life were spent entirely in the rue de Varenne; and all those years rise up to meet me whenever I turn the corner of the street. Rich years, crowded and happy years; for though I should have preferred London, I should have been hard to please had I not discovered many compensations in my life in Paris.

I found myself at once among friends, both old and knew. The Bourgets always spent a part of the winter in the quiet and leafy rue Barbet de Jouy, a short walk from our door; and in other houses of the old Faubourg I found three or four of the French girl friends I had known in my youth at Cannes, and who had long since married, and settled in Paris. Their welcome, and that of the Bourgets, at once made me feel at home, and thanks to their kindness I soon enlarged my circle of acquaintances. My new friends came from worlds as widely different as the University, the literary and Academic *milieux*, and the old and aloof society of the Faubourg Saint-Germain, to which my early companions at Cannes all belonged. As a stranger and newcomer, not only outside of all groups and coteries, but hardly aware of their existence, I enjoyed a freedom not possible in those days to the native-born, who were still enclosed in the old social pigeon-holes, which they had begun to laugh at, but to which they still flew back.

If in those days any authentic member of the Faubourg Saint-Germain had been asked what really constituted Paris society, the answer would undoubtedly have been: 'There is no Paris society any longer – there is just a welter of people from heaven knows where.' In a once famous play by Alexandre Dumas fils, 'L'Etrangère', written, I suppose, in the 'sixties, the Duke (a Duke of the proudest and most ancient nobility) forces his equally proud and perfectly irreproachable wife to invite his foreign mistress (Mrs Clarkson) to an evening party. The Duchess is seen receiving her guests in the high-ceilinged *salon* of their old *hôtel*, with tall French windows opening to the floor. Mrs Clarkson arrives, elegant, arrogant and nervous; the Duchess receives her simply and courteously; then she rings for the major-domo, and gives the order: '*Ouvrez les fenêtres! Que tout le monde entre maintenant!*'

In the Paris I knew, the Paris of twenty-five years ago, everybody would have told me that those windows had remained wide open ever since, that *tout le monde* had long since come in, that all the old social conventions were tottering or already demolished, and that the Faubourg had become as promiscuous as the Fair of Neuilly. The same thing was no doubt said a hundred years earlier, and two hundred years even, and probably something not unlike it was heard in the more exclusive *salons* of Babylon and Ur.

At any rate, as I look back at it across the chasm of the war, and all the ruins since heaped up, every convention of that compact and amiable little world seems still to have been standing, though few were rigid enough to hinder social enjoyment. I remember, however, one amusing instance of this rigidity. Soon after coming to Paris my husband and I, wishing to make some returns for the welcome my old friends had given us, invited a dozen of them to dine. They were all intimate with each other, and members of the same group; but, being new to the job, and aware of the delicate problems which beset the question of precedence in French society, I begged one of the young women I had invited to advise me as to the seating of my guests. The next day she came to me in perplexity.

'My dear, I really don't know! It's so difficult that I think I'd better consult my uncle, the Duc de D.' That venerable nobleman, who had represented his country as Ambassador to one or two of the great powers, was, I knew, the final authority in the Faubourg on ceremonial questions, and though surprised that he should be invoked in so unimportant a matter, I gratefully awaited his decision. The next day my friend brought it. 'My uncle was very much perplexed. He *thinks* on the whole you had better place your guests in this way.' (She handed me a plan of the table.) 'But he said: "My dear child, Mrs Wharton ought *never* to have invited them together"' – not that they were not all good and even intimate friends, and in the habit of meeting daily, but because the shades of difference in their rank were so slight, and so difficult to adjust, that even the diplomatist Duke recoiled from the attempt.

It took me, naturally, some time to acquire even the rudiments of this 'unwritten law'; to remember, for instance, that an Academician takes precedence of every one but a Duke or an Ambassador (though what happens if he is both a Duke and an Academician I can't remember, if I ever knew); that the next-but-two most honoured guest sits on the right of the lady who is on the host's right; that a foreigner of no rank whatever takes precedence of every rank but that of an Academician, a Cardinal or an Ambassador (or does he? Again I can't remember!); and that, under the most exquisite surface urbanity, resentment may rankle for years in the bosom of a guest whose claims have been disregarded. As almost all the rules are exactly the opposite of those prevailing in England, my path was no doubt strewn with blunders; but such indulgence as may have been needed was accorded because of my girlish intimacy with a small group belonging to the inner circle of the Faubourg, and because I had written a successful novel, a translation of which had recently appeared, with a flattering introduction by Bourget. Herein lay one of the many distinctions between the social worlds of New York and Paris. In Paris no one could live without literature, and the fact that I was a professional writer, instead of frightening my fashionable friends, interested them. If the French Academy had served no other purpose than the highly civilizing one of linking together society and letters, that service would justify its existence. But it is a delusion to think that a similar institution could render the same service in other societies. Culture in France is an eminently social quality, while in Anglo-Saxon countries it might also be called anti-social. In France, where politics so sharply divide the different classes and coteries, artistic and literary interests unite them; and wherever two or three educated French people are gathered together, a *salon* immediately comes into being.

2

In the numberless books I had read about social life in France – memoirs, history, essays, from Sainte-Beuve to Jules Lemaître and after – I had been told that the *salon* had vanished forever, first with the famous *douceur de vivre* of the Old Régime, then with the downfall of the Bourbons, then with the end of the House of Orleans, and finally on the disastrous day of Sedan. Each of these catastrophes doubtless took with it something of the exclusiveness, the intimacy and continuity of the traditional *salon*; but before I had lived a year in Paris I had discovered that most of the old catchwords were still in circulation, most of the old rules still observed, and that the ineradicable passion for good talk, and for seeing the same people every day, was as strong at the opening of the twentieth century as when the *Précieuses* met at the Hôtel de Rambouillet. When I first went to live in Paris, old ladies with dowdy cashmere 'mantles', and bonnets tied under their chins, were pointed out to me as still receiving every afternoon or evening, at the same hour, the same five or six men who had been the 'foundation' of their group nearly half a century earlier. Though circles as small as these scarcely formed a *salon*, they were composed of the same elements, and capable of the same expansion. Occasionally even the most exclusive felt the need of a blood-transfusion, and more than once it happened to me to be invited, and as it were tested, by the prudent guardian of the hearth.

The typical *salon*, the *salon* in action, was of course a larger and more elastic organization. It presupposed a moderate admixture of new elements, judiciously combined with the permanent ones, those which were called *de fondation*. But these recognized *salons* were based on the same belief that intimacy and continuity were the first requisites of social enjoyment. To attain the perfection of this enjoyment the Parisian hostess would exercise incessant watchfulness over all the members of her own group, as well as over other groups which might supply her with the necessary new blood, and would put up with many whims and humours on the part of her chief performers; and I remember, when I once said to a French friend: 'How can Madame A endure the crotchets of Monsieur X? Why doesn't she stop inviting him?' his astonished reply: '*Mais elle ne veut pas dégarnir son salon!*'

This continuity of social relations was what particularly appealed to me. In London, where another ideal prevailed, and perpetual novelty was sought for, the stream of new faces rushing past me often made me feel as if I were in a railway station rather than a drawing-room; whereas after I had got my bearings in Paris I found myself, as usual, settling down into a small circle of friends with whom, through all my years in the rue de Varenne, I kept up a delightful intimacy.

Paul Bourget was then at the height of his social popularity. He was one of the most interesting and versatile of talkers, and much in demand by ambitious hostesses; but he too preferred a small group to general society, and was always at his best among his intimates. Far more than I was aware of at the time, he smoothed my social path in Paris, bringing me into contact with the people he thought most likely to interest me, and putting me at once on a footing of intimacy in the houses where he was most at home. Through all the changes which have since befallen us both, his friendship has never failed me; and in looking back at those mirage-like years I like to think how much of their happiness I owed to him and to his wife.

Early in our first winter he did me an exceptionally good turn. A new Academician – I forget who – was to be received under the famous 'Cupola', and Bourget invited me to the ceremony. I had never seen an Academic reception – still one of the most unchanged and distinctive events of Parisian life – and was naturally delighted, as invitations are few, and much sought after if the candidate happens to be (as he was in this case) a familiar and popular Parisian figure. For some reason Minnie Bourget could not go with me, and as I had never been to the Institut, and did not know how to find my way in, or to manoeuvre for a seat, Bourget asked an old friend of his, the Comtesse Robert de Fitz-James, to take me under her wing. She invited me to luncheon, I think – or came to lunch with us; at any rate, before we had struggled to our places through the fashionable throng battling in the circuitous corridors of the Institut, she and I had become friends.

The widowed Comtesse de Fitz-James, known as 'Rosa' among her intimates, was a small thin woman, then perhaps forty-five years old, with a slight limp which obliged her to lean on a stick, hair prematurely white, sharp features, eager dark eyes and a disarmingly guileless smile. Belonging by birth to the wealthy Viennese banking family of the Gutmanns, she had the easy cosmopolitanism of a rich Austrian Jewess, and though she had married early, and since her marriage had always lived in Paris, she spoke English almost perfectly, and was always eager to welcome any foreigners likely to fit into the carefully-adjusted design of her *salon*, which, at that time, was the meeting-place of some of the most distinguished people in Paris. There were still, among the irreducibles of the Faubourg, a few who held out, declined to risk themselves among such international promiscuities, and received the mention of the hostess's name with raised eyebrows, and an affectation of hearing it for the first time. But they were few even then, and now that the world we then knew has come to an end, even they would probably agree that in the last ten or fifteen years before the war Madame de Fitz-James's *salon* had a prestige which no Parisian hostess, since 1918, has succeeded in recovering.

When I first knew it, the *salon* in question looked out on the mossy turf and trees of an eighteenth century *hôtel* standing between court and garden in the rue de Grenelle. A few years later it was transferred to a modern building in the Place des Invalides, to which Madame de Fitz-James had moved her fine collection of eighteenth century furniture and pictures at the suggestion of her old friends, the Comte and Comtesse d'Haussonville, who lived on the floor above. The rue de Grenelle apartment, which had much more character, faced north, and her Anglo-Saxon friends thought she had left in search of sunlight, and congratulated her on the change. But she looked surprised, and said: 'Oh, no; I hate the sun; it's such a bore always having to keep the blinds down.' To regard the sun as the housewife's enemy, fader of hangings and devourer of old stuffs, is common on the continent, and Madame de Fitz-James's cream-coloured silk blinds were lowered, even in winter, whenever the sun became intrusive. The three drawing-rooms, which opened into one another, were as commonplace as rooms can be in which every piece of furniture, every picture and every ornament is in itself a beautiful thing, yet the whole reveals no trace of the owner's personality. In the first drawing-room, a small room hung with red damask, Madame de Fitz-James, seated by the fire, her lame leg supported on a foot-rest, received her intimates. Beyond was the big drawing-room, with pictures by Ingres and David on the pale walls, and tapestry sofas and arm-chairs; it was there that the dinner guests assembled. Opening out of it was another small room, lined with ornate Louis XV bookcases in which rows of rare books in precious bindings stood in undisturbed order – for Madame de Fitz-James was a book-collector, not a reader. She made no secret of this – or indeed of any of her idiosyncrasies – for she was one of the most honest women I have ever known, and genuinely and unaffectedly modest. Her books were an ornament and an investment; she never pretended that they were anything else. If one of her guests was raised to Academic honours she bought his last work and tried to read it – usually with negative results; and her intimates were all familiar with the confidential question: 'I've just read So-and-So's new book. *Tell me, my dear: is it good?*'

This model hostess was almost always at home; in fact she very nearly realized the definition of the perfect hostess once given me by an old frequenter of Parisian *salons*. 'A woman should never go out – *never* – if she expects people to come to her,' he declared; and on my protesting that this cloistered ideal must, on merely practical grounds, be hard for a Parisian hostess to live up to, he replied with surprise: 'But why? If a woman once positively resolves never to go to a funeral or a wedding, why should she ever leave her house?'

Why indeed? And Madame de Fitz-James, though she fell short of this counsel of perfection, and missed few funerals and weddings, and occasionally went to an afternoon tea, seldom lunched or dined out. When she did, she preferred big banquets, where the food and the plate were more interesting than the conversation. This, I am sure, was not because she was unduly impressed by the display of wealth, but because it was less of an effort to talk to the fashionable and the overfed, and the crowd gave her the shelter of anonymity which she seemed to crave outside of her own doors. Occasionally – but very seldom – she came to dine with us; and these small informal parties, though always composed of her own friends, seemed to embarrass and fatigue her. She appeared to feel that she ought to be directing the conversation, signing to the butler to refill the wine-glasses, trying to reshape the groups into which the guests had drifted after dinner; and the effort to repress this impulse was so tiring that she always fled early, with an apologetic murmur. As with most of the famous hostesses I have known, her hospitality seemed to be a blind overpowering instinct, hardly ever to be curbed, and then only with evident distress. When I saw her in other people's houses she always made me think of the story of the English naturalist who kept two tame beavers, and one day, having absented himself for an hour or two, found on his return that the dear creatures had built a dam across the drawing-room floor. That is exactly what Madame de Fitz-James blindly yearned to do in other people's drawing-rooms.

3

She and Bourget had a real regard for each other, and it was thanks to him that I soon became an habitual guest at her weekly lunches and dinners. These always took place on fixed days; a dinner of fourteen or sixteen, with a small reception afterward, on a certain evening of the week, a smaller dinner on another, and on Fridays an informal and extremely agreeable luncheon, at which her accomplished cook served two *menus* of equal exquisiteness, one for those who abstained from meat on Fridays, the other for heretics and non-conformers. More than once, in the excitement and delight of the good talk, I have eaten my way unknowingly through the fat and the lean *menus*, with no subsequent ill-effects beyond a slight reluctance to begin again at dinner; and I was not the only guest whom intellectual enjoyment led into this gastronomic oversight.

Certainly, in my limited experience, I have never known easier and more agreeable social relations than at Rosa de Fitz-James's. Lists of names are not of much help in evoking an atmosphere; but the pre-war society of the Faubourg Saint-Germain has been so utterly dispersed and wiped out that as a group the frequenters of Madame de Fitz-James's drawing-room have an almost historic interest. Among the academicians – in such cases, I suppose, entitled to be named first – were, of course, Bourget himself, the Comte d'Haussonville (Madame de Staël's grandson and biographer), the two popular playwrights, Paul Hervieu and the Marquis de Flers, the former gaunt, caustic and somewhat melancholy, the latter rotund, witty and cordial to the brink of exuberance; the poet and novelist Henri de Régnier, and my dear friend the Marquis de Ségur, a charming talker in his discreet and finely-shaded way, and the author, among other historical studies, of a remarkable book on Julie de Lespinasse. The Institut was represented by two eminent members, the Comte Alexandre de Laborde, the learned bibliophile and authority on illuminated manuscripts, whom his old friend, Gustave Schlumberger, has characterized as 'the most worldly of scholars, and the most scholarly of men of the world'; the other, also a friend of mine, the Baron Ernest Seillière, a tall quiet man with keen eyes under a vertical shock of white hair, who had studied in a German University, and whose interest in the *Sturm-und-Drang* of the German Romantics, and its effect on European culture, has resulted in a number of erudite and interesting volumes.

Diplomacy (combined with the Academy) shone at Madame de Fitz-James's in the person of the French Ambassador in Berlin, the wise and witty Jules Cambon, whom I had known since his far-off days in Washington, and who was a much sought-for guest whenever his leave brought him to Paris; by Maurice Paléologue, who, after filling important posts at the Foreign Office, was to be the last French Ambassador at St Petersburg before the war, and soon after its close to enter the Academy; by the German and Austrian Ambassadors, Prince Radolin and Count Czechen; by Don Enrique Larreta, the Argentine Ambassador, a real lover of letters, and author of that enchanting chronicle-novel, 'The Glory of Don Ramiro' (of which Rémy de Gourmont's French version is a triumph of literary interpretation); and, among Secretaries of Embassy, by Mr George Grahame, attached to the British Embassy in Paris, the cultivated and indefatigably brilliant

Charles de Chambrun (now French Ambassador to the Quirinal), and the gay and ironic Olivier Taigny, whose ill-health unfortunately shortened his diplomatic career, but left him his incisive wit.

I have probably left out far more names than I have recorded; but I am impatient to escape from the seats of honour to that despised yet favoured quarter of the French dining-room, the *bout de table*. As I have already said, in France, where everything connected with food is treated with a proper seriousness, the seating of the guests has a corresponding importance – or had, at any rate, in pre-war days. In London, even in those remote times, though the old rules of precedence still prevailed at big dinners (and may yet, for all I know), they were relaxed on intimate occasions, and one of the first to go was that compelling host and hostess always to face each other from the head and foot of the table. In France, all this is reversed. Host and hostess sit opposite one another in the middle of the table (a rule always maintained, in my time, at whatever cost to the harmonious grouping of the party), and the guests descend right and left in dwindling importance to the table-ends, where the untitled, unofficial, unclassified, but usually young, humorous and voluble, are assembled. These *bouts de table* are at once the shame and glory of the French dinner-table; the shame of those who think they deserve a better place, or are annoyed with themselves and the world because they have not yet earned it; the glory of hostesses ambitious to receive the quickest wits in Paris, and aware that most of the brilliant sallies, bold paradoxes and racy anecdotes emanate from that cluster of independents.

The Parisian table-end deserves a chapter to itself, so many are the famous sayings originating there, and so various is the attitude of the table-enders. At first, of course, it is good fun to be among them, and a sought-after table-ender has his own special prestige; but as the years pass, he grows more and more ready to make way for the rising generation, and work upward to the seats of the successful. Not long ago I met at dinner a new Academician, elected after many efforts and long years of waiting, and who had risen without intermediate stages from the table-end to his hostess's right hand. As the guests seated themselves, an old and unpromoted table-ender, passing behind the new Academician, laid a hand on his shoulder, and said: 'Ah, my dear B, after so many years of table-end I shall feel terribly lonely without my old neighbour!' Every one burst out laughing except the Academician, who silently unfolded his napkin with an acid smile, and the mistress of the house, who was flurried by this free-and-easy treatment of a guest now raised to the highest rank. A good story is told of the Comte A de R, a nobleman known as a fierce stickler for the seat to which his armorial bearings entitled him, and who on one occasion was placed, as he thought, too near the table-end. He watched for a lull in the talk, and then, turning to the lady next to him, asked in a piercing voice: 'Do you suppose, *chère Madame*, the dishes will be handed as far down the table as this?' (It was this same Comte de R who, on leaving another dinner, said to a guest of equally aristocratic descent, who lived in his neighbourhood: 'Are you walking home? Good! Let us walk together, then, *and talk of rank.*')

In those old days at Madame de Fitz-James's there were, I imagine, few malcontents at the table-ends, for the great rushes of talk and laughter that swept up from there sent a corresponding animation through all the occupants of the high seats. The habitual holders of the ends were the young André Tardieu, then the masterly political leader-writer of the *Temps*, his govern-mental honours still far ahead of him, the young André Chaumeix, in those days also of the *Temps*, Abel Bonnard, almost the only talker I have known in a French *salon* who was allowed to go on talking as long as he wanted on the same subject (the conventional time-allowance being not more than five minutes), Etienne Grosclaude, the well-known journalist and wit, and only a seat or two farther up (when the company was small) Alexandre de Gabriac, Charles de Chambrun, Taigny and the Marquis du Tillet, each alert to catch and send back the ball flung by their irrepressible juniors.

The whole *raison d'être* of the French *salon* is based on the national taste for general conversation. The two-and-two talks which cut up Anglo-Saxon dinners, and isolate guests at table and in the drawing-room, would be considered not only stupid but ill-bred in a society where social intercourse is a perpetual exchange, a market to which every one is expected to bring his best for barter. How often have I seen such transactions blighted by the presence of an English or American guest, perhaps full of interesting things to say, but unpractised in the accustomed sport, and blocking all circulation by imprisoning his or her restive but helpless neighbour in a relentless duologue!

At Madame de Fitz-James's the men always outnumbered the women, and this also helped to stimulate general talk. The few women present were mostly old friends, and *de fondation*; none very brilliant talkers, but all intelligent, observant and ready to listen. In a French *salon* the women are expected to listen, and enjoy doing so, since they love good talk, and are prepared by a long social experience to seize every allusion, and when necessary to cap it by another. This power of absorbed and intelligent attention is one of the Frenchwoman's greatest gifts, and makes a perfect background for the talk of the men. And how good that talk is – or was, at any rate – only those can say who have frequented such a *salon* as that of Madame de Fitz-James. Almost all the guests knew each other well, all could drop into the conversation at any stage, without groping or blundering, and each had something worth saying, from Bourget's serious talk, all threaded with golden streaks of irony and humour, to the incessant fire-works of Tardieu, the quiet epigrams of Henri de Régnier, the anecdotes of Taigny and Gabriac, the whimsical and half-melancholy gaiety of Abel Bonnard.

The creator of a French *salon* may be moved by divers ambitions; she may wish to make it predominantly political, or literary and artistic, or merely mundane – though the worldly *salon* hardly counts, and is, at any rate, not worth commemorating. Any hostess, however, who intends to specialize, particularly in politics, runs the risk of making her *salon* dull; and dullest of all is that exclusively devoted to manufacturing Academicians, an industry inexhaustibly fascinating to many Frenchwomen. Few can resist political or academic intrigues as an ingredient in their social mixture; but the great art is to combine the ingredients so that none predominates, and to flavour the composition with an occasional dash of novelty. The transients introduced as seasoning must not be too numerous, or rashly chosen; they must be interesting for one reason or another, and above all they must blend agreeably with the 'foundation' mixture. In describing French society one has to borrow one's imagery from the French *cuisine*, so similar are the principles involved, and so equally minute is the care required, in preparing a *soufflé* or a *salon*.

Madame de Fitz-James chose her transients with exceptional skill. The few women she added now and then to her habitual group usually possessed some striking quality. The most stimulating and vivid was the Princesse Lucien Murat, and the two most charming were the daughter and the sister of famous poets; the subtle and exquisite Madame Henri de Régnier (one of the three daughters of Hérédia) and my dear friend Jeanne de Margerie, sister of Edmond Rostand, and an intimate of old days, for her husband, until recently French Ambassador in Berlin, had been for many years secretary of Embassy in Washington. Jeanne de Margerie's gifts were of a quieter order, but she was exceptionally quick and responsive, with an unfailing sense of fun; and when she died, not long after the war, a soft but warm radiance vanished from the Parisian scene, and from the lives of her friends.

I do not remember ever seeing Madame de Noailles, the poetess, at Madame de Fitz-James's. Poets are usually shy of *salons*, and so are monologuists like Madame de Noailles, whose dazzling talk was always intolerant of the slightest interruption. Among the women I met there by far the most remarkable was Matilde Serao, the Neapolitan novelist and journalist. She was an old friend of Bourget's, by whom she was first introduced to Madame de Fitz-James, who at once recognized her in spite of certain external oddities, as an invaluable addition to her parties. Matilde Serao, for a number of years before the war, made an annual visit to Paris, and had many friends there. She was a broad squat woman, with a red face on a short red neck between round cushiony shoulders. Her black hair, as elaborately dressed as a Neapolitan peasant's, looked like a wig, and must have been dyed or false. Her age was unguessable, though the fact that she was accompanied by a young daughter in short skirts led one to assume that she was under fifty. This strange half-Spanish figure, oddly akin to the *Meniñas* of Velasquez, and described by Bourget as 'Dr Johnson in a ball-dress', was always arrayed in low-necked dresses rather in the style of Mrs Tom Thumb's – I remember in particular a spreading scarlet silk festooned with black lace, on which her short arms and chubby hands rested like a cherub's on a sunset cloud. With her strident dress and intonation she seemed an incongruous figure in that drawing-room, where everything was in half-shades and semi-tones – but when she began to speak we had found our master. In Latin countries the few women who shine as conversationalists often do so at the expense of the rapid give-and-take of good talk. Not so Matilde Serao. She never tried to vaticinate or to predominate; what interested her was exchanging ideas with intelligent people. Her training as a journalist, first on her husband Edoardo Scarfoglio's newspaper, *Il Mattino*, and later as editor of a sheet of her own, *Il Giorno*, had given her a rough-and-ready knowledge of life, and an experience of public affairs, totally lacking in the drawing-room Corinnes whom she outrivalled in wit and eloquence. She had a man's sense of fair play, listened attentively, never dwelt too long on one point, but placed her sallies at the right moment, and made way for the next competitor. But when she was encouraged to talk, and given the field – as, alone with Abel Bonnard, she often was – then her monologues rose to greater heights than the talk of any other woman I have known. The novelist's eager imagination (two or three of her novels are masterly) was nourished on wide reading, and on the varied experience of classes and types supplied by her journalistic career; and culture and experience were fused in the glow of her powerful intelligence.

Another of Madame de Fitz-James's distinguished transients was Count Keyserling, who came often to her house when he was in Paris, as did his charming sister. There were also not a few agreeable Austrians, Count Fritz Hoyos and his sisters among them; none perhaps particularly interested in ideas, but all with that gift of ease and receptivity which made the pre-war Austrian so accomplished a social being. I remember, by the way, asking Theodore Roosevelt, at the end of his triumphal passage across Europe, what type of person he had found most sympathetic on his travels, and my momentary surprise at his unexpected reply: 'The Austrian gentlemen'.

Henry James was another outlander who, when he came to stay with us, at once became *de fondation*, as did Walter Berry and my friend Bernard Berenson; and from Rumania came Princess Marthe Bibesco and her cousin Prince Antoine (afterward Rumanian Minister in Washington) – but the list is too long to be continued. Instead, I wish to evoke at its close the figure of the most beloved, the kindliest and one of the wittiest of Madame de Fitz-James's 'foundation' guests – the Abbé Mugnier (afterward made a Canon of Notre Dame), without whom no reunion at Rosa's would have been complete. The Abbé's sensitive intelligence was a solvent for the conflicting ideas and opinions of the other visitors, since no matter how much they disagreed with each other, they were one in appreciating 'Monsieur l'Abbé', and at the approach of his small figure, with eyes always smiling behind their spectacles, and a tuft of gray hair vibrating flame-wise above his forehead, every group opened to welcome him.

Even for those who know the Abbé Mugnier well, it is not easy to define the qualities which thus single him out. Profound kindness and keen intelligence are too seldom blent in the same person for a word to have been coined describing that rare combination. I can only say that as vicar of the ultra-fashionable church of Sainte Clotilde, and then as chaplain of a convent in a remote street beyond Montparnasse, he seemed equally in his proper setting; and his quick sense of fun and irony is so lined with tender human sympathy that the good priest is always visible behind the shrewd social observer.

The Abbé Mugnier had an hour of celebrity when he converted Huysmans; he has since made other noted converts, and his concern for souls, and his wise dealings with them, cause him to be much sought after as the consoler of the dying, though those who have met him only in the world would not at first associate him with such scenes – at least not until they catch the tone of his voice in speaking of grief and suffering. His tolerance and sociability have indeed occasionally led people to risk in his presence remarks slightly inappropriate to his cloth; and it is good to see the quiet way in which, without the least air of offence, he gives the talk a more suitable turn.

His wise and kindly sayings – so quietly spoken that they sometimes escape the inattentive – are celebrated in Paris; but they have doubtless been recorded by many, and I will cite only two or three, which were said in my hearing. The Abbé, in spite of his social leanings, has a Franciscan soul, and is one of the few Frenchmen I have known with a genuine love of trees and flowers and animals. Before his sight began to fail he used to come out every year in June to my little garden near Paris, to see the long walk when the Candidum lilies were in bloom; and he really *did* see them, which is more than some visitors do, who make the pilgrimage for the same purpose. His tenderness for flowers and birds is so unFrench that he might have imbibed it in the Thuringian forests where he used to wander on his summer holidays in the path of Goethe (Goethe and Châteaubriand, both forest-lovers, are his two literary passions); and it seems appropriate, therefore, that two of his sayings to me should be about birds.

We were speaking one day of the difficult moral problems which priests call *cas de conscience*, and he said: 'Ah, a very difficult one presented itself to me once, for which I knew of no precedent. I was administering the Sacrament to a dying parishioner, and at that moment the poor woman's pet canary escaped from its cage, and lighting suddenly on her shoulder, pecked at the Host.'

'Oh, Monsieur l'Abbé – and what did you do?'

'I blessed the bird,' he answered with his quiet smile.

Another day he was talking of the great frost in Paris, when the Seine was frozen over for days, and of the sufferings it had caused among the poor. 'I shall never forget the feeling of that cold. On one of the worst nights – or rather at three in the morning, the coldest hour of the twenty-four – I was called out of bed by the sacristan of Sainte Clotilde, who came to fetch me to take the viaticum to a poor parishioner. The sick man lived a long way off, and oh, how cold we were on the way there, Lalouette and I – the old sacristan's name was Lalouette (the lark),' he added with a reminiscent laugh.

The play on the name was irresistible, and I exclaimed: 'Oh, how tempted you must have been, when he came for you, to cry out: "'Tis not the lark, it is the nightingale"—' I broke off, fearing that my quotation might be thought inappropriate; but with his usual calm smile the Abbé answered: 'Unfortunately, Madame, we were not in Verona.'

Once, in another vein, he was describing the marriage of two social 'climbers' who had invited all fashionable Paris to their nuptial Mass, and had asked the Abbé (much sought after on such occasions also) to perform the ceremony. At the last moment, when the guests were already assembled, he discovered (what had perhaps been purposely slurred over), that the couple were in some way technically disqualified for a church marriage. 'So,' said the Abbé drily, 'I blessed them in the sacristy, between two sterilized palms; and of course I could not prevent their assisting afterward at Mass with the rest of the company.'

Another day we were lunching together at a friend's house, and the talk having turned on the survival in the French provinces of the old-fashioned village atheist and anti-clerical (in the style of Flaubert's immortal Monsieur Homais), our hostess told us that she had known an old village chemist near her father's place in the Roussillon who was a perfect type of this kind. His family were much distressed by his sentiments, and when he lay on his death-bed besought him to receive the parish priest; but he refused indignantly, and to his wife's question: 'But what can you have against our poor *Curé*?', replied with a last gust of fury: 'Your *curés* – your *curés*, indeed! Don't tell me! I know all about your *curés*—'

'But what do you know against them?'

'Why, I read in a history book long ago that ten thousand *curés* died fighting for the beautiful Helen under the walls of Troy.'

A shout of mirth received this prodigious bit of history, and as our laughter subsided we heard the Abbé's chuckle, and saw the little flame-like tuft quiver excitedly on his crest.

'Well, Monsieur l'Abbé, what do you think of that?'

'Ah, would to heaven it were true!' the Abbé murmured sadly.

The war broke up that company of friendly people; death followed on war, and now the whole scene seems as remote as if it had belonged to a past century, and I linger with a kind of piety over the picture of that pleasant gray-panelled room, with its pictures and soft lights, and arm-chairs of faded tapestry. I see Bourget and James talking together before the fire, soon to be joined by the Abbé Mugnier, Bonnard and Walter Berry; Monsieur d'Haussonville, Hervieu and Larreta listening to Matilde Serao, and Chambrun, Berenson and Tardieu forming another group; and in and out among her guests Madame de Fitz-James weaving her quiet way, leaning on her stick, watching, prodding, interfering, re-shaping the groups, building and re-building her dam, yet somehow never in the way, because, in spite of her incomprehension of the talk, she always manages to bring the right people together and diffuses about her such an atmosphere of kindly hospitality that her very blunders add to the general ease and good humour.

4

I have dwelt so long on one pre-war *salon* that it might seem as if the greater part of my life in Paris had been spent in it; but I risked producing this impression because I wished to put first among my Parisian glimpses the vision of a little society in which the old *douceur de vivre* was combined with an intelligent interest in current ideas and events.

Naturally, in the course of my Parisian years, I saw other typical scenes, and came to know many people in other circles, and to form friendships quite outside of Madame de Fitz-James's agreeable drawing-room; but hers remains with me as peculiarly characteristic of a vanishing order.

One of the first friends I made was Jacques-Emile Blanche, the distinguished painter and man of letters, in whose house one met not only most of the worthwhile in Paris, but an interesting admixture of literary and artistic London. Blanche speaks and writes English fluently, and he and Madame Blanche often went to London, and had many English friends in the world of society and letters, as well as among painters; and before the war their picturesque half-timbered house at Auteuil welcomed all that was newest and most amusing in cosmopolitan society. In such houses as the Blanches', and that of another friend, Monsieur André Chevrillon (the nephew of Taine), pre-war Paris was first brought into familiar contact with English artists, savants and men of letters, and made aware of the riches of intellectual and artistic life in England. It is hard to realize now how few those contacts were before the war, and how completely, except for a handful of Parisians, France remained enclosed in her own culture.

Blanche, besides being an excellent linguist, and a writer of exceptional discernment on contemporary art, is also a cultivated musician; and in those happy days painters, composers, novelists, playwrights – Diaghilew, the creator of the Russian *ballet*, Henry Bernstein, whose plays were the sensation of the hour, George Moore, André Gide, my dear friend Mrs Charles Hunter, the painters Walter Sickert and Ricketts, and countless other well-known people, mostly of the cosmopolitan type – met on Sundays in the delightful informality of his studio, or about a tea-table under the spreading trees of the garden. The lofty studio-living-room (his real painting room is tucked away in a corner upstairs) was in those days the most perfect setting for such meetings. Everything in it was harmonious in colour and tone, from the tall Coromandel screens, the old Chinese rugs on the floor, and the early Chinese bronzes and monochrome procelains, to the crowning glory of the walls, hung with pictures by Renoir, Degas, Manet, Corot, Boudin, Alfred Stevens and Whistler – the 'Bathing Women' of Renoir, the sombre and powerful 'Young Woman with the Glove' of Manet (a portrait of one of Madame Blanche's aunts in her youth), and an early Gainsborough landscape of a peculiar hazy loveliness; and among them, or else in the upper gallery, some of the most notable of our host's own portraits; the perfect study of Thomas Hardy, the Degas, the Debussy, the

Aubrey Beardsley, the George Moore and the young Marcel Proust – for Blanche, with singular insight, began long ago that unique series of portraits of his famous contemporaries which ought some day to be permanently grouped as a whole.

On other afternoons there met at the Blanches' a small company of music-lovers ('Les Amis de la Musique', I think they were called), and it was enchanting to listen to Bach and Beethoven, Franck, Debussy or Chausson, with those great pictures looking down from the walls, and the glimpse of lawn and shady trees deepening the impression of the music by enclosing it in a country solitude.

The Blanches, for years, have spent their summers in a charming little stone manor-house in the village of Offranville, near Dieppe. A garden bursting with flowers divides the house from the village street, and at the back the windows look out on a beautiful orchard where the calves from the neighbouring farm caper under the apple-blossoms. I used to go there often to stay, and the first time I went I met a young man of nineteen or twenty, who at that time vibrated with all the youth of the world. This was Jean Cocteau, then a passionately imaginative youth to whom every great line of poetry was a sunrise, every sunset the foundations of the Heavenly City. Excepting Bay Lodge I have known no other young man who so recalled Wordsworth's 'Bliss was it in that dawn to be alive'. Every subject touched on – and in his company they were countless – was lit up by his young enthusiasm, and it is one of the regrets of later years to have watched the fading of that light. Life in general, the Parisian life in particular, is the cause of many such effacements – or defacements; but in Cocteau's case the pity is particularly great because his gifts were so many, and his fervours so genuine. For many years I saw a great deal of him; he came often to the rue de Varenne, and to many of my friends' houses; but I never enjoyed his talk as much as in the leafy quiet of Offranville. I wish now that I had set down a thousand of his sayings; but all have vanished, save one strangely beautiful story, which he told me he had read somewhere, but which I have never been able to trace.

One day when the Sultan was in his palace at Damascus a beautiful youth who was his favourite rushed into his presence, crying out in great agitation that he must fly at once to Baghdad, and imploring leave to borrow his Majesty's swiftest horse.

The Sultan asked why he was in such haste to go to Baghdad.

'Because,' the youth answered, 'as I passed through the garden of the Palace just now, Death was standing there, and when he saw me he stretched out his arm as if to threaten me, and I must lose no time in escaping from him.'

The young man was given leave to take the Sultan's horse and fly; and when he was gone the Sultan went down indignantly into the garden, and found Death still there. 'How dare you make threatening gestures at my favourite?' he cried; but Death, astonished, answered: 'I assure your Majesty I did not threaten him. I only threw up my arms in surprise at seeing him here, because I have a tryst with him tonight in Baghdad.'

Many of my other encounters at the Blanches' were full of interest; and so were other adventures in the more specialized world of letters, and of the University. Bourget one day brought to see me (two years or more before we came to live in Paris) a young friend of his, Charles Du Bos, who was anxious to translate my recently published novel, 'The House of Mirth'. Charles Du Bos, being Anglo-American on his mother's side, was exceptionally proficient in English, and he desired to follow a literary career without yet knowing precisely what turn it would take. Bourget, who was an old friend of his family, and naturally in sympathy with this ambition, suggested his getting his hand in by translating my book; and so it happened that 'The House of Mirth' was given to French readers by the future literary critic, and biographer of Byron, who in the course of the work became one of my closest friends.

5

When we finally settled in the rue de Varenne 'The House of Mirth,' then appearing in the *Revue de Paris*, was attracting attention in its French dress, partly because few modern English and American novels had as yet been translated, but chiefly because it depicted a society utterly unknown to French readers. The success of the book was so great that translations of my short stories (I had as yet written but two novels) were in great demand in the principal French reviews, and to this I owe an interesting glimpse of the Parisian life of letters. Those were the days when the *Revue de Paris*, edited by that remarkable man, Louis Ganderax, rivalled (if it did not out-rival) the *Revue des Deux*

Mondes in interest and importance, and I was lucky enough to be made welcome in the editorial groups of both reviews, and to be much invited out in those agreeable circles.

Oddly enough, it was an old American friend of my husband's who enlarged my range in this direction. Archibald Coolidge (future Librarian of Harvard) was giving the Hyde Lectures that winter at the Sorbonne, and as soon as he found we were in Paris he decided that I must be made known to his friends in the University. So indefatigable was this kindly being in bringing to the house the most agreeable among his colleagues, as well as other acquaintances, that my husband and I christened him 'the retriever'. It was thanks to him, I think, that I first met Monsieur André Chevrillon, the author of a number of delightful books on English literature, and two or three exceptionally sensitive records of travel in India and North America. All the Taine nephews and nieces inherited the great man's English culture, spoke the language fluently, and were thoroughly versed in English literature; and it was Monsieur Chevrillon who first made not only Ruskin but Kipling known to French readers. It was in the cosmopolitan atmosphere of his house at Saint Cloud that I first met, among other interesting people, the Comte Robert d'Humières, whose translations of Kipling rank with Scott Moncrieff's of Proust. Robert d'Humières was one of the most versatile of that alert and cultivated group; an admirable linguist, quick, well-read and responsive to new ideas, he combined great social gifts with a real love of letters. He wrote a brilliant little volume on the English in India, and another, equally remarkable, on contemporary England. He and his charming wife went often to England, and on one of their visits I gave them a letter for James. He asked them down to Lamb House, and a letter to me (published in Percy Lubbock's edition of the Letters) records his delighted impression of the pair. Robert d'Humières and I became great friends. He came very often to the rue de Varenne, and in 1914 he began a translation of my recently published novel, 'The Custom of the Country'. I had had many offers to translate this book, but had always refused, as I thought it almost impossible to make a tale so intensely American intelligible to French readers. But Robert d'Humières was perfectly fitted for the task, and judging from the first chapters his translation would have been masterly. The war sent him at once to the front; but in 1916 a bad attack of rheumatism obliged him to return to Paris, and he sent me word to come and see him. I found him, though very ill and worn, hard at work again on 'The Custom of the Country'; but as soon as he was discharged he asked to go back to the trenches, and almost immediately fell in leading an attack. His broken-hearted wife died soon afterward.

Another friend whom I got to know through the devoted 'retriever' was Victor Bérard, the eminent director of the *Ecole des Hautes Etudes*, whose speculative and picturesque interpretation of the Odyssey (*Les Phéniciens et l'Odyssée*) had aroused great interest far beyond University circles. Victor Bérard was a big handsome man, with a brain bursting with intellectual enthusiasms and rash hypotheses. He had the indefatigable activity, the almost limitless powers of work, of the typical French scholar, and his wife told me that, winter and summer, he was always at his desk at five in the morning, and that his working and teaching day often did not end till midnight. In spite of this he and Madame Bérard dispensed a tireless hospitality, receiving in their big old-fashioned house, which overlooked the neighbouring gardens of the Observatoire, many of the most distinguished men of letters, historians and archæologists of the day – and eminent painters as well, for Bérard was the intimate friend of Lucien Simon, Cottet and René Ménard, who were also great friends of each other, and consequently often to be seen together at his house.

These gatherings at the Bérards', and also at the Ganderaxes', the René Doumics', and other houses in the old closely-shut Parisian world of science and letters, were naturally of great interest to a stranger like myself; but they lacked – as such societies have wherever I have known them – the ease and amenity to be found only where intelligent people of various callings, with a few cultivated idlers among them, predominate over the highly-trained specialist. The only completely agreeable society I have ever known is that wherein the elements are selected and blent by a woman of the world, instinctively alert for every shade of suitability, and whose light hand never suffers the mixture to stiffen or grow heavy. At that time in Paris the appearance of a 'foreigner' in any society not slightly cosmopolitanized still caused a certain constraint, especially among its womenkind; and I gradually perceived that in University circles the presence of an American woman was almost paralyzing to the ladies of the party. As the men, immediately after the meal was over, always fled with coffee and cigarettes to the farthest corner of the room, leaving the women to themselves, I was subjected on such occasions to an hour's desolating conversation, which invariably began with the three questions: 'Are you soon to give us the pleasure of reading another of your wonderful novels?', 'Do you write in French, and then have your books translated into English?' and 'Have you already seen all the new plays?' – after which the talk languished into silence, my burdensome presence preventing the natural interchange of remarks on children, servants and prices which would otherwise have gone on between the ladies.

In many different sets I continued to make friends, and I keep a special niche in my memory for some of these. Among the dearest was Gustave Schlumberger, the celebrated archæologist and historian of the Byzantine Empire, who looked like a descendant of one of the Gauls on the arch of Titus, and who was cherished by a large group of devoted friends for the inexhaustible interest of his talk as much as he was dreaded by others for his uncurbed violence of speech. To me he was invariably kind, partly no doubt because of my interest in the archæological wonders of his beloved country; and during the last years of his life I saw him frequently. Another dear friend, very different in character though they shared certain artistic interest, was Auguste Laugel, whose acquaintance I made through Etta Reubell, my old friend, and Henry James's. Monsieur Laugel, the devoted friend of the Orléans family, who was especially attached to the Duc d'Aumale, and to whose learning and taste the Duke was indebted for the creation of the famous library at Chantilly, was an old man when I first knew him, and lived a quiet meditative life among his books and his friends. But his early years had been full of distinguished and successful activities, as a graduate of *Polytechnique*, as civil engineer, and professor at the *Ecole des Mines*, as a linguist, a traveller, and a writer on scientific subjects. To these interests he added a keen love of art and letters, and that highly specialized knowledge of books and of their makers which made of him one of the most accomplished bibliophiles of his day.

During a long sojourn in America, at the time of our Civil War, he was in frequent and intimate contact with the leading Northern generals and statesmen, and the result of those experiences was summed up in a series of notable articles in the Parisian press. Subsequently he followed the fortunes of the Duc d'Aumale, twice accompanying him into exile, and returning to France only when the Prince was finally allowed to re-establish himself at Chantilly.

Of all these years of labour and adventure there remained, when I knew him, only the mellowing influences left by a life of fruitful activity. Monsieur Laugel had married an American lady who had been very beautiful. They were a devoted couple, and after her death he had privately printed a small volume of poems, not addressed to the young bride in her freshness, but to the old and dying wife, as she lay helpless and motionless, for months, like the statue on her own grave. He did me the honour of giving me this book, as well as other treasures from his private library, and in particular one of its most precious volumes. I happened one day to mention that another of my friends, also a learned bibliophile, knowing my admiration for Racine, had given me the rare first editions of 'Athalie' and 'Esther', but had never been able to add to them a copy of the far rarer, the almost unfindable, 'Phèdre'. The next day Monsieur Laugel sent me the missing treasure; and I never look at the slim exquisite volume without a grateful thought for my delightful old friend, the perfect model of the distinguished and cultivated French gentleman of his day.

Chapter Twelve
Widening Waters

I

These new friendships, and many others, added much to my enjoyment of Paris; but the core of my life was under my own roof, among my books and my intimate friends. Above all it was in my work, which was growing and spreading, and absorbing more and more of my time and my imagination.

I had continued steadily at my story-telling, from which nothing could ever distract me for long, and during the busy happy Parisian years, and especially after the appearance of 'The House of Mirth', a growing sense of mastery made the work more and more absorbing. In 1908 I published 'The Hermit and the Wild Woman', a volume of short stories, in 1910 another, called 'Tales of Men and Ghosts', and between the two the record of some of our early motor journeys in France.

But the book to the making of which I brought the greatest joy and the fullest ease was 'Ethan Frome'. For years I had wanted to draw life as it really was in the derelict mountain villages of New England, a life even in my time, and a thousandfold more a generation earlier, utterly unlike that seen through the rose-coloured spectacles of my predecessors, Mary Wilkins and Sarah Orne Jewett. In those days the snow-bound villages of Western Massachusetts were still grim places, morally and physically: insanity, incest and slow mental and moral starvation were hidden away behind the paintless wooden house-fronts of the long village street, or in the isolated farm-houses on the neighbouring hills; and Emily Brontë would have found as savage tragedies in our remoter valleys as on her Yorkshire moors. In this connection, I may mention that every detail about the colony of drunken mountain outlaws described in 'Summer' was given to me by the rector of the church at Lenox (near which we lived), and that the lonely peak I have called 'the Mountain' was in reality Bear Mountain, an isolated summit not more than twelve miles from our own home. The rector had been fetched there by one of the mountain outlaws to read the Burial Service over a woman of evil reputation; and when he arrived every one in the house of mourning was drunk, and the service was performed as I have related it. The rector's predecessor in the fashionable parish of Lenox had, I believe, once been called for on a similar errand, but had prudently refused to go; my friend, however, thought it his duty to do so, and drove off alone with the outlaw – coming back with his eyes full of horror and his heart of anguish and pity. Needless to say, when 'Summer' appeared, this chapter was received with indignant denial by many reviewers and readers; and not the least vociferous were the New Englanders who had for years sought the reflection of local life in the rose-and-lavender pages of their favourite authoresses – and had forgotten to look into Hawthorne's.

'Ethan Frome' shocked my readers less than 'Summer'; but it was frequently criticized as 'painful', and at first had much less success than my previous books. I have a clearer recollection of its beginnings than of those of my other tales, through the singular accident that its first pages were written – in French! I had determined, when we came to live in Paris, to polish and enlarge my French vocabulary; for though I had spoken the language since the age of four I had never had much occasion to talk it, for any length of time, with cultivated people, having usually, since my marriage, wandered through France as a tourist. The result was that I had kept up the language chiefly through reading, and the favourite French authors of my early youth being Bossuet, Racine, Corneille and La Bruyère, most of my polite locutions dated from the seventeenth century, and Bourget used to laugh at me for speaking 'the purest Louis Quatorze'. To bring my idioms up to date I asked Charles Du Bos to find, among his friends, a young professor who would come and talk with me two or three times a week. An amiable young man was found; but, being too amiable ever to correct my spoken mistakes, he finally hit on the expedient of asking me to prepare an 'exercise' before each visit. The easiest thing for me was to write a story; and thus the French version of 'Ethan Frome' was begun, and carried on for a few weeks. Then the lessons were given up, and the copy-book containing my 'exercise' vanished forever. But a few years later, during one of our summer sojourns at the Mount, a distant glimpse of Bear Mountain brought Ethan back to my memory, and the following winter in Paris I wrote the tale as it now stands, reading my morning's work aloud each evening to Walter Berry, who was as familiar as I was with the lives led in those half-deserted villages before the coming of motor and telephone. We talked the tale over page by page, so that its accuracy of 'atmosphere' is doubly assured – and I mention this because not long since, in an article by an American literary critic, I saw 'Ethan Frome' cited as an interesting example of a successful New England story written by some one who knew nothing of New England! 'Ethan Frome' was written after I had spent ten years in the hill-region where the scene is laid, during which years I had come to know well the aspect, dialect, and mental and moral attitude of the hill-people. The fact that 'Summer' deals with the same class and type as those portrayed in 'Ethan Frome', and has the same setting, might have sufficed to disprove the legend – but once such a legend is started it echoes on as long as its subject survives.

2

Almost all my intimate friends from England and America used to come to stay with us in Paris; Walter Berry, whenever he could escape from his hard work as one of the Judges of the International Tribunal at Cairo; Henry James, Howard Sturgis, Percy Lubbock, Gaillard Lapsley, Robert Norton and John Hugh-Smith. I also continued to see a great deal of Egerton Winthrop, Robert Minturn, and many other old friends from America, who came annually to Paris; and usually, before going back to the Mount for the summer, or on my return from America in the autumn, I snatched a few weeks in England, dividing them between Lamb House, Queen's Acre, and Hill Hall, Mrs Charles Hunter's place in Essex.

Mrs Charles Hunter was so much a part of my annual English holiday, so much the centre of my picture of the English world, that when she died the other day, for me at least, almost the whole fabric went with her. Henry James, who was her devoted friend, had long wanted us to meet; but knowing of her only as a fashionable hostess and indefatigable entertainer, and not wishing to plunge again into the world of big house-parties and London 'crushes', I had evaded all suggestions and invitations.

And then suddenly – I forgot when or where – we met, and became friends.

Sargent's portrait (given by her to the Tate Gallery) renders Mary Hunter's fair abundant beauty in all its harvest brightness; and it was thus that I first knew her – still beautiful, wealthy, hospitable and boundlessly generous, with no clear idea about money except that, if one had it, it was to be spent for the pleasure of others. Later, when her fortune, which was entirely in coal, dwindled to nothing with the other great English mining-fortunes, she bore the loss with dauntless good humour, a spirit of 'the Lord gave, and the Lord hath taken away', of which I know few finer examples; but her notion of money remained as hazy when every penny mattered as when wealth poured uncounted through her lavish hands. As one of her friends said: 'Mary is a cornucopia'; and to the end of her life generosity, pity, eagerness to help and to make happy, kept spilling out of her in words and deeds when they could no longer be expressed in cheques.

A year or two before her death we were staying at the same house in the country, and having broken her motoring spectacles she asked me to take her to an optician's to buy another pair. She was already ruined, and living in such narrow circumstances that I thought it quite natural for her to consider the price. 'How much do you suppose they'll cost, my dear? Not above two or three pounds?' she asked anxiously. I burst out laughing. 'Bless you, no! Not above two or three shillings.' I expected a sigh of relief; but she gave no sign of seeing any difference, and to the very end such shades of more-or-less remained too microscopic for her notice.

The golden waves of prosperity were rolling higher and higher about her when our acquaintance began. Her husband, who adored her, wished her to enjoy every luxury; but he had always refused to give her a town house, fearing, as he said, that life in London would lead to extravagance beyond even his resources. He bestowed on her, instead, Hill Hall, a William-and-Mary house of stately proportions, built about a great interior quadrangle, and dominating the blue distances of Essex; and for the London season she hired one of the ornate seventeenth century houses attached to the Burlington Hotel. This she furnished luxuriously, and lived in it exactly as if it were her own – save that the upkeep stopped when she was not in town.

At Hill no limits were set, but the house was not expensively furnished, though arranged with much taste, and containing a few good pictures. Life there was on a large scale, for there were many rooms, and in addition to the perpetual come-and-go of married daughters, grandchildren and other relations, there was a succession of friends for a good part of the year, and a big house-party for every week-end.

I used sometimes to wonder what Rosa de Fitz-James, with her careful sense of conformity, of selection, her French cult of the *ce-qui-se-fait*, would have thought of those happy-go-lucky week-ends, with friends tumbling in unexpectedly from everywhere, extra seats being hastily crowded into the long dining-room, fresh provisions hurried to the already groaning tea-table, spare-rooms prepared, messages telephoned, people passing in and out with a sort of smiling fatalism, no questions asked, no explanations expected, just a continuous surge of easy good-humoured life through the big house, the broad flagged terraces and the crowded tennis-courts. I was about to add 'and the gardens' when I remembered that, oddly enough for an Englishwoman, Mary Hunter was congenitally incapable of interesting herself in horticulture, her only attempt in that line at Hill being a made-to-order rose-garden of which Percy Lubbock remarked that it looked 'as if no one had ever said a kind word to it'.

Mary Hunter's hospitality was more comprehensive than Madame de Fitz-James's, not only because her nature was larger and more impetuous, but because all the meticulous French discriminations would have been meaningless to her, and to her world, where numbers had a secret magic, and even to the intelligent the sense of being in a crowd was more stimulating than that of being too carefully shielded from it. Mrs Hunter's guests, however, were combined with unusual discrimination, for though she herself had – as far as I could see – no particular pleasure in good talk, she enjoyed it vicariously, as a good hostess, and, as a clever one, managed to get together the elements to create it. Even her most haphazard parties contained a nucleus of intimate friends with literary and artistic tastes, and this saved the week-ends of Hill from the dullness usual in such assemblages. Moreover, Mrs Hunter's watchful solicitude made her combine her inner group with a view to the enjoyment of all its members, and when I went to Hill I usually found there some of my own friends, among whom Henry James, Percy Lubbock and Howard Sturgis were the most frequent.

In earlier days she had gathered about her many painters and musicians, and more than once, especially among the painters, her generous encouragement gave the first impetus to a successful career. Sargent's portrait of herself, and the famous one of her three daughters (now in the National Gallery), are known to every one; but she and her family were also repeatedly painted by Mancini, and by Mrs Swinnerton; and she was the life-long friend of Sargent, Walter Sickert, Rodin (who made a fine bust of her), Professor Tonks, Mr Steer, Claude Monet and Jaques-Emile Blanche. As is usual with hostesses of her kind, the thought of the illustrious unsociable would not let her sleep, and she was determined not only to admire and help her celebrities (and help them she did, in every possible way) but to enjoy their society on her own terms; that is, in the crowd and tumult of the Hill week-ends. She had all the tenacity and inventiveness of the celebrity-collector, and there is a tale of her, already a legend when I heard it, but so characteristic that it may well be true. She was a great admirer of Mancini's art, and hearing that he was staying in London she immediately introduced herself by telephone, and besought him to come down to Hill for the following Sunday. But he was poor, solitary-minded, and unable to speak English; and to excuse himself he enumerated all these objections. Go to stay with Mrs Hunter – but he couldn't possibly! Why, to begin with, he didn't even own a dress-coat.

'Is that all? Nonsense! My husband'll lend you one.'

'Oh, but that's nothing. I don't speak English – not more than two words. And I don't understand anything that is said to me.'

'Well, that doesn't matter either. So-and-so and so-and-so, who are coming, both speak Italian perfectly.'

'Ah, but you don't understand. I couldn't even buy my railway-ticket, or find my way from my hotel to the station.'

'My dear Signor Mancini, don't worry about that. I have an Italian footman – a perfect genius of a footman. He'll be at your hotel with a cab tomorrow afternoon at four; he'll pack your things, take you to the train, bring you down, and wait on you while you're here.'

There was a faint murmur of surrender from Mancini, and Mary Hunter instantly called up a London tailoring establishment and ordered a dress-suit (it is not recorded how she obtained the measures). She then telephoned to an employment agency for an Italian footman, and on being told that they had none on their list, and could not possibly engage to produce one at such short notice, replied calmly: 'You *must* find me one at any price, and he must bring Signor Mancini down to Hill tomorrow afternoon.' And he was found, and brought Mancini down – with the dress-clothes smuggled into the latter's suit-case.

When I first went to Hill those epic days were over. Most of the painter friends of my hostess's youth were already middle-aged and illustrious, and except in two or three cases the intimacy, though not the friendship, had probably declined; or else Mrs Hunter may have divided her friends into separate groups, for I seldom met any painters or musicians at Hill, and the 'nucleus' in my time was usually literary. James was, of course, its central figure, welcomed and delighted in by all the family, and enveloped by the most discerning affection. The rival luminary, who hated and envied James, and missed no chance to belittle and sneer at him, was George Moore. I shall never forget a luncheon at Hill when John Hugh-Smith with seeming artlessness drew Moore out on his great contemporaries, and James, Conrad, Hardy, and all others of any worth, were swept away on a torrent of venom. It was the tone of 'The Dunciad' without its wit. But that was George Moore's way; and I recall another instance of it at the house of Jacques Blanche, one of his most devoted and long-suffering friends. My husband and I often went to the Blanches' literary and artistic luncheons, and one day George Moore was of the party. When we returned to the big studio after luncheon, and coffee and cigarettes were served, Moore ostentatiously drew out his cigar-case, lit a big cigar, and offered one to my husband. The latter, though he loved a good cigar, declined, and Moore said in a loud voice: 'If you haven't brought any of your own you'd better take one of mine. They never give them here.' 'I know,' replied my husband quietly; 'that's why I never bring one.'

Mary Hunter could not resist baiting her hospitable hook with a name like James's. She loved and admired him so much that she wanted his glory to shine over as many of her parties as possible, and forgetting that its light, if intense, was not far-spread, she sometimes mentioned him as an inducement to guests who had never even heard his name. I was at Hill on one such occasion, when, on the arrival of a fashionable beauty, her hostess welcomed her with: 'And tomorrow, you know, you're going to see Henry James!'

The lady's perplexity was great, but so also was her frankness. Who in the world, she asked, was Henry James, and why should she particularly want to see him? Mrs Hunter was dumbfounded: was it possible that dear Lady— really didn't know? No; she really didn't. But she was goodnaturedly ready to be enlightened, and having been told that Henry James was one of the greatest of living novelists, she suffered 'The Wings of the Dove' and 'The Golden Bowl' to be pressed into her submissive hands, and obediently agreed to read them both before the next afternoon!

When she came down the following day, just before luncheon, I was sitting in the hall. The four fat volumes were under her arm, and she thumped them down on the table, and turned her lovely smile on me. 'Well – of all the *tosh*!' she said gaily.

Knowing that Henry James, though he suffered acutely from the criticisms of the literary, would enjoy this fresh breeze out of Philistia, I told him the tale as soon as he arrived. He welcomed it with a joyful chuckle; and when he and the lady met that evening they at once became the best of friends.

This anecdote leads me to two others which I may as well insert at this point into my English picture. Once when James and I were staying together in the country our host suggested taking us to call on a charming neighbour, formerly, I think, a celebrated music-hall artist. James, I believe, had met the lady at a theatrical supper some twenty years earlier, and he declared himself delighted to renew the acquaintance. The lady, who also remembered the far-off supper, welcomed him cordially; and in the course of the visit, drawing me aside, she expressed her pleasure at seeing dear Mr James again after so many years, and added: 'I've so often wondered what had happened to him since. Do tell me – *has he kept up his writing?*'

My other tale concerns Lamb House, but at a much later time, when, after James's death, it was tenanted for some years by Robert Norton, who had known James well, and treated the house and its contents with the same veneration as the guardian of 'The Birthplace' treated that shrine in James's story. Robert Norton happened one day to run across a London great lady, an old acquaintance of his, who was staying near Rye. She told him she had been longing for years to visit Lamb House, of which she had heard so much, and begged him to let her come to see it. She came, and he took her all over, showing each room, each piece and furniture, each relic, and explaining: 'Here James dictated to his secretary every morning; under this weeping ash he used to sit in hot weather; this silver-point was done of him by Sargent before he shaved his beard; this is a replica of his bust by—', till finally the great lady, grateful but bewildered, interrupted him to ask: 'I've heard so much of Lamb House, as a particularly charming specimen of a small Georgian house – but *would* you mind telling me who this Mr Henry James is, who appears to have lived here?'

The keeper of the 'Birthplace' remembered 'The Death of the Lion', and answered her question with a smile.

3

Henry James's visits to the rue de Varenne were always a busy time for me. He had been much in Paris in his youth, had frequented the great generation of the Goncourt 'garret', met Flaubert frequently, and been intimate with Turgeniev, and later with Alphonse Daudet, and of course with Bourget. His description of taking Daudet down to Box Hill to see Meredith, and of the two great writers, both stricken with the same fatal malady, advancing painfully toward each other across the platform of the little country station, was one of the most moving things I ever heard him relate. He also piloted Bourget about London and Oxford, on the latter's first visit to England, when he was preparing the English impressions afterward included in *Etudes et Portraits*; and all these contacts had made James's name familiar among French intellectuals long before they struggled to decipher his books.

James's unusual social gifts, and keen enjoyments of society (once he had escaped from its tyrannous routine), lent a schoolboy's zest to his Paris visits. The first time he stayed with us there must have been in 1905, before the rue de Varenne days, when my brother Harry, who had a flat in Paris, lent it to us during a temporary absence. It was in that year, I think, that James, through my intervention, sat to Blanche for the admirable portrait which distressed the sitter because of the 'Daniel Lambert' curve of the rather florid waist-coat; and during those sittings, and on other occasions at the Blanches', he made many new acquaintances, and renewed some old friendships.

James's simple cordiality would have made him welcome anywhere; but he was particularly popular among his French friends, not only on account of his quickness and adaptability, but because his youthful frequentations in the French world of letters, following on the school-years in Geneva, had so steeped him in continental culture that the cautious and inhospitable French intelligence felt at once at ease with him. This feeling was increased by his mastery of the language. French people have told me that they had never met an Anglo-Saxon who spoke French like James; not only correctly and fluently, but – well, just as they did themselves; avoiding alike platitudes and pomposity, and using the language as spontaneously as if it were his own.

It was no wonder therefore that James enjoyed his French holidays. He was invited out continually, and the only difficulty was to capture him now and then for an evening in the rue de Varenne. The contrast to the severe winter routine of Rye, the change of scene, of food, of point of view – the very differences in the houses and streets, in the mental attitude and the moral conventions – of all these nothing escaped him, nothing failed to amuse him. In the intervals between dining out he liked a dash in the motor; and among other jolly expeditions, I remember a visit to Nohant, when he saw for the first time George Sand's house. I had been there before, and knew how to ingratiate myself with the tall impressive guardian of the shrine, a handsome *Berrichonne* who could remember, as a very little girl, helping 'Madame' to dress Maurice's marionettes, which still dangled wistfully from their hooks in the little theatre below stairs.

James, who shared my delight in the enchanting *Histoire de ma Vie* and the *Lettres d'un Voyageur*, had known personally a number of the illustrious pilgrims – Flaubert, Maupassant, Alexandre Dumas fils and others – who used to come to Nohant in the serene old age of its tumultuous châtelaine. He was therefore fascinated by every detail of the scene, deeply moved by the inscriptions on the family grave-stones under the wall of the tiny ancient church – especially in the tragic Solange's: *La Mère de Jeanne* – and absorbed in the study of the family portraits, from the Elector of Saxony and the Mlles Verrier to Maurice and his children. He lingered delightedly over the puppet theatre with Maurice's grimacing dolls, and the gay costumes stitched by his mother; then we wandered out into the garden, and looking up at the plain old house, tried to guess behind which windows the various famous visitors had slept. James stood there a long time, gazing and brooding beneath the row of closed shutters. 'And in which of those rooms, I wonder, did George herself sleep?' I heard him suddenly mutter. 'Though in which, indeed –' with a twinkle – 'in which indeed, my dear, did she *not*?'

A vision especially dear to me is associated with one of James's visits to the rue de Varenne. It is that of the exquisite picture of Paris by night in the tale – perhaps the most beautiful of his later short stories – called 'The Velvet Glove'. He and I had often talked over the subject of this story, which was suggested by the fact that a very beautiful young Englishwoman of great position, and unappeased literary ambitions, had once tried to beguile him into contributing an introduction to a novel she was writing – or else into reviewing the book; I forget which. She had sought from him, at any rate, a literary 'boost' which all his admiration and liking for her could not, he thought, justify his giving; and they parted, though still friends, with evidences on her part of visible disappointment – and surprise. The incident certainly gave him a theme 'to his hand'; but it lay unused for lack of a setting, for he wanted to make of it, not a mere ironic anecdote – that was too easy – but a little episode steeped in wistfulness and poetry. And then, one soft spring evening, after we had dined somewhere out of town – possibly at Versailles, or at a restaurant in the Bois – knowing his love for motoring at night, I proposed a circuit in the environs, which finally brought us home by way of Saint Cloud; and as we hung there, high above the moonlit lamplit city and the gleaming curves of the Seine, he suddenly 'held' his setting, as the painters say, and, though I knew nothing of it till long afterward, 'The Velvet Glove' took shape that night.

The theatre was of course one of James's great interests when he was in Paris; but he was so much invited out, and so much amused by his glimpses of a new and stimulating social scene, that he could seldom spare an evening. When he did, it was usually for the first night of some well-known dramatist, such as Paul Hervieu, or in later years Henry Bataille or Henry Bernstein. James's interest in the theatre was sustained by the conviction (which it took so many bitter disappointments to eradicate) that he would one day achieve popular success as a playwright. It is an illusion often nursed by novelists, especially those who, like James, are gradually dominated by the sense of 'situation', the strictly scenic element, in their subjects. It is difficult to understand that there is little connection between the novelist's sense of a situation and that of the playwright, and James was persuaded to the end that his constructive instinct ought to have served in play-building as well as in story-telling. Perhaps it might have, if he had not been so oddly enslaved by what might be called the Dumas-fils convention (a tradition from which the French have now so wholly emancipated themselves). The typical Dumas-fils play was a miracle of neat joinery, culminating in a 'moral' of which all his characters were merely the subservient tools. It seems odd that James, whose conception of the novel was so independent and original, regarded these stage conventions as inevitable. He admired Ibsen, but seems never to have felt any incongruity between the two conceptions of the theatre, much less to have contemplated the possibility of creating a formula of his own for his plays, as he had for his novels.

James's interest in the stage naturally included the world of the theatre, with its rivalries and scandals, its generosities and absurdities, and all its *grandeurs et misères*. He was always particularly amused by anecdotes about theatrical people, and I remember a report of one conversation with a retired actress which delighted his listeners. The lady in question, in far-off days, had had a brief career on the London stage in classical tragedy, but long before James's coming to England she had married a man who had given her a place in the most conservative circles of early Victorian London. Always irreproachable in conduct and reputation, she yet yearned now and then for an opportunity to speak of her theatrical years, and especially to dwell on the perils to which the virtuous actress is exposed. On one occasion she had been detailing these at some length to James, and after complacently enumerating the various forms of temptation she had successfully resisted, she added: 'And would you believe it, Mr James? *One fiend in human shape actually offered me cameos.*'

There were many amusing incidents connected with Henry James's visits to Paris. I was the object of much attention on the part of hostesses who wished to use him as a social 'draw', and of literary ladies who aspired to translate his novels; and among the advances made by the latter I remember two over which, when they were reported to him, his chuckles were particularly prolonged. In one case a fervent translatress besought me to recommend her to the Master as particularly qualified to translate 'The Golden Bowl' because she had just dealt successfully with a work called 'The Filigree Box'; while another tried to ingratiate herself by assuring me that her deep appreciation of my own great work, 'The House of the Myrtles', was surpassed only by her unbounded admiration for that supreme anatomical masterpiece, 'The Golden Bowel'.

Ah, how we used to come back from those parties bearing our sheaves of laughter – and how the laughter still rings in my ears as I call up the scenes that provoked it!

4

'Well, I *am* glad to welcome to the White House some one to whom I can quote "The Hunting of the Snark" without being asked what I mean!'

Such was my first greeting from Theodore Roosevelt after his accession to the Presidency – a date so much earlier than that of my sojourn in Paris that I ought to have introduced it before, had it not seemed simpler to gather into one chapter the record of our too infrequent meetings. Though I had known Theodore Roosevelt since my first youth, and though his second wife is my distant cousin, I had met him only at long intervals – usually at my sister-in-law's, in New York – and we had never 'hooked' (in the French sense of the *atômes crochus*) until after the publication of 'The Valley of Decision'. He had a great liking for the book, which he wanted, after his usual fashion, to rearrange in conformity with his theory of domestic morals and the strenuous life; but when I pointed out that these ideals did not happen to prevail in the decadent Italian principalities which Napoleon was so soon to wipe out or to remodel, he laughingly acknowledged the fact, and thereafter we became great friends. My intimacy with Bay Lodge, and with the Jusserands, with whom my friendship dated back to my childhood, created other links between the Roosevelts and myself, and the first time I went to Washington after they were installed in the White House I was promptly summoned to lunch, and welcomed on the threshold by the President's vehement cry: 'At last I can quote "The Hunting of the Snark"'!

'Would you believe it,' he added, 'no one in the Administration has ever heard of Alice, much less of the Snark, and the other day, when I said to the Secretary of the Navy: "Mr Secretary, *What I say three times is true*", he did not recognize the allusion, and answered with an aggrieved air: "Mr President, it would never for a moment have occurred to me to impugn your veracity"!'

These whirlwind welcomes were very characteristic, for

Theodore Roosevelt had in his mind so clear a vision of each interlocutor's range of subjects, and his own was so extensive and so varied, that when he met any one who interested him he could never bear to waste a moment in preliminaries.

I remember another instance of this impatient desire to get to his point, however remote from the topics of the moment. Many years ago, that charming old institution, Williams College, conferred an honorary degree on Roosevelt, and the college authorities invited me to the Commencement ceremonies. I motored from the Mount to Williamstown, and when I appeared at the reception, which took place after the conferring of the degrees, the President, who probably did not expect to meet me there, uttered an exclamation of surprise, and cried out: 'But you're the very person I wanted to see! Of course you've read that wonderful new book of de la Gorce's, the "History of the Second Empire"? What an amazing thing! Let's go off into a corner at once and have a good talk about it.'

And go off into a corner we did, and talked about it at some length, to the visible interruption of the academic formalities; but that was the President's way, and as everybody loved him, everybody forgave him; and moreover they all knew that in another ten minutes he would be cornering somebody else on some other equally absorbing subject. What he could not and would not endure was talking about things which did not interest him when there were so many that *did* – so far too many for the brief time he had to spare for them. One feels, in looking back, something premonitory in this impatience, this thirst to slake an intellectual curiosity almost as fervent as his moral ardours.

With his faculty of instantly extracting the best that each person had to give, he seldom failed, when we met, to turn the talk to books. So much of his time was spent among the bookless that many people never suspected either the range of his literary culture or his learned interest in the natural sciences; and in Washington they were probably fully known only to the small group of people to whom he turned for intellectual stimulus – such as the Cabot Lodges, Henry Adams, Walter Berry, the Jusserands and Spring-Rice.

But there was another tie between us. Theodore Roosevelt was one of the most humorous *raconteurs* I ever knew, and a very good mimic; and when we were among a little band of fun-lovers – say with Bay Lodge, the President's sister, Mrs Douglas

Robinson, and a few other collectors of good nonsense – he kept us rocking with his cow-boy tales and his evocations of White House visitors. His liberty of speech, even in mixed company, was startling. Once, at a moment of acute tension between the President and the Senate, I was lunching at the White House with a big and haphazard party, among whom were several guests who had never before met the President, and at least one journalist; and suddenly I heard him break out to the assembled table: 'Well, yes, I'm tired; I'm terribly tired. I don't know exactly what's the matter with me; but if only we could revive the good old Roman customs, I know a bath in Senator —'s blood would set me right in no time.'

He was noted for speaking recklessly before people incapable of appreciating either his humour or his irony, and to whom it must often have been a temptation to quote his personal comments; yet it was always said that during his two terms of office no public advantage was ever taken of these indiscretions, and in a country like ours there could be no greater proof of the degree to which he was loved and respected.

One of our last meetings was in the rue de Varenne, in the course of the astonishing world-tour of 1909–10, when, after completing his second term of office as the most famous man in America, he discovered that his celebrity also embraced the other side of the globe. On this tour, during which, in spite of his repeated protests that he was only a private citizen, he was received with sovereign honours by every European government, he came to Paris to give a lecture at the Sorbonne. Through his old friend Jusserand, then Ambassador to Washington, who had arranged to meet him in Paris, I was notified that he would like to come to the rue de Varenne. He sent me word to invite a few people to meet him – not governmental or 'universitaire', since he was sure to see them elsewhere, but my own group of friends; and every one I summoned answered to the call, for the desire to meet him was intense. I tried to choose, in the literary and academic line, principally those who spoke English; but unhappily they were few; and though Roosevelt knew French well, he spoke it badly, and with a rather bewildering pronunciation. The consequence was that, having found among my guests an Academician (I forget who) who was a specialist on some subject which particularly interested him, and could talk to him about it in English, he broke up the royal 'circle' (of which he was of course expected to go the round), and by isolating himself too long with this particular interlocutor caused much disappointment to some of my other guests.

Such an omission was not easily understood or forgiven; but it was difficult to stem the current of the President's eloquence, and the President he still was, to all intents and purposes. I was made to feel afterward that Jusserand and I had failed in our duty in not organizing the party in such a way that each guest should have a few minutes' talk with the great man; for it was inconceivable to my amiable but highly disciplined guests that either the President or his hostess should unintentionally omit a single move of the traditional game they had been invited to play with him.

I was only once at Sagamore – and I think it was there that I saw Theodore Roosevelt for the last time. There could not have been a fitter setting for what turned out to be our goodbye; for it was only at Sagamore that the least known side of his character was revealed, and *ranchero* and statesman both made way for the private man, absorbed in books and nature, and in the quiet interests of a country life.

What a good day that was! My husband and I went down to lunch, and found no one but the family (a term which, as in my own house, always included two or three busy and extremely interested dogs). The house was like one big library, and the whole tranquil place breathed of the love of books and of the country, so that I felt immediately at home there. After luncheon Mr Roosevelt, with a good deal of simple amusement, showed us the photographs taken of himself and the Emperor William during the famous German manœuvres. He was perfectly aware of the studied impertinence of the Kaiser's famous inscription on one of the photographs – it read, I think: 'President Roosevelt shows the Emperor of Germany how to command an attack', or something of the kind – but he treated it as an imperial appeal to his sense of humour, which indeed it probably was.

In looking back over my memories of Theodore Roosevelt I am surprised to find how very seldom I saw him, and yet how sure I am that he was my friend. He had the rare gift of bridging over in an instant those long intervals between meetings that so often benumb even the best of friends, and he was so alive at all points, and so gifted with the rare faculty of living intensely and entirely in every moment as it passed, that each of those encounters glows in me like a tiny morsel of radium.

5

During our first years in Paris the friend of my childhood, Henry
White, was our Ambassador there. He had married our beautiful
neighbour at Newport, Margaret Rutherfurd, whose two equally
beautiful young brothers, Lewis and Winthrop, had been (with
the exception of Madame Jusserand and Daisy Terry) my earliest
playmates. The intimacy between the two families had never
relaxed, and during the years when Henry White was first
Secretary at our London Embassy he and his wife were the means
of my meeting many interesting people whenever I went to
England. The Whites, in their youth, and even in their middle age,
were one of the handsomest couples I have ever seen, and on the
Rutherfurd side the beauty of the whole family was proverbial.
The story was told of an Englishman and an American who were
strolling down Piccadilly together, and discussing the relative
degree of good looks of their respective compatriots. 'I grant you,'
the Englishman said, 'that your women are lovely; perhaps not as
regularly beautiful as ours, but often prettier and more graceful.
But your men – yes, of course, I've seen very good-looking
American men; but nothing – if you'll excuse my saying so – to
compare with our young Englishmen of the Public School and
University type, our splendid young athletes: there, like these two
who are just coming toward us—' and the two in question were
Margaret White's brothers, the young Rutherfurds.

Another story, also turning on young masculine beauty, was
told to me by one of two other proverbially handsome brothers,
Grafton and Howard Cushing of Boston. Once, when these two
ambrosial youths were staying in London, the eldest, Grafton,
was asked by Queen Victoria's niece, the Countess Feo Gleichen,
who was a sculptor of talent, to sit to her for a bust. The sittings
took place in Countess Gleichen's apartment in Saint James's
Palace; and Howard, who lived in lodgings with his brother, told
me how one morning very early he was awakened by a hammer-
ing at the door, and heard the excited voice of the lodging-house
buttons crying out: 'If you please, sir, her Majesty has sent word
to say that she expects you at Buckingham Palace this morning at
nine o'clock sharp, and you're to wear the same shirt that you
wore yesterday.'

In Paris our Embassy, as long as the Whites were there, was a
second home to me, and Harry, who was never happier than in

contriving happiness for others, was always arranging for me to meet interesting people. I remember, in particular, lunching at the Embassy one day with Orville Wright, the survivor of the two famous brothers, who had come to Paris, I think, for the inauguration of the statue at Le Mans commemorative of their first flight on French soil. Walter Berry, who was also at the lunch, had for many years been the counsel of the French Embassy in Washington. He was the intimate friend of Jusserand, and when, in 1905, or there abouts, the French Government sent a military mission to America to investigate the queer new 'flying machine' which two unknown craftsmen of Dayton, Ohio, had invented, Walter Berry was requested by the Ambassador to accompany the mission to Dayton as legal adviser. He stayed there for three weeks, saw the machine 'levitate' a few inches above the earth, and came back awed by the possibility of the 'strange futures beautiful and new' folded up within those clumsy wings, and much impressed by the two shy taciturn men who had called the monster into being. I remember his telling me that when he discussed with Wilbur Wright the future of aviation, the latter said: 'I can conceive that aeroplanes might possibly be of some use in war, but never for any commercial purpose, or as a regular means of communication.'

It must have been about the same time that I was invited by the Marquis de Polignac to see an exhibition of flying in the aerodrome he had constructed at Reims. I went there with Walter Berry, and in the presence of a large assemblage of scientific notabilities we saw several glorious 'aces' (whose names, alas, I have forgotten) execute, at a height of a few yards above the ground, non-stop flights around the aerodrome, which, as I remember it, must have had about the dimensions of an ordinary polo-field. And that was only two or three years before the war!

6

Fate seemed to have conspired to fill those last years of peace with every charm and pleasure. 'Eyes, look your last' – in and about Paris all things seemed to utter the same cry: the smiling suburbs unmarred by hideous advertisements, the unravaged cornfields of Millet and Monet, still spreading in sunny opulence to the city's edge, the Champs-Elysées in their last expiring elegance, and the great buildings, statues and fountains withdrawn at dusk into silence and secrecy, instead of being torn from their mystery by the vulgar intrusion of flood-lighting.

One of the loveliest flowers on the bough so soon to be broken was the dancing of Isadora Duncan. Hardly any one in Paris had heard of her when she first appeared there, but in me her name woke an old memory. Years before, a philanthropic Boston lady who spent her summers at Newport had invited her friends to a garden party at which Isadora Duncan was to dance. 'Isadora Duncan?' People repeated the unknown name, wondering why it had been used to bait Miss Mason's invitation. Only two kinds of dancing were familiar to that generation: waltzing in the ball-room and pirouetting on the stage. I hated pirouetting, and did not go to Miss Mason's. Those who did smiled, and said they supposed their hostess had asked the young women to dance out of charity – as I daresay she did. Nobody had ever seen anything like it; you couldn't call it dancing, they said. No other Newport hostess engaged Miss Duncan, and her name vanished from everybody's mind. And then, nearly twenty years later, I went one night to the Opera in Paris, to see a strange new dancer about whom the artists were beginning to talk . . .

I suppose that liking or not liking the conventional form of ballet-dancing is as little to be accounted for as one's feeling about olives or caviar. To me the word 'dancing' had always suggested a joyful *abandon*, a plastic improvisation, the visual equivalent of

> Like to a moving vintage down they came,
> Crowned with green leaves, and faces all on flame . . .

in Keats's glorious bacchanal. The traditional ballet-dancing, the swollen feet in ugly shoes performing impossible *tours de force* of poising and bounding, reminded me, on the contrary, of 'But, oh, what labour – Prince, what pain!', and except in Carpeaux's intoxicating group, and Titian's 'Triumph of Bacchus', I had never seen dancing as I inwardly imagined it. And then, when the curtain was drawn back from the great stage of the Opera, and before a background of grayish-green hangings a single figure appeared – a tall, rather awkwardly made woman, dragging a scarf after her – then suddenly I beheld the dance I had always dreamed of, a flowing of movement into movement, an endless interweaving of motion and music, satisfying every sense as a flower does, or a phrase of Mozart's.

That first sight of Isadora's dancing was a white milestone to me. It shed a light on every kind of beauty, and showed me for the first time how each flows into the other as the music merged with her dancing. All through the immense rapt audience one felt the rush of her inspiration, as one feels the blowing open of the door in the 'Walkyrie', when Sieglinde cries out: '*Wer ging?*' and Sigmund answers: '*Einer kam. Es war der Lenz!*'

Yes; it was the spring, the bursting into bloom of acres and acres of silver fruit-blossom where a week before there had been only dead boughs. And I believe it was that fertilizing magic which evoked our next and last vision of beauty before the war: the Russian Ballet. Every one who saw the Imperial ballet in St Petersburg, in its official setting, has assured me that when Diaghilew brought his dancers to Paris he infused new life into them, broke down old barriers of convention, and taught their exquisitely disciplined steps to flow into wild free measures. It is hard to believe that Isadora's inspiration had no part in the change.

It seemed as if those years contained some generative fire which called forth masterpieces; for close on Isadora, and on Diaghilew's dancers, came Proust's first volume. Proust – a name almost as unfamiliar as Isadora's, and destined, like hers, to fly through our imaginations on a shower of spring blossoms: the hawthorn hedge of *Du Côté de chez Swann*. At the moment it merely recalled to me some clever skits on contemporary writers which I had glanced at from time to time in the *Figaro*. I forget who first spoke to me about the book, but it may have been Blanche, who was one of Proust's earliest friends and admirers. I began to read languidly, felt myself, after two pages, in the hands of a master, and was presently trembling with the excitement which only genius can communicate.

I sent the book immediately to James, and his letter to me shows how deeply it impressed him. James, at that time, was already an old man and, as I have said, his literary judgments had long been hampered by his increasing preoccupations with the structure of the novel, and his unwillingness to concede that the vital centre (when there was any) could lie elsewhere. Even when I first knew him he read contemporary novels (except Wells's and a few of Conrad's) rarely, and with ill-concealed impatience; and as time passed, and intricate problems of form and structure engrossed him more deeply, it became almost impossible to persuade him that there might be merit in the work of writers apparently insensible to these sterner demands of the art. I remember, for instance, that when he published his 'Notes on Novelists', one of our friends, who had been greatly struck by Lawrence's 'Sons and Lovers', reproached James for having dealt so summarily with a new novelist who was beginning to attract the attention of intelligent readers. James's reply was evasive and unsatisfactory, and at last his interlocutor exclaimed: 'Come, now! Have you ever read any of Lawrence's novels – really read them?' James's most mischievous smile crept down from his eyes to his lips. 'I – I have trifled with the exordia,' he murmured with a wicked twinkle.

No one but a novelist knows how hard it is for one of the craft to read other people's novels; but in the presence of a masterpiece all of James's prejudices and reluctances vanished. He seized upon *Du Côté de chez Swann* and devoured it in a passion of curiosity and admiration. Here, in the first volume of a long chronicle-novel – the very type of the unrolling tapestry which was so contrary to his own conception of form – he instantly recognized a new mastery, a new vision, and a structural design as yet unintelligible to him, but as surely there as hard bone under soft flesh in a living organism. I wonder if in any other art the joy of such recognition is as great as it is to the born novelist who loves his craft, and sees its subtle and Protean form so often stretched out of shape by insensitive hands. I look back with peculiar pleasure at having made Proust known to James, for the encounter gave him his last, and one of his strongest, artistic emotions.

Neither James nor I ever met Proust. In my case the meeting could have been easily arranged, for he was the friend of some of my most intimate friends. But what I heard about him, even from the people who were fondest of him, did not increase my desire to meet him. I did not then know how ill he already was – at that time even his intimates scarcely guessed it – and to be told that the only people who really interested him were Dukes and Duchesses, and that the only place where one could hope to find him was at the Ritz, after midnight, was enough to put me off. When I first read *Du Côté de chez Swann* I was on the point of pouring out my admiration in a letter; but supposing that many readers must have yielded to the same impulse, I remained silent. When I read Proust's correspondence, and discovered that *Swann* (on the whole the most perfect of the series) had fallen flat even among his intimates, and that a word of praise, though from a casual stranger, would have been priceless to him, I bitterly regretted my discretion. But by the time I had found out who he was, and through whom I could have made his acquaintance, his books were already the fashion in the very circles least capable of reading or understanding him – and on the whole I am glad I did not try to pursue him there. His greatness lay in his art, his incredible littleness in the quality of his social admirations. But in this, after all, he merely exemplified the tendency not infrequent in novelists of manners – Balzac and Thackeray among them – to be dazzled by contact with the very society they satirize. If it is true that *pour comprendre il faut aimer* this seeming inconsistency may, in some, be a deep necessity of the creative imagination.

7

We still went home every summer to the Mount, and all our old friends returned year after year to stay with us: chief among them, as usual, Egerton Winthrop, Walter Berry, Robert Minturn, the Jusserands from Washington, Robert Grant and his wife from Boston, Bay Lodge and his beautiful Bessy, and another old Boston friend, William Richardson. But much as I loved the place, the glowing summer weeks, and the woodland pageantry of our matchless New England autumn, it was all darkened by my husband's growing ill-health. Since the first years of our marriage his condition, in spite of intervals of apparent health, had become steadily graver. His sweetness of temper and boyish enjoyment of life struggled long against the creeping darkness of neurasthenia, but all the neurologists we consulted were of the opinion that there could be no real recovery; and time confirmed their verdict. Such borderland cases are notoriously difficult, and for a long time my husband's family would not see, or at any rate acknowledge, the gravity of his state, and any kind of consecutive treatment was therefore impossible. But at length they understood that he could no longer lead a life of normal activity, and in bringing them to recognize this I had the help of some of his oldest friends, whose affectionate sympathy never failed me in those difficult years.

The care of the Mount had been my husband's chief interest

and occupation, and the place had now to be sold, for much as I loved it the burden would have been too heavy for me to carry alone. It was sad to leave that lovely country, and for the moment I did not feel like making another country home for myself; so I lingered on in the rue de Varenne during the last two or three years before the war, going away only for a few weeks now and then, to visit friends or to travel.

Among the friends made at this time I must put first the Berensons. I had known them slightly for some years, but our real friendship dated from my first visit to their villa near Florence, in 1910, or thereabouts; and since then a pilgrimage to I Tatti has been one of my annual joys. I had never before stayed in a house where I could lead exactly the same life as in my own; working in the morning, and browsing at all hours in a library which, though incalculably bigger and more important than mine, was based on the same requirements; a broad and firm foundation of books of reference constantly replenished and kept up to date; all the still *living* classics, in Greek, Latin and the principal modern languages, and an annual influx of the best in current letters. Henry James and Howard Sturgis had nothing nearer to a library than a few dozen shelves of heterogeneous volumes; and indeed, even in houses commonly held to be 'booky' one finds, nine times out of ten, not a library but a book-dump. But such a library as that of I Tatti is the book-worm's heaven: the fulfilment of all he has dreamed that a great working library ought to be, continually weeded out and renewed, 'not made of spent deeds but of doing', not a dusty mausoleum of dead authors but a glorious assemblage of eternally living ones.

This 'great good place', which at first consisted in one noble room, lined with books to the high vaulted ceiling, and used not only as a library but as a living-room, was added to the original house by my dear friend Geoffrey Scott, and Cecil Pinsent, his partner; and they presently built out from it a wing containing two long conventual book-rooms with tall doors leading out to a terrace of clipped box.

When I first knew Geoffrey Scott he was still practising as an architect, and not long afterward he brought out that perfect book – or shall I say, that perfect introduction to a book? – 'The Architecture of Humanism'. My interest in the Italian architecture of the Renaissance, and the styles deriving from it, created one of the first links between us, and led to many delightful pilgrimages. Geoffrey Scott was at that time established in Florence with his partner, and whenever I went to stay with the Berensons we used to go off on architectural excursions and garden hunts, to Siena, Montepulciano, and all through Tuscany and Umbria. But one of our most amusing journeys took us to the Emilia, when I introduced Geoffrey to the little fairytale town of Sabbioneta, then so far from the beaten track that it had remained undisturbed in its decaying beauty. There are people who, wherever they go, attract droll adventures, little lurking picturesquenesses of incident. Geoffrey was one of them, and all our excursions were spangled with laughter. At Sabbioneta, when we arrived, the village boys were having a bicycle race about the green facing the little garden-palace of the Dukes of Sabbioneta (a junior branch of the Mantuan Gonzagas). The instant we appeared racers and spectators abandoned the track for the more novel sport of hunting us through the deserted grassy streets, yelling out comments on our nationality, speech and appearance, crowding in upon us in the crumbling palaces and hushed church, and rudely breaking the spell of the sleepy place.

Finally I could stand it no longer, and having run down in his den the local *carabiniere*, I besought him to come to our protection. Such was my respect for those beautifully uniformed and highly varnished guardians of the peace that I doubted not but one word from him would scatter our enemies; but he was alone, and could not leave his post. He assured me, however, that he would send his comrade to our relief as soon as the latter returned.

So on we surged, the mob triumphant at our discomfiture, and finally, in despair, ended up at the little garden-palace. There, just as our persecutors were crowding in with us, the promised *carabiniere* did appear. He wore spectacles, he carried a book in his hand – but still, he represented the law in a land accustomed (as I thought) to respect it. '*Now* you'll see!' I triumphed to Geoffrey.

The *carabiniere* saluted us and turned to face the pack. He looked at them over his spectacles, he opened his mouth, and spoke. '*Bisogna*,' he said, '*adoperare un po' più di prudenza*.' ('You must really try to conduct yourselves with more circumspection'.) Whereupon he stretched one arm across the threshold, pulled us in with the other, and hastily locked out the yelping band. In the palace he followed us about, listened attentively to the explanations of the custodian, and studied his little volume – which was apparently a local guide-book!

During those last pre-war years I travelled more, and in more different directions than ever before. Breaking with the seductive habit of going always and only to Italy, I made, one spring, a motor-trip to Spain with Madame de Fitz-James and a dear friend of hers and mine, Jean du Breuil de Saint Germain. Before the war motoring in Spain was still something of an adventure; the roads were notoriously bad, motor-maps were few and unreliable, the village inns dubious. However, we set forth, and having carefully worked out our itinerary I was delighted to find that we were following, stage by stage, Théophile Gautier's route of sixty or seventy years earlier, and that so little was changed in the character of the towns and villages through which we passed that his charming *Voyage en Espagne* was still a perfect guide-book. We went by way of Pamplona, Burgos, Avila and Salamanca to Madrid; but there we were held up by the impossibility of going farther south on wheels. Even the few miles from Madrid to Toledo were impassable, and we were warned that we must make the trip by train!

Spain was enriched for me by a rush of juvenile memories which made me exclaim at each step: 'But I've been here before! I've seen this already!' Whenever I go back there everything I see is suffused in this faint glow of old associations, as if my receptive faculties were afloat in a rich thick medium like the *fond de cuisson* without which no good French cook will practise his art. A child of four stores up by anticipation so much of what the mature self is later to enjoy that the adventures of a little girl may incalculably enrich the inner life of an old woman.

I was eager to return to Spain in more adventurous company, and go to more out-of-the-way places; and I made two more Spanish journeys before 1914. Each year the roads were improving, and it was becoming easier to get information about their condition; and being with a companion who was not afraid of the unknown, and wanted to see what I did, I managed to enlarge my map very considerably. These travels took in, on the east coast, the Seo d'Urgel, Ripoll, Gerona and Barcelona; and we even motored to Montserrat, though at that time the road thither from Barcelona was so hard to find, and so nearly impracticable, that the ascent took the best part of a day, and we had to spend the night at the monastery. Foreign visitors, other than pilgrims, were still infrequent, and the brother who received us explained that there were two hostelries for pilgrims, and asked us to choose between the one with a communal kitchen, where we could cook our own food, and the other, and more expensive one, to which a restaurant was attached. Feeling rather vulgar and purse-proud, we chose the latter, and having asked for four rooms were shown into an icy vaulted chamber with a stone floor, and four niches in the walls, each containing a bed. Our Spanish was not adequate to dealing with this difficulty, but supplementing it by pantomime we finally induced the brother to give us two four-niched rooms instead of one! I have never since cared to return to Montserrat, which may now be reached from Barcelona in an hour, by a perfect road lined with cafés and places of amusement, and leading to the luxurious hotels on the summit.

Thence we went to Jaca and Huesca, returned to Burgos and Avila, and managed, on the way back, to get from the Alcalde of Santillana the keys of the prehistoric cave of Altamira, then still abandoned to the care of a local peasant, who guided us through it with one smoky candle, which he held up recklessly to show the brilliant and delicate paintings. I think it was only after the war that the Duke of Alba succeeded in convincing King Alfonso of the necessity of giving proper protection to this incomparable treasure, and lighting it with electricity.

In the summer of 1912 or 1913 I went to Germany with Bernard Berenson. We motored to Berlin by the lovely route of the Rhine and the Thuringian forest, and for the first time I saw Weimar, so small and smiling in its leafy quiet, and Wetzlar, with Lotte's quaint wedge-shaped house, unchanged without and within since she lived there. In Berlin we spent eight crowded days, during which I trotted about the great Museums after my learned companion (who has always accused me of not properly appreciating the privilege), and was rewarded by a holiday in Dresden, and a day's dash to the picturesque heights of Saxon Switzerland. But the evenings in Berlin also brought their reward, for we not only heard 'The Ring' admirably given at the Opera but saw a memorable performance of Tolstoy's 'Living Corpse', and an enchanting one of the first part of Faust at the *Kleines Theater*, with charming scenery by Reinhardt, a Gretchen of eighteen, a Faust to match, and a Mephistopheles of twenty-five – budding understudies of the stars who were away on their summer holidays. But the crowning joy was *Der Rosenkavalier*, which neither Berenson nor I had yet heard, even in snatches on the gramophone. The sensations of that evening rank with my first sight of Isadora's dancing, my first Russian ballet, my first reading of *Du Côté de chez Swann*. They were vernal hours – *es war der Lenz!* But already the sickles were sharpening for the harvest . . .

One afternoon at the Adlon, just before leaving Berlin, we came upon a quietly dressed elderly lady who greeted Berenson as an old friend, and introduced to us the silent and rather sad-looking young man who was with her. The lady was the Princess of Thurn and Taxis, and the young man Rainer Maria Rilke, the exquisite poet, whose work I already knew and admired, though his greatest poems, the *Duineser Elegien*, written at the Princess's castle of Duino, near Trieste, were still in manuscript. She spoke to me, I remember, of their remote and mysterious beauty, while Berenson was talking to Rilke; and I longed for a better chance of seeing him than that hurried encounter over clattering teacups. The better chance never came. Rilke died soon after the war, and once more I cursed the shyness which had prevented my telling him then and there how much I cared for his writings.

I had the luck, in those years, to make two other enchanting journeys. The first, in 1913, took us through the length and breadth of Sicily, of which hitherto I had seen only Palermo and the towns of the east coast. Now we explored also the great central ridge across which Goethe laboured on horse-back, and from there went to Segesta, Trapani and Selinonte, then still a desert beach strewn with prone columns and mighty architectural fragments. The other tour, in the early spring of 1914, was made with Percy Lubbock and Gaillard Lapsley. We started by motor from Algiers, and after a day at the exquisite oasis of Bou-Saada, in southern Algeria, turned eastward across the mountains of Kabylia to Timgad, Constantine and Tunis, and from Tunis, by Sfax and Souss, to Kairouan the fabulous, and thence to El Djem, Gabès (whence we tried in vain to cross to Djerba, the Lotus-eaters' island), and southward to the mysterious town of Médénine, beyond which there were then no roads for motor-travel.

I have yielded to the temptation of setting down these names for the sake of their magic properties; but such a journey is now a commonplace of North African travel, and a dash across the desert from Tozeur to Gardaïa less of an adventure than our run from Gabès to Médénine. Though such recollections constitute the traveller's joy they may easily become the reader's weariness. In writing one's personal reminiscences it is not always easy to discriminate between one's self and one's audience, and the peril of prolixity lies in wait for the writer who begins his first paragraph with 'I remember'. As long as the scenes or incidents remembered are distant enough to revive a lost touch of local colour, or of vanished customs, to enlarge on them may be excusable; and if I could recall the details of my *diligence* journey through Spain at the age of four I might conceivably produce a tale as captivating as Théophile Gautier's or Washington Irving's. But to readers who may fly to Ur, or motor across the Atlas to Timbuctoo, in the course of an ordinary holiday excursion, it can be of little interest to learn how Timgad looked to me under a full moon, or what song the siren sang when I tried to pick up a passage from Gabès to the Lotus-eaters. All this is locked away in me in a safe place; but I must go there alone to count my treasures, for if I offered them to other eyes they might turn into a pinch of dust, like that beautiful Etruscan queen too rashly dragged from her painted tomb into the daylight.

Chapter Thirteen
The War

I

One beautiful afternoon toward the end of June 1914, I stopped at the gate of Jacques Blanche's house at Auteuil. It was a perfect summer day; brightly dressed groups were gathered at tea-tables beneath the over-hanging boughs, or walking up and down the flower-bordered turf. Broad bands of blue forget-me-nots edged the shrubberies, old-fashioned *corbeilles* of yellow and bronze wall-flowers dotted the lawn, the climbing roses were budding on the pillars of the porch. Outside in the quiet street stood a long line of motors, and on the lawn and about the tea-tables there was a happy stir of talk. An exceptionally gay season was drawing to its close, the air was full of new literary and artistic emotions, and that dust of ideas with which the atmosphere of Paris is always laden sparkled like motes in the sun.

I joined a party at one of the tables, and as we sat there a cloud-shadow swept over us, abruptly darkening bright flowers and bright dresses. 'Haven't you heard? The Archduke Ferdinand assassinated . . . at Sarajevo . . . where *is* Sarajevo? His wife was with him. What was her name? Both shot dead.'

A momentary shiver ran through the company. But to most of us the Archduke Ferdinand was no more than a name; only one or two elderly diplomatists shook their heads and murmured of Austrian reprisals. What if Germany should seize the opportunity—? There would be more particulars in next morning's papers. The talk wandered away to the interests of the hour . . . the last play, the newest exhibition, the Louvre's most recent acquisitions . . .

I was leaving in a day for a quick dash to Barcelona and the Balearic islands, before going to England, where I had taken a house in the country, carrying out at last my life-long dream of a summer in England. All my old friends had promised to come and stay; we were to motor to Scotland, to Wales, to all the places I had longed to see for so many years. How happy and safe the future seemed!

After some radiant days among the Pyrenees we descended into the burning summer of Catalonia. Even the transparent Spanish air had never seemed so saturated with pure light. I remember a day when we picnicked in the scant shade of a group of cork-trees above a vineyard where an iridescent heat-shimmer hung visibly over the fiery red earth. But at Barcelona we had a disappointment. For three weeks ahead not a berth was to be had on the little boat crossing every night from there to Majorca. The Balearics had not yet been discovered by foreign trippers, but Spanish holiday-makers took possession of the islands in summer. It was too sultry to linger in Barcelona, and the few hotels then existing at Palma were sure to be crammed with excursionists; so we wandered about in the Spanish Pyrenees, and then made for the Atlantic coast at Bilbao. The days were long and shining, the new roads lured us on. We gave little thought to the poor murdered Archduke, and international politics seemed as remote as the moon. My servants had already closed my apartment in Paris, and gone to the house I had taken in England, and I was to follow early in August. Slowly we began to loiter northward.

During the last days in Spain we felt the chill of the same cold cloud which had darkened the Blanches' garden-party. The belated French newspapers were beginning to be disquieting, and we decided to hasten our return. On July 30th we slept at Poitiers, and all night long I lay listening to the crowds singing the *Marseillaise* in the square in front of the hotel. 'What nonsense! It can't be war,' we said to each other the next morning; but we started early and rushed through to Paris, where the air was already thick with rumours. Everything seemed strange, ominous and unreal, like the yellow glare which precedes a storm. There were moments when I felt as if I had died, and waked up in an unknown world. And so I had. Two days later war was declared.

2

When I am told – as I am not infrequently – by people who were in the nursery, or not born, in that fatal year, that the world went gaily to war, or when I have served up to me the more recent legend that France and England actually wanted war, and forced it on the peace-loving and reluctant Central Empires, I recall those first days of August 1914, and am dumb with indignation.

France was paralyzed with horror. France had never wanted war, had never believed that it would be forced upon her, had proved her good faith by the absurd but sublime act of ordering her covering troops ten miles back from the frontier as soon as she heard of Austria's ultimatum to Servia! It may be useless to revive such controversies now; but not, I believe, to put the facts once more on record for a future generation who may study them with eyes cleared of prejudice. The criminal mistakes made by the Allies were made in 1919, not in 1914.

I have related, in a little book written during the first two years of the war, the impressions produced by those dark and bewildering days of August 1914, and I will not return to them here, except to describe my personal situation. This was rather absurdly conditioned by the fact that I had no money – a disability shared at the moment by many other foreigners in France. When I reached Paris I had about two hundred francs in my pocket, and was preparing to call at the bank for my usual remittance when I learned that the banks would make no payments. I borrowed a small sum from Walter Berry, who happened to have some cash in hand; but other penniless friends assailed him, and I could not ask for enough to send my servants in England, who were expecting me to arrive with funds to pay the previous month's expenses. My old friend Frederick Whitridge was staying at his house in Hertfordshire, close to the place I had hired, and I wired him to give my servants enough to go on with. He replied: 'Very sorry. Have no money.' I cabled to my bank in New York to send me at least a small sum, and the bank cabled back: 'Impossible.'

At last, after a long delay – I forget how many days it took – I managed to get five hundred dollars from New York, by paying another five hundred for the transmission! To re-transmit to England what remained would have been, if not impossible, at any rate so costly that little would have been left to settle my tradesmen's bills. I had never had a house in England before, and accustomed to the suspiciousness of French tradespeople I was wondering how much longer my poor servants, who were totally unknown in the neighbourhood, would be able to obtain credit, and I realized that the only thing to do was to get to England myself as quickly as possible – not an easy undertaking either.

As I had no money to pay any more hotel bills I moved back to my shrouded quarters in the rue de Varenne, and camped there until I could get a permit to go to England. At that time it was believed in the highest quarters that the war would be fought out on Belgian soil, that it would last at the longest not more than six weeks, and that one decisive battle might probably end it sooner. My friends all advised me, if I could get to England, to stay there 'till the war was over' – that is, presumably, till some time in October; and the first news of the battle of the Marne made it seem for two or three delirious days as though this prediction might come true.

While I was waiting to get to England I was asked by the Comtesse d'Haussonville, President of one of the branches of the French Red Cross (*Secours aux Blessés Militaires*) to organize a work-room for such work-women of my *arrondissement* as were not yet receiving government assistance. Almost all the hotels, restaurants, shops and work-rooms had closed with the drafting of the men for the army, and there remained a large number of women and children without means of livelihood, for whom immediate provision had to be made. I was totally inexperienced in every form of relief work, and not least in the management of anything like a work-room for seamstresses and *lingères*; and I had no money to do it with! But by this time it was possible for those who had a deposit in a French bank (which at the moment I had not), to draw it out in small amounts, and I assailed all my American friends who were either living in Paris, or still stranded there. I collected about twelve thousand francs (the first of many raids on the pockets of my compatriots), some one lent us a big empty flat in the Faubourg Saint-Germain, and luckily I came across two clever sisters (nieces of Professor Landormy, the well-known musical critic), who gave the aid of their quick wits and youthful energy. All this did not teach me how to run a big work-room, where we soon had about ninety women; but there was an ardour in the air which made it seem easy to accomplish whatever one attempted. There were several skilled *lingères* among our workers, and we decided to try for orders for fashionable *lingerie*, instead of competing with the other *ouvroirs* by making hospital supplies; and by dint of badgering my friends I extracted from them a rush of orders later supplemented by more from America. Our *lingerie* soon became well-known, and as I had told my assistants never on any account to refuse an order, whatever might be asked for, we were soon doing a thriving trade in unexpected lines, including men's shirts (in the low-neck Byronic style) for young American artists from Montparnasse!

This work was barely started when I got my visa for England, and a permit from the French War Office to motor to Calais (trains being slow and uncertain). At Folkestone Henry James met me and took me back to Lamb House for the night; then I hurried on to Stocks, the place I had hired. It was a charming old house in beautiful gardens, belonging at that time to the Humphry Wards. I knew the place well, and had looked forward to seeing all my friends about me in those pleasant rooms. How little could I have imagined in what conditions I was to arrive there! The country was deserted, and I was alone in the big echoing rooms, looking out on gardens radiant with flowers which I had no heart to enjoy. To the honour of the British race let it be recorded that all through those agonizing days Mrs Ward's upper housemaid (whom I had taken on with the house) kept every room filled with bowls of flowers arranged with the most exquisite art; also that the local tradesmen had given my butler and cook unlimited credit, and would probably have gone on trusting them to the end of the summer. In what other country could such faith in an unknown customer have been found?

The loneliness of those days at Stocks was indescribable. The wireless was not yet, and for news we had to await the arrival of the London papers, which came late and irregularly. Every day I walked to the village post office to fetch the papers. The hours were endless – for the first time in my life I could not read, and sat unoccupied in Mrs Ward's pleasant library. Henry James came to stay for a day or two; so, I think, did Percy Lubbock and Gaillard Lapsley. But no one could bear to remain – it was too far from London and the news, and there was something oppressive, unnatural, in the serene loveliness of the old gardens, the cedars spreading wide branches over deserted lawns, the borders glowing with unheeded flowers. Besides, our separate lonelinesses seemed to merge in one great sense of solitude, of being cut off forever from the old untroubled world we had always known, so that my friends and I felt that our being together was really not much help to any of us.

I had never intended to follow the advice to stay in England 'till the end of the war'. I meant to pay my bills, hand back Stocks to its owners, and return immediately to Paris, where I could be of use, and should have the blessed drug of hard work. But suddenly the way back was barred. I went up to London, I saw Mr Page at our Embassy, and Monsieur Paul Cambon at his, and both could only bid me be patient. For the moment, they told me, even if I succeeded in crossing to Calais I should not be allowed to go a yard farther. There began to be rumours of a big battle – *the* decisive battle – not far from Paris. As soon as that was over it might be possible to give me my permit.

My solitude at Stocks became more and more unbearable. Mrs Ward, who was at her house in London, understood this, and as she, on the other hand, had assumed war duties in the country, she proposed that we should exchange houses, and I gratefully installed myself under her roof in Grosvenor Place. There at least I could see people who fancied themselves well-informed, could pick up scraps of news, and could importune my Embassy and Monsieur Cambon. So the days dragged on, lit up for a moment by the glorious news of the Marne, but darkened again – only too soon – by the indecisive results of an action which was at first believed to have been a final victory. I have but a blurred memory of those weeks of suspense, and recall distinctly only the last days of my stay in England. From the moment when I was summoned by Mr Page, and told that my return to Paris was authorized, the rushing back and forth to the two Embassies kept me blissfully busy. Ours was crammed with travellers waiting for similar permissions, and it was hard to fix the attention of the overworked officials. At last one of them told me that I must have myself photographed for my permit (I imagine there were no regular passports as yet). He hurriedly gave me the address of the photographer usually employed by the Embassy, who, he said, being used to the job, would deliver my photograph the same day.

I hastened to the address given – a vague street somewhere in Millbank. The houses were all exactly alike, but on the one bearing the number given me I read the sign 'Photographer', and confidently rang the bell. A small shy man with pale hair and eyes admitted me, and showed me into a parlour furnished with aspidistras and antimacassars. Thence, after a long delay, he summoned me with the request to follow him to the roof. I was slightly surprised; but in those days everything was unexpected, and I climbed obediently up a ladder to the top of an outbuilding behind the house. Here this strange photographer seated me on a kitchen chair, and ducking under his voluminous black draperies took aim. But apparently something did not work, and after repeated duckings, and rumpled reappearances, he said in a tone of apology: 'I'm so sorry, madam; but the truth is, I've always specialized in photographing wild beasts, and this is the first time I've ever done a human being.'

I had evidently come to the wrong address; but there was nothing for it but to receive his excuses with a shout of laughter, and implore him to go on all the same. He did, and the portrait bore painful witness to the truth of his statement; but though it looked like a wild-cat robbed of her young it was sufficiently like to get me safely through to Paris.

3

On leaving Paris I had entrusted all the money I had collected to a young lady recommended to me by the Red Cross for the post of treasurer. During the German advance before the Marne many people had followed the example of the government, and moved rapidly in the direction of Bordeaux. Our treasurer was among them – and in the haste of departure she carried off all our funds! Ready money being still difficult to obtain, or to transmit, long and complicated negotiations were necessary before the Red Cross could recover my capital; and thereafter I acted as my own treasurer. But meanwhile the German advance, which had sent so many rich residents out of Paris, had driven into it the lamentable horde of the Belgian and French refugees. The Red Cross was engrossed by its immense task in the field and in the military hospitals, the government relief services were disorganized and totally unprepared for the sudden influx of refugees, and immediate help had to be given. Charles Du Bos, with a group of French and Belgian friends, had improvised an emergency work called *L'Accueil Franco-Belge*, which had already rendered great service, but risked being swamped by the increasing throng of applicants, and the lack of funds. I was asked to form an American committee, and to raise money; I did both, and speedily found myself, inexperienced as I was, unable to carry this new burden as well as my big *ouvroir*. But friends came to my aid, giving money and time, and before many months the relief work was on a sound basis, though none of us (luckily) foresaw the huge proportions it was to assume, and the repeated appeals for financial aid that our overworked committee would have to make.

It is unnecessary to chronicle our labours in detail. The *Accueil Franco-Belge* (afterward the *Accueil Franco-Américain*) was only one among many war-charities to supplement the inadequate and over-tasked administrative effort; but a few points in its growth and organization are worth recording. When it became necessary to divide the work into separate departments – registration bureau, centre for distribution of clothing, medical dispensary, cheap restaurants, etc., – we installed our central bureau in the large and handsome business offices in the Champs-Elysées which were put at our disposal by the Comtesse de Béhague. Here the refugees were registered, and given tickets for food, clothing and lodging; and among the hard-worked functionaries who performed this drudgery were not only Charles Du Bos himself, but Darius Milhaud, the well-known composer, Geoffrey Scott, André Gide and Percy Lubbock. These were among our punctual and faithful volunteers; but others – how many! – came and went, speedily overcome by the boredom of the task, or the inability to keep regular hours (and what hours! – our office was often open from 9 a.m. till after midnight).

My greatest difficulty was that of divining beforehand on which of our volunteers we should be able to count. Some would drift in vaguely, saying: 'I'll try for a few days – but don't expect too much from me,' and would turn out to be the future corner-stones of the building. Others, lucid, precise and self-confident, would point out our deficiencies, offer to remedy them, and fade away after a week. I recall one rich compatriot, long established in Paris, who offered to take over the management of our chaotic clothes-distribution, where, as she pointed out, everything needed sorting, listing and superintending. I was enchanted! Here at last, I thought, is a practical intelligence, some one who knows instinctively all that I am vainly trying to learn. I drew a deep breath of relief, and made an appointment to meet her the next morning at the *Vestiaire*. She came for about a week, increased the confusion she had offered to dispel – and then disappeared.

Such experiences were discouraging, and I was beginning to fear that my lack of discernment in choosing my helpers, and my innate distaste for anything like 'social service', were a hopeless handicap to my usefulness. But by this time I was President of our committee, and the work had to be kept going.

One day Mrs Royall Tyler came to see me. I had met her husband before the war at the house of my friend Raymond

Koechlin, the distinguished archæologist and collector, but my acquaintance with her was very slight. Royall Tyler, already an accomplished archivist, was at that time employed by the British Record Office in editing the State Papers bearing on the diplomatic relations between England and Spain in the sixteenth century. Soon after the outbreak of the war he and his wife came to Paris, and Mrs Tyler called on me, and said simply: 'My husband and I want to help you. How can you use us?' I was touched by the offer, but uncertain what to say. I knew them both too little to guess at their capacity, and above all at their staying powers. But I had begun to suspect that intelligence is a valuable asset even in assigning lodgings and food-tickets to refugees, and I liked the simple way in which the offer was made. I 'took on' both husband and wife, and Royall Tyler rendered me immense help until our entry into the war enrolled him in the United States Intelligence service; while of his wife I can only say that she found the *Accueil* a tottering house of cards, and turned it into solid bricks and mortar. Never once did she fail me for an hour, never did we disagree, never did her energy flag or her discernment and promptness of action grow less through those weary years. The real 'Magic City' was that which her inexhaustible resourcefulness raised out of our humble beginnings, and it was thanks to her that each fresh emergency was met by new and far-seeing measures of relief, so that in 1918, when the war ended, we had, in addition to five thousand refugees permanently cared for in Paris, and four big colonies for old people and children, four large and well-staffed sanatoria for tuberculous women and children. The most important of these, *La Tuyolle*, was handed over in 1920 to the Department of the Seine and is still running under the staff originally selected and trained by Mrs Tyler; and it still has the reputation of being one of the best sanatoria in France.

More and more funds had to be raised for our ever-growing work, and when the ardour of our supporters began to flag Mrs Tyler offered to go to America and beg for more. Beg she did, valiantly and successfully, returning with spoils beyond my hopes, and the lasting good-will of the friends to whom I had commended her. Another effort was presently required, and this time it fell to my lot to put together 'The Book of the Homeless', a collection of original poems, articles and drawings, contributed by literary and artistic celebrities in Europe and America. I appealed right and left for contributions, and met with only one refusal – but I will not name the eminent and successful author who went by on the other side.

'The Book of the Homeless', and the subsequent auction sale in New York of the original manuscripts and sketches, brought us in another large sum; but I ached with the labour of translating (in a few weeks' time) all but one of the French and Italian contributions! I am at best a slow worker, and with all the other tasks I had shouldered I could have cried for weariness at the mere thought of taking up my pen; but the overwhelming needs of the hour doubled every one's strength, and the book was ready on time.

I cannot end this summary of our war-labours without speaking of the response from America which alone made it possible for me to go on with the work. From my cousin Lewis Ledyard and his friend Payne Whitney, whose generosity built for us the sanatorium of *La Tuyolle*, to the woman doctor who sold her tiny scrap of radium because she had no other means of helping, and the French and English servants in New York who again and again sent us their joint savings, we met on every side with inexhaustible encouragement and sympathy. 'Edith Wharton' committees were formed in New York, Boston, Washington, Philadelphia and Providence, and friends and strangers worked with me at a distance as untiringly as those who were close at hand. I should like to tell them all now that I have never forgotten what they did.

4

A year or two ago my friend Madame Octave Homberg, President of the Mozart Society of Paris, brought out to dine with me one summer evening that most magical of flute-players, René Leroy, and Félix Raugel, the distinguished organizer and conductor of the Mozart Society's concerts.

René Leroy I knew already; Raugel was a stranger, except by reputation, and when he entered the room I had no sense of ever having seen him before. But he came straight up to me with beaming smile and hands outstretched. 'Madame! What an age since we last met! Do you remember? It was in August 1915, when you rode up a mountain in the Vosges, astride on an army mule, and suddenly appeared in the camp of the Blue Devils [*Chasseurs Alpins*] on top of the Col de la Chapelotte!'

I stared at him in wonder; and as he spoke the peaceful room vanished, and the twilight shadows of my suburban garden, and I saw myself, an eager grotesque figure, bestriding a mule in the long tight skirts of 1915, and suddenly appearing, a prosaic Walkyrie laden with cigarettes, in the heart of the mountain fastness held by the famous *Chasseurs Alpins*, already among the legendary troops of the French army. Seeing Félix Raugel again brought back to me with startling vividness the scenes of my repeated journeys to the front; the scarred torn land behind the trenches, the faces of the men who held it, the terrible and interminable epic of France's long defence. I remembered the emotion of my arrival at the posts I was permitted to visit, the speechless astonishment of officers and men at the sight of a wandering woman, their friendly greetings, the questions, the laughter, the jolly picnic lunches around boards resting on trestles, the reluctant goodbyes, the burden of messages to wives and mothers with which I returned to the rear . . .

Early in 1915 the French Red Cross asked me to report on the needs of some military hospitals near the front. Common prudence should have made me refuse to beg for more money; but in those days it never occurred to any one to evade a request of that kind. Armed with the needful permits, and my car laden to the roof with bundles of hospital supplies, I set out in February 1915 to inspect the fever-hospital at Châlons-sur-Marne. What I saw there made me feel the urgency of telling my rich and generous compatriots something of the desperate needs of the hospitals in the war-zone, and I proposed to Monsieur Jules Cambon to make other trips to the front, and recount my experiences in a series of magazine articles.

Foreign correspondents were still rigorously excluded from the war-zone; but Monsieur Cambon, after talking the matter over with General Joffre's chief-of-staff, General Pellé, succeeded in convincing him that, even if in my ignorance I should stumble on some important military secret, there would be little risk of its betrayal in articles which could not possibly be ready for publication until several months later; while the description of what I saw might bring home to American readers some of the dreadful realities of war. I was given leave to visit the rear of the whole fighting line, all the way from Dunkerque to Belfort, and did so in the course of six expeditions, some of which actually took me into the front-line trenches; and, wishing to lose no time

in publishing my impressions, I managed to scribble the articles
between my other tasks, and they appeared in 'Scribner's
Magazine' in 1915, and immediately afterwards in a volume
called 'Fighting France'.

When the book was published it was not permissible to give too
precise details about places or people, and I have sometimes
thought of bringing out a new edition in which the gaps should be
filled in with more personal touches: such as the moment when I
was received at La Panne, in a little wind-rocked sand-girt villa, by
the Queen of the Belgians, who had summoned me to talk of the
Belgian child-refugees committed to our care; or the day when
Monsieur Paul Boncour (afterward French Minister of Foreign
Affairs), in a particularly impeccable uniform, escorted me to the
first-line trenches in Alsace; or the other when Monsieur Henry de
Jouvenel (lately French Ambassador to Italy), receiving at Sainte
Menehoulde my request to go on to Verdun, at first positively
refused, and then, returning from a consultation with the General
of the division, said with a smile: 'Are you the author of "The
House of Mirth"? If you are, the General says you shall have a
pass: but for heaven's sake drive as fast as you can, for we don't
want any civilians on the road today.' (It was on February 28,
1915, the day the French retook the heights of Vauquois, on the
road to Verdun; and, as I have related in my book, we actually
witnessed the victorious assault from a cottage garden at
Clermont-en-Argonne.)

In Lorraine I was guided by an old friend, Raymond Recouly,
then on the staff of General Humbert, one of the heroes of the
Marne; and it was thanks to Recouly's disobedience of his chief's
orders that we had a risky and exciting hour at Pont-à-Mousson,
then close under the German guns, and rigorously closed to
civilians. Nor, if I am giving thanks, must I omit to record my
gratitude to another friend, Jean-Louis Vaudoyer, the well-
known poet and novelist, whom I had already visited somewhere
in a shelter at the rear of the front lines, I think in Alsace. On our
return to Châlons-sur-Marne, after a second trip to Verdun, it
chanced that we found Vaudoyer on the staff of the General in
command in that region. It was a bitter winter evening when we
arrived at Châlons, where we were to spend the night before
returning to Paris. To our dismay we found the place thronged
with troops, and were not surprised to hear, on applying at the
hotel of the Haute Mère Dieu, the only one open, that there was

not a single room free. We insisted, and the landlady at last replied: 'We are under military orders always to keep two rooms at the disposal of staff-officers. If they are not required tonight you may induce the General in command to let you have them.'

At Headquarters, in the stately Préfecture of Châlons, we found the great hall and monumental staircase swarming with officers, messengers and orderlies, and in spite of our high recommendations we were told that the rooms were not available, and that probably we should not find one in all Châlons. The only alternative was to sleep in the motor on a night of bitter frost (as my good chauffeur eventually did), for no civilian car was allowed on the roads after dark, and we were prisoners till the next day. Never shall I forget the relief of running across Jean-Louis Vaudoyer at the very moment when we were disconsolately leaving the Préfecture, and hearing him hurriedly whisper: 'I know what has happened, and I can lend you my little lodging for the night, for I'm on duty here at Headquarters. You ought not to be in the streets at this hour, but I'll give you the password. If you can manage to wake up the landlady she'll let you in; if you can't —well,' his shrug seemed to say, 'there is really nothing else that I can do for you.'

We did get to the door of his lodgings unchallenged, we did rouse the landlady without making too much noise; and oh, the sight of those peaceful rooms, the clean sheets, the warm stove! I don't think I ever slept as deeply and completely as that night in Vaudoyer's blessed bed.

The noting of my impressions at the front had the effect of rousing in me an intense longing to write, at a moment when my mind was burdened with practical responsibilities, and my soul wrung with the anguish of the war. Even had I had the leisure to take up my story-telling I should have had no heart for it; yet I was tormented with a fever of creation.

After two years of war we all became strangely inured to a state which at first made intellectual detachment impossible. It would be inexact to say that the sufferings and the suspense were less acutely felt; but the mysterious adaptability of the human animal gradually made it possible for war-workers at the rear, while they went on slaving at their job with redoubled energy, to create within themselves an escape from the surrounding horror. This was possible only to real workers, as it is possible for a nurse on a hard case to bear the sight of the patient's sufferings because she is doing all she can to relieve them. All the pessimism and the lamentations came from the idlers, while those who were labouring to the limit possessed their souls, and faced the future with confidence.

Gradually my intellectual unrest sobered down into activity. I began to write a short novel, 'Summer', as remote as possible in setting and subject from the scenes about me; and the work made my other tasks seem lighter. The tale was written at a high pitch of creative joy, but amid a thousand interruptions, and while the rest of my being was steeped in the tragic realities of the war; yet I do not remember ever visualizing with more intensity the inner scene, or the creatures peopling it.

Many women with whom I was in contact during the war had obviously found their vocation in nursing the wounded, or in other philanthropic activities. The call on their co-operation had developed unexpected aptitudes which, in some cases, turned them forever from a life of discontented idling, and made them into happy people. Some developed a real genius for organization, and a passion for self-sacrifice that made all selfish pleasures appear insipid. I cannot honestly say that I was of the number. I was already in the clutches of an inexorable calling, and though individual cases of distress appeal to me strongly I am conscious of luke-warmness in regard to organized beneficence. Everything I did during the war in the way of charitable work was forced on me by the necessities of the hour, but always with the sense that others would have done it far better; and my first respite came when I felt free to return to my own work.

Such freedom was seldom to be achieved during those terrible years, and between 1914 and 1918 I had time only for 'Fighting France', 'Summer', a short tale called 'The Marne', and a series of articles, 'French Ways and Their Meaning', which I was asked to write after our entry into the war, with the idea of making France and things French more intelligible to the American soldier. These articles appeared in a volume in 1919.

In 1917 I had my only real holiday. General Lyautey, then Resident General in Morocco, had held since 1914, in one or another of the Moroccan cities, an annual industrial exhibition, destined to impress upon France's North African subjects the fact that the war she was carrying on in no way affected her normal activities. The idea was admirable, the result wholly successful. To these exhibitions, which were carried out with the greatest taste and intelligence, the Resident annually invited a certain number of guests from allied and neutral countries. I was among those who were asked to visit the exhibition at Rabat; and General Lyautey carried his kindness to the extent of sending me on a three weeks' motor tour of the colony. The brief enchantment of this journey through a country still completely untouched by foreign travel, and almost destitute of roads and hotels, was like a burst of sunlight between storm clouds. I returned from it to the crushing gloom of the last dark winter, to the night which was not to lift again until the following September, and I had no time to set down the story of my wonderful journey until 1920, when it appeared in a volume called 'In Morocco'.

5

One evening at the end of July 1918 Royall Tyler and I were sitting in my drawing-room in the rue de Varenne. He had been staying with me for a few days; and I suppose that as usual we were talking of the war, though his responsible position in our Paris Intelligence Bureau made confidential communications impossible. At any rate, as we sat there our talk was suddenly interrupted by the sound of a distant cannonade. We broke off and stared at each other.

Four years of war had inured Parisians to every kind of noise connected with air-raids, from the boom of warning maroons to the smashing roar of the bombs. The rue de Varenne was close to the Chamber of Deputies, to the Ministries of War and of the Interior, and to other important government offices, and bombs had rained about us and upon us since 1914; and as we were on Big Bertha's deathly trajectory her evil roar was also a well-known sound.

But this new noise came neither from maroon, from aeroplane nor from the throat of the dark Walkyrie; it was the level throb of distant artillery, a sound with which my expeditions to the front had made me painfully familiar. And this was the first time that I had heard it in Paris! The firing along the front was often distinctly audible on the south coast of England, and sometimes, I believe, at certain points in Surrey; but though familiar to dwellers in the south-western suburbs of Paris, it had never before, to my knowledge, reached the city itself. My guest and I sprang up and rushed to a long window opening on a balcony. There we stood and listened to that far-off rumour, relentless, unbroken, portentous; and suddenly Tyler turned to me with an illuminated face. 'It's the opening of Foch's big offensive!'

Some three months later, on a hushed November day, another unwonted sound called me to the same balcony. The quarter I lived in was so quiet in those days that, except for the crash of aerial battles, few sounds disturbed it; but now I was startled to hear, at an unusual hour, the familiar bell of our nearest church, Sainte Clotilde. I went to the balcony, and all the household followed me. Through the deep expectant hush we heard, one after another, the bells of Paris calling to each other; first those of our own quarter, Saint Thomas d'Aquin, Saint Louis des Invalides, Saint François Xavier, Saint Sulpice, Sainte Etienne du Mont, Saint Séverin; then others, more distant, joining in from all around the city's great periphery, from Notre Dame to the Sacré Cœur, from the Madeleine to Saint Augustin, from Saint Louis-en-l'Ile to Notre-Dame de Passy; at first, as it seemed, softly, questioningly, almost incredulously; then with a gathering rush of sound and speed, precipitately, exultantly, till all their voices met and mingled in a crash of triumph.

We had fared so long on the thin diet of hope deferred that for a moment or two our hearts wavered and doubted. Then, like the bells, they swelled to bursting, and we knew the war was over.

Chapter Fourteen
And After

I

On the 14th of July 1919 I stood on the high balcony of a friend's house in the Champs Elysées, and saw the Allied Armies ride under the Arch of Triumph, and down the storied avenue to the misty distance of the Place de la Concorde and its obelisk of flame.

As I stood there, high over the surging crowds and the great procession, the midsummer sun blinding my eyes and the significance of that incredible spectacle dazzling my heart, I remembered what Bergson had once said of my inability to memorize great poetry: 'You're dazzled by it.'

Yes, I thought; I shan't remember all this except as a golden blur of emotion. Even now I can't catch the details, I can't separate the massed flags, or distinguish the famous generals as they ride by, or the names of the regiments as they pass. I remember thankfully that a *grand mutilé* for whom I have secured a wheeled chair must have received it just in time to join his group in the Place de la Concorde . . . The rest is all a glory of shooting sun-rays reflected from shining arms and helmets, from the flanks of glossy chargers, the dark glitter of the 'seventy-fives, of machine-guns and tanks. But all those I had seen at the front, dusty, dirty, mud-encrusted, blood-stained, spent and struggling on; when I try to remember, the two visions merge into one, and my heart is broken with them.

2

The war was over, and we thought we were returning to the world we had so abruptly passed out of four years earlier. Perhaps it was as well that, at first, we were sustained by that illusion.

My chief feeling, I confess, was that I was tired – oh, so tired! I wanted first of all, and beyond all, to get away from Paris, away from streets and houses altogether and for always, into the country, or at least the near-country of a Paris suburb. In motoring out to visit our group of refugee colonies to the north of Paris I had sometimes passed through a little village near Ecouen. In one of its streets stood a quiet house which I had never noticed, but which had not escaped the quick eye of my friend Mrs Tyler. She stopped one day and asked the concierge if by chance it were for sale. The answer was a foregone conclusion: of course it was for sale. Every house in the northern suburbs of Paris was to be bought at that darkest moment of the spring of 1918. They had all been deserted by their owners since the last German advance, for they were in the direct line of the approach to Paris, and the little house in question was also on Bertha's trajectory. But Mrs Tyler, the next day, told me she had found just the house for me, and we drove out to see it. The way there – now, alas, disfigured by the growth of Paris – was through pleasant market-gardens, and acres of pear and apple orchard. The orchards were just bursting into bloom, and we seemed to pass through a rosy snow-storm to reach what was soon to be my own door. I saw the house, and fell in love with it in spite of its dirt and squalour – and before the end of the war it was mine. At last I was to have a garden again – and a big old kitchen-garden as well, planted with ancient pear and apple trees, espaliered and in cordon, and an old pool full of fat old gold-fish; and silence and rest under big trees! It was Saint Martin's summer after the long storm.

The little house has never failed me since. As soon as I was settled in it peace and order came back into my life. At last I had leisure for the two pursuits which never palled, writing and gardening; and through all the years I had gone on gardening and writing. From the day when (to the scandal of the village!) I chopped down a giant araucaria on the lawn, until this moment, I have never ceased to worry and pet and dress up and smooth down my two or three acres; and when winter comes, and rain and mud possess the Seine Valley for six months, I fly south to another garden, as stony and soilless as my northern territory is moist and deep with loam. But to do justice to my two gardens, or at least to my enjoyment of them, would require not a chapter but a book; and pending that I must pass on to the other branch of my activity.

3

The brief rapture that came with the cessation of war – the blissful thought: 'Now there will be no more killing!' – soon gave way to a growing sense of the waste and loss wrought by those irreparable years. Death and mourning darkened the houses of all my friends, and I mourned with them, and mingled my private grief with the general sorrow. I myself had lost a charming young cousin, Newbold Rhinelander, shot down in an aeroplane battle in September 1917, and three dear friends. Of these, Jean du Breuil de Saint Germain and Robert d'Humières both fell leading their men though in each case their age would have assured them a safe berth as staff officers, had they been willing to accept it. The third of my friends was a young American, Ronald Simmons, excluded from active service by a weak heart, and appointed head of the American Intelligence service at the important post of Marseilles. He did admirable work there till the Spanish grippe swept over France; then his heart gave way, and he died in three days.

But sorrows come 'not single spies but in battalions', and while I was mourning the friends killed in the war, more intimate griefs befell me. In 1916 died Henry James, the perfect friend of so many years, and in 1920 my beloved Howard Sturgis. By the loss of these two friends, and that of Egerton Winthrop, who died suddenly at about the same time, my life was greatly impoverished. In recent years I had seen less of Egerton Winthrop; but a friendship such as ours is made of many elements, and there remained, I believe, on his side a great affection, and on mine a gratitude which went back to the first days of what I might call my conscious life. To the purblind creature he had found me he had been the first to hold out a wise and tender hand; and the loss of his wisdom and tenderness made a darkness in my life.

But with Henry James and Howard Sturgis the sorrow was present, was poignant. They were part of my daily thoughts and plans, and my roots were torn up with theirs. In Howard Sturgis's case a fatal illness had declared itself, and much suffering was inevitable; so that his best friends could only pray for the end to come quickly. Happily it did, and he faced it with lucid serenity. It added to my grief that it was impossible for me to go to him; not that a last meeting would have helped either of us much, but simply because I knew he would have liked the fact of my coming.

In Henry James's case, though he was so much older, it was

harder for his friends to resign themselves, for it seemed as though a man of his powerful frame and unimpaired intellectual vitality ought to have lived longer. We all knew that for years he had suffered from the evil effects of a dangerous dietary system, called (after the name of its egregious inventor) 'Fletcherizing'. The system resulted in intestinal atrophy, and when a doctor at last persuaded him to return to a normal way of eating he could no longer digest, and his nervous system had been undermined by years of malnutrition. The Fletcher fad, moreover, had bred others, as usually happens; and James's incessant preoccupation with his health gradually led to periods of nervous depression. The death of his brother William shook him to the soul, not only because of their deep attachment to each other, but because Henry, following the phases of his brother's fatal malady, had become convinced that he had the same organic heart-disease as William. The intense disappointment caused by his successive theatrical failures may also have had a share in weakening his health. Mr Leon Edel, in his suggestive essay on James's play-writing, has made out so good a case for him as a dramatist (if only circumstances had been more favourable) that I sometimes wonder if I was not wrong in thinking these theatrical experiments a mistake. James, at any rate, never thought them so. He believed himself gifted for the drama, and, apart from the creative joy that the writing of his plays gave him, he longed intensely, incurably, for the shouting and the garlands so persistently refused to his great novels, and which, had he succeeded in his theatrical venture, would have come to him in a grosser but more substantial form. I once said that Anglo-Saxons had no notion of what the French mean when they speak of *la gloire*; but in that respect James was a Latin, and the last infirmity of noble minds was never quite renounced by his.

His dying was slow and harrowing. The final stroke had been preceded by one or two premonitory ones, each causing a diminution just marked enough for the still conscious intelligence to register it, and the sense of disintegration must have been tragically intensified to a man like James, who had so often and deeply pondered on it, so intently watched for its first symptoms. He is said to have told his old friend Lady Prothero, when she saw him after the first stroke, that in the very act of falling (he was dressing at the time) he heard in the room a voice which was distinctly, it seemed, not his own, saying: 'So here it is at last, the

distinguished thing!' The phrase is too beautifully characteristic
not to be recorded. He saw the distinguished thing coming, faced
it, and received it with words worthy of all his dealings with life.

But what really gave him his death-blow was the war. He
struggled through two years of it, then veiled his eyes from the
endless perspective of destruction. It was the gesture of
Agamemnon, covering his face with his cloak before the unbearable.

Before James died he bore witness, in his own moving way, to
the depth of his grief. He loved England, naturally, as his home of
many years, as the scene of his greatest work, and of his dearest
friendships; but he loved America also, and the longing for a
better understanding between his native and his adopted
countries possessed him more and more as the war dragged on.
His one consolation was the knowledge that Mr Page, for whom
he had a great regard, was fighting valiantly in the same cause; but
after the 'Lusitania', and the American government's supine
attitude at that time, James felt the need to make manifest by some
visible, symbolic act, his indignant sympathy with England. The
only way open to him, he thought, was to renounce his American
citizenship and be naturalized in England; and he did this. At the
time I considered it a mistake; it seemed to me rather puerile, and
altogether unlike him. Not knowing what to say I refrained from
writing to him: and I regret it now, for I think the act comforted
him, and it deeply touched his old friends in England.

I have never seen any one else who, without a private personal
stake in that awful struggle, suffered from it as he did. He had not
my solace of hard work, though he did all he had strength for, and
gave all the pecuniary help he could. But it was not enough. His
devouring imagination was never at rest, and the agony was more
than he could bear. As far as I know the only letters of mine which
he kept were those in which I described my various journeys to the
front, and when these were sent back to me after his death they
were worn with much handing about. His sensitiveness about his
own physical disabilities gave him an exaggerated idea of what his
friends were able to do, and he never tired of talking of what he
regarded as their superhuman activities. But still the black cloud
hung over the world, and to him it was soon to be a pall. Perhaps it
was better so. I should have liked to have him standing beside me
the day the victorious armies rode by; but when I think of the
years intervening between his death and that brief burst of

radiance I have not the heart to wish that he had seen it. The
waiting would have been too bitter.

4

My spirit was heavy with these losses, but I could not sit still and
brood over them. I wanted to put them into words, and in doing
so I saw the years of the war, as I had lived them in Paris, with a
new intensity of vision, in all their fantastic heights and depths of
self-devotion and ardour, of pessimism, triviality and selfishness.
A study of the world at the rear during a long war seemed to me
worth doing, and I pondered over it till it took shape in 'A Son at
the Front'. But before I could settle down to this tale, before I
could begin to deal objectively with the stored-up emotions of
those years, I had to get away from the present altogether; and
though I began planning and brooding over 'A Son at the Front' in
1917 it was not finished until four years later. Meanwhile I found
a momentary escape in going back to my chidish memories of a
long-vanished America, and wrote 'The Age of Innocence'. I
showed it chapter by chapter to Walter Berry; and when he had
finished reading it he said: 'Yes; it's good. But of course you and I
are the only people who will ever read it. We are the last people
left who can remember New York and Newport as they were
then, and nobody else will be interested.'

I secretly agreed with him as to the chances of the book's
success; but it 'had its fate', and that was – to be one of my rare
best-sellers! I still had the writing-fever on me and the next
outbreak came in 1922, when I published 'The Glimpes of the
Moon', a still further flight from the last grim years, though its
setting and situation were ultra-modern. After that I settled down
to 'A Son at the Front'; and although I had waited so long to begin
it, the book was written in a white heat of emotion, and may
perhaps live as a picture of that strange war-world of the rear,
with its unnatural sharpness of outline and over-heightening of
colour.

After 'A Son at the Front' I intended to take a long holiday –
perhaps to cease from writing altogether. It was growing more
and more evident that the world I had grown up in and been
formed by had been destroyed in 1914, and I felt myself incapable
of transmuting the raw material of the after-war world into a

work of art. Gardening, reading and travel seemed the only solace left; and during the first years after the war I did a good deal of all three.

Years earlier, the reading of Monsieur Joseph Bédier's famous book, 'Les Chansons Epiques', had roused in me a longing to follow the mediaeval pilgrims across the Pyrenees to the glorious shrine of Compostela; and after the war this desire, and the resolve to satisfy it, were reawakened by the appearance of two new books, Kingsley Porter's 'Romanesque Sculpture of the Pilgrimage Roads', and Miss Georgina King's 'The Way of St James'.

We began our pilgrimage at Saint Jean-Pied-de-Port, in the western Pyrenees, and descended thence into Spain by Roncevaux and Jaca. We were resolved to miss no stage of the ancient way, and from Jaca we went to Burgos, and thence, by way of Fromista, Carrión de los Condes and Sahagun, to León, and across the Cantabrian Mountains to Oviedo. The roads in the Asturias and Galicia were still mediaeval, and our progress was slow; but our determination to carry out the pilgrimage to its end (or, I should rather say, to its beginning) bore us on over interminable humps and bumps to La Coruña, and thence to the solitary and mysterious point of Finisterre (*Nuestra Señora de Finibus Terrae*), where, as readers of the Golden Legend know, the decapitated body of St James the Greater landed in the boat carved out of stone in which it had been reverently laid on the distant shore of Palestine. From Finisterre, with imaginations raised to a high pitch of expectancy, we followed the saint back, past his halting-place at Padròn, to the mighty church which enshrines him; and on arriving at Santiago de Compostela we found that our expectations had not been pitched high enough! Perhaps because this was the first journey of any length which I had made since the war, every mile of the way seemed fabulous and beautiful. But even the impression left by the Panteòn de los Reyes at Leon, and the incomparable Camara Santa of Oviedo, faded in the radiance which streams from the singing sculptures of the Portico de la Gloria. Yet when I returned to Compostela a few years later, over smooth roads, and without the excitement of plunging into the unknown, the strange grandeur of that isolated city of palaces and monasteries, and the glory of its great church, impressed me more deeply than ever, and I rank Compostela not far behind Rome in the mysterious power of drawing back the traveller who has once seen it.

5

For years and years – ever since our first cruise in the Ægean – I had dreamed the impossible dream of going on another. Youth had passed, and middle-age was going, in the vain cherishing of that dream, when suddenly, unexpectedly, a stroke of literary luck made it seem that I might repeat the adventure. In going on our first cruise we had been reckless to the point of folly; but we were young, we were two, we were ready to face any financial consequences. Now I was old, I was alone, and I had learned the necessity of living within one's means. But when a friend wrote me that he had seen at Southampton a delightful little yacht of the same tonnage and draft as our dear old 'Vanadis', my prudence vanished like a puff of smoke, and I felt as reckless (and as young!) as when I had first set foot on the deck of the latter, nearly forty years earlier.

So the yacht 'Osprey' was chartered, and we set out from the Old Port of Hyères, the same from which Saint Louis, King of France, sailed forth on his last crusade. The date was March 31 1926, the day serene and sunny, and we were a congenial party, with lots of books, a full set of Admiralty charts, a stock of good provisions and *vins du pays* in the hold, and happiness in our hearts. From that day until we disembarked at the same port, two months and one week later, I lived in a state of euphoria which I suppose would seem inconceivable to most people. But I am born happy every morning, and during the magical cruise nothing ever seemed to occur during the day to diminish my beatitude, so that it went on rolling up like the interest on a millionaire's capital. Now and then, it is true, a twinge passed through me at the thought of the reckoning; but I said to myself: 'Never mind! As soon as I get home I'll write the story of the cruise, and call it "The Sapphire Way", and it will be such enchanting reading that it will immediately become a best-seller, and pay all the expenses of the journey.'

Would it have, I wonder? The book is not yet written, and probably never will be; for I returned to fiction as soon as I got home, as I always do when no more pressing task prevents. Yet what a charming book it would have been – like so many that have never been written!

At any rate, the intention of doing it sent my conscience to sleep, and I lived in unbroken bliss as we wandered from island to island, from shore to shore, always 'under a roof of blue Ionian weather', retracing the stages of the former cruise, and seeing many new wonders which had then been difficult of access, such as Delphi, Mistra, Cyprus and Crete. Not the least interesting part of the adventure was the following out, stage by stage, of our old itinerary, and noting the changes produced either by the hand of man (as at Rhodes and the renovated islands of the Dodecanese), or by that other Hand, always written with a capital, which scatters earth-quakes and volcanic eruptions throughout those lovely lands as freely as man distributes his administrative changes.

At Rhodes, which I had seen in the depths of Turkish squalour and *laissez-faire*, we now found a city magically restored to its ancient beauty, without the overdoing so irresistible to most restorers; and in the islands of the Dodecanese, taken over with Rhodes by Italy, the same touch has given order and cleanliness even to such human rabbit-warrens as the mediaeval citadel of Astypalaea.

A fortunate change in our travelling equipment was the substitution of oil for coal as fuel; so that, instead of having to lose hours in coaling, the 'Osprey' glided from port to port without delay or discomfort; and had her oil-tank been slightly larger we should not even have had the small inconvenience of replenishing it. Even the Hand of God fell on us lightly and as it were playfully; for we had the luck to slip into Santorin and Crete between two earthquakes of considerable violence, one of which occurred only a few weeks before our visit, and the other just afterwards. So it was that in Santorin's mysterious harbour we lay close to a new lava-island still visibly edged with subterranean fires, and at Candia, in Crete, beheld in all their plastic perfection the glorious Minoan jars garlanded with seaweed and sea-monsters, the slim Prince Charming of the lilies, and the frivolous young ladies leaning from their box above the arena to watch the young acrobats leap from bull to bull, where, a few weeks after our visit, the Museum floor was strewn with their shattered fragments.

But I am writing my reminiscences, and not that memorable work, 'The Sapphire Way', which, if ever it is done, will require several hundred pages, and all the colours of Turner's palette; so I will conclude by saying that this cruise proved to me again what the first had so fully shown: that *Kein Genuss ist vorübergehend*, and that no treasure-house of Atreus was ever as rich as a well-stored memory.

6

These and other wanderings have been the high lights of the last years; when I turn from them the sky darkens. The disappearance of one dear friend after another must always be the chief sadness of a life bound up in a few close personal ties. Such losses seem doubly poignant in the brave new world predicted by Aldous Huxley, and already here in its main elements – a world in which so many sources of peace and joy are already dried up that the few remaining have a more piercing sweetness. Saddest of all is it, as the years pass, to see the premature ending of lives which seemed meant to widen into usefulness and beauty. Such a life I had hoped Geoffrey Scott's would be. Since our first meeting, more than twenty years earlier, I had always found him a delightful comrade. I had rejoiced, with his other friends, in the appearance of those two well-nigh perfect books, 'The Architecture of Humanism' and 'The Portrait of Zélide,' so little appreciated at first beyond a small circle of readers, so tardily discovered by the general public; yet, accomplished as these books were, I felt in him something dispersed and tentative, as though the balance between his creative and critical faculties had not yet been struck. This discord ran through his whole character, and though no one could be gayer, more flashingly responsive to every appeal of life's ironies and beauties (and for him, as for all subtler intelligences, the two were always interwoven), yet under this laughing surface lay a desert of gloom and despondency –

> A country where the lights are low,
> And where the roads are hard to find,

as he once wrote of his own mind. Even his work, though he brought to it such a scrupulous art, ceased to interest him as soon as he had exteriorized the emotions producing it; and I used to tell him he was like an over-fed squirrel, who only cared to crack every nut, and then threw them away. But I was mistaken; he was not over-fed, but only groping for the right nourishment.

After the war he used to stay with me for long weeks, and we made various motor-flights together in Umbria and the North of Italy. In 1926, when he spent a month with me in the country near Paris, he was planning a book on Benjamin Constant – and what a book it would have been! I can imagine no subject better suited to him, and no one better fitted to interpret that unquiet and elusive character. I took him to the drowsy hill-village of Saint Michel-du-Tertre, where Benjamin Constant had once lived, and to the Abbaye d'Hérivaux, which he had bought after the Revolution; but all through Geoffrey's eager inquiries, and his keen interest in the projected work, ran the same streak of agitation and uncertainty. He had been asked for a life of Boswell for the English Men of Letters series, and the suggestion delighted him. But he was reluctant to begin the book because he knew of the existence, in private hands, of a quantity of unexplored Boswellian material, as yet inaccessible to scholars, but which, through the friendly intervention of Sir Edmund Gosse, he hoped one day to examine. I remember his once saying sadly: 'If I put off the Boswell in the hope of seeing those papers, some one else will write the book instead, and every one will say, as they always do, that I'm lazy and undecided; yet to set to work without being able to use this new material seems hardly worth while. What do you advise?'

I answered at once: 'Never mind what people say. Don't do the book till you can consult all the material available. Never do anything against your better judgment simply to prove that you're not lazy.' As far as his own welfare was concerned, it might have been better for him to tie himself down to any definite task, rather than drift longer on the old sea of alternatives; but since the question was one of literary probity it seemed impossible to hesitate.

I have never seen him more adrift, more undecided and disenchanted, than during those weeks; and it was a relief to hear, I think that same autumn, that the Boswell documents had been bought by an American collector who, at Geoffrey's request, had agreed to let him examine them. The rest of the story is known; the unforeseen importance of the discovery, the new owner's invitation to Geoffrey to return to America with him and edit the whole collection, and Geoffrey's immediate acceptance. To his friends there is a certain irony in the fact that the sensitive and imaginative art-critic and biographer, master of a perfect prose and of a delicate lyrical gift, should have become known to the general public only through an editorial task. The first Boswell volumes met with unqualified praise, and Geoffrey's letters showed the steadying effect of the welcome given to his labours. I had feared the strain, and the long exile from Europe, in conditions scarcely made for peace of mind; but I soon felt that he was gaining strength from the effort. His letters were not altogether happy, but they gave no hint of uncertainty; he was determined to carry the work through, and buoyed up by knowing that the need to be near the British Museum must soon bring him back to England.

One day in London, in July 1929, I suddenly came across Geoffrey. There was so little trace in his strong erect figure and smiling face of the worn unquiet being I had parted from three years earlier that at first I hardly recognized him. He had taken an unexpected holiday from his work, and as he was not to be in England more than a fortnight he had notified no one in advance. He told me he was to sail in two days for America, where he intended to settle down again to a year's work, with the hope, after that, of continuing his labours in England. We spent the afternoon together, wandering from one picture gallery to another in happy talk – the happiest I ever had with him. He had found his work, and himself. The old irony, the old mockery and subtlety were there, but tempered by a new and confident hope in the future. He felt his strength equal to his task, and was happy with that best happiness, the sense of mastery over one's work. We parted full of plans for the future, and the next morning he sailed for New York – and ten days later lay there dead.

But he had felt his hand on the wheel, had guided Fortune where he chose; and his friends, when they remembered him, must think of that.

7

The world is a welter and has always been one; but though all the cranks and the theorists cannot master the old floundering monster, or force it for long into any of their neat plans of readjustment, here and there a saint or a genius suddenly sends a little ray through the fog, and helps humanity to stumble on, and perhaps up.

The welter is always there, and the present generation hears close underfoot the growling of the volcano on which ours danced so long; but in our individual lives, though the years are sad, the days have a way of being jubilant. Life is the saddest thing there is, next to death; yet there are always new countries to see, new books to read (and, I hope, to write), a thousand little daily wonders to marvel at and rejoice in, and those magical moments when the mere discovery that 'the woodspurge has a cup of three' brings not despair but delight. The visible world is a daily miracle for those who have eyes and ears; and I still warm my hands thankfully at the old fire, though every year it is fed with the dry wood of more old memories.

SUGGESTIONS FOR FURTHER READING

Ammons, Elizabeth, *Edith Wharton's Argument with America*, Athens: University of Georgia Press, 1980. Considers EW's critique of American culture, focussing on her treatment of the plight of women.

Auchincloss, Louis, *Edith Wharton*, Minneapolis: University of Minnesota Press, 1961. Short critical survey.

Bell, Millicent, *Edith Wharton and Henry James: The Story of their Friendship*, New York: George Braziller, 1965. An account of their relationship based on their correspondence, in which EW's achievement starts to emerge from James's shadow.

Bloom, Harold (ed.), *Edith Wharton*, in Modern Critical Views Series, New York and Philadelphia: Chelsea House, 1986. Eleven authoritative articles, covering biographical and critical topics.

Erlich, Gloria C., *The Sexual Education of Edith Wharton*, Berkeley: University of California Press, 1992. Considers the effects of 'double-mothering' (the presence of a nanny and a biological mother) on EW's life and her fiction.

Fryer, Judith, *Felicitous Spaces: The Imaginative Structures of Edith Wharton and Willa Cather*, Chapel-Hill: University of North Carolina, 1986. Considers EW's concern with spatial relations in her fiction, non-fiction and life.

Gimbel, Wendy, *Edith Wharton: Orphancy and Survival*, New York: Praeger, 1984. Considers life and work in close association, emphasising symbolic value of EW's houses in her development.

Goodman, Susan, *Edith Wharton's Women: Friends and Rivals*, Hanover and London: University Press of New England. Reassesses EW's attitude to other women, formerly regarded as hostile and competitive.

Goodwyn, Janet, *Edith Wharton: Traveller in the Land of Letters*, London: Macmillan, 1990. Discusses EW's sense of place and landscape, actual and metaphorical.

Joslin, Katherine, *Edith Wharton*, in Women Writers series, London: Macmillan, 1991. Short discussion of life and major works from feminist standpoint, including summary of EW's fluctuating critical reputation.

Lewis, R. W. B., *Edith Wharton: A Biography*, New York: Harper and Row, 1975. The authorised biography, the first to make use of the private papers at Yale, unsealed in 1969. Inaugurates a new phase of scholarship, in which EW's private life is treated extensively in relation to her fiction.

Lewis, R. W. B., and Nancy, *The Letters of Edith Wharton*, London: Simon and Schuster, 1988. Four hundred letters to her chief correspondents. Widens picture of EW by including letters to Morton Fullerton which emerged only in 1980. Includes detailed chronology of life.

Lindberg, Gary H., *Edith Wharton and the Novel of Manners*, Charlottesville: University of Virginia Press, 1975. Detailed readings of EW's work placing it in the tradition of the novel of manners.

Lubbock, Percy, *Portrait of Edith Wharton*, London: Cape, 1947. Informal and unsympathetic memoir based on contributions by her friends.

Nevius, Blake, *Edith Wharton: A Study of her Fiction*, Berkeley: University of California Press, 1953 (repr. 1976). The first full-length study of EW's work. Highlights her preoccupation with individual freedom versus the demands of society.

Powers, Lyall (ed.), *Letters of Henry James and Edith Wharton, 1900–1915*, London: Weidenfeld & Nicolson, 1990.

Vita-Finzi, Penelope, *Edith Wharton and the Art of Fiction*, London: Pinter, 1990. Discusses EW's theory of literature, in fiction and non-fiction.

Wagner-Martin, Linda, *The House of Mirth: A Novel of Admonition*, Boston: Twayne, 1990. Detailed discussion of EW's first bestseller in its historical context.

Waid, Candace, *Edith Wharton's Letters from the Underworld: Fictions of Women and Writing*, Chapel-Hill: University of North Carolina Press, 1991. Analyses EW's concern in her fiction and poetry with the place of the woman writer in the context of her own ambivalent relation to American literature.

Wershovan, Carol, *The Female Intruder in the Novels of Edith Wharton*, Rutherford, N. J.: Fairleigh Dickinson Press, 1982. Identifies motif in EW's work of the female outsider whose intervention stimulates moral development in a static culture.

Wolff, Cynthia Griffin, *A Feast of Words: The Triumph of Edith Wharton*, New York, Oxford University Press, 1977. Psychoanalytically-orientated treatment of the life and works, using (like R. W. B. Lewis above) the newly revealed biographical material.

INDEX

CLASSIC NOVELS
IN EVERYMAN

A SELECTION

The Way of All Flesh
SAMUEL BUTLER
A savagely funny odyssey from joy-less duty to unbridled liberalism **£4.99**

Born in Exile
GEORGE GISSING
A rationalist's progress towards love and compromise in class-ridden Victorian England **£4.99**

David Copperfield
CHARLES DICKENS
One of Dickens' best-loved novels, brimming with humour **£3.99**

The Last Chronicle of Barset
ANTHONY TROLLOPE
Trollope's magnificent conclusion to his Barsetshire novels **£4.99**

He Knew He Was Right
ANTHONY TROLLOPE
Sexual jealousy, money and women's rights within marriage – a novel ahead of its time **£6.99**

Tess of the D'Urbervilles
THOMAS HARDY
The powerful, poetic classic of wronged innocence **£3.99**

Wuthering Heights and Poems
EMILY BRONTE
A powerful work of genius – one of the great masterpieces of literature **£3.50**

Tom Jones
HENRY FIELDING
The wayward adventures of one of literatures most likable heroes **£5.99**

The Master of Ballantrae and Weir of Hermiston
R. L. STEVENSON
Together in one volume, two great novels of high adventure and family conflict **£4.99**

£3.99

£2.99

£3.99

AVAILABILITY

All books are available from your local bookshop or direct from
Littlehampton Book Services Cash Sales, 14 Eldon Way, LinesideEstate, Littlehampton, West Sussex BN17 7HE. PRICES ARE SUBJECT TO CHANGE.

To order any of the books, please enclose a cheque (in £ sterling) made payable to Littlehampton Book Services, or phone your order through with credit card details (Access, Visa or Mastercard) on 0903 721596 (24 hour answering service) stating card number and expiry date. Please add £1.25 for package and postage to the total value of your order.

CLASSIC FICTION
IN EVERYMAN

A SELECTION

Frankenstein
MARY SHELLEY
A masterpiece of Gothic terror in its
original 1818 version **£3.99**

Dracula
BRAM STOKER
One of the best known horror stories
in the world **£3.99**

The Diary of A Nobody
GEORGE AND WEEDON
GROSSMITH
A hilarious account of suburban life
in Edwardian London **£4.99**

Some Experiences
and Further Experiences
of an Irish R. M.
SOMERVILLE AND ROSS
Gems of comic exuberance and
improvisation **£4.50**

Three Men in a Boat
JEROME K. JEROME
English humour at its best **£2.99**

Twenty Thousand Leagues
under the Sea
JULES VERNE
Scientific fact combines with
fantasy in this prophetic tale of
underwater adventure **£4.99**

The Best of Father Brown
G. K. CHESTERTON
An irresistible selection of crime
stories – unique to Everyman **£3.99**

The Collected Raffles
E. W. HORNUNG
Dashing exploits from the most glam-
orous figure in crime fiction **£4.99**

£2.99

£5.99

£5.99

AVAILABILITY
All books are available from your local bookshop or direct from
**Littlehampton Book Services Cash Sales, 14 Eldon Way, LinesideEstate,
Littlehampton, West Sussex BN17 7HE.** PRICES ARE SUBJECT TO CHANGE.

To order any of the books, please enclose a cheque (in £ sterling) made payable to
Littlehampton Book Services, or phone your order through with credit card details (Access,
Visa or Mastercard) on 0903 721596 (24 hour answering service) stating card number and
expiry date. Please add £1.25 for package and postage to the total value of your order.

WOMEN'S WRITING
IN EVERYMAN

A SELECTION

Female Playwrights of the Restoration
FIVE COMEDIES
Rediscovered literary treasures in a unique selection **£5.99**

The Secret Self
SHORT STORIES BY WOMEN
'A superb collection' *Guardian* **£4.99**

Short Stories
KATHERINE MANSFIELD
An excellent selection displaying the remarkable range of Mansfield's talent **£3.99**

Women Romantic Poets 1780-1830: An Anthology
Hidden talent from the Romantic era, rediscovered for the first time **£5.99**

Selected Poems
ELIZABETH BARRETT BROWNING
A major contribution to our appreciation of this inspiring and innovative poet **£5.99**

Frankenstein
MARY SHELLEY
A masterpiece of Gothic terror in its original 1818 version **£3.99**

The Life of Charlotte Brontë
MRS GASKELL
A moving and perceptive tribute by one writer to another **£4.99**

Vindication of the Rights of Woman and The Subjection of Women
MARY WOLLSTONECRAFT
AND J. S. MILL
Two pioneering works of early feminist thought **£4.99**

The Pastor's Wife
ELIZABETH VON ARNIM
A funny and accomplished novel by the author of *Elizabeth and Her German Garden* **£5.99**

£4.99

£2.99

£5.99

SHORT STORY COLLECTIONS IN EVERYMAN

A SELECTION

The Secret Self
Short Stories by Women
'A superb collection' *Guardian* **£4.99**

Selected Short Stories
and Poems
THOMAS HARDY
The best of Hardy's Wessex in a unique selection **£4.99**

The Best of
Sherlock Holmes
ARTHUR CONAN DOYLE
All the favourite adventures in one volume **£4.99**

Great Tales of Detection
Nineteen Stories
Chosen by Dorothy L. Sayers **£3.99**

Short Stories
KATHERINE MANSFIELD
A selection displaying the remarkable range of Mansfield's writing **£3.99**

Selected Stories
RUDYARD KIPLING
Includes stories chosen to reveal the 'other' Kipling **£4.50**

The Strange Case of
Dr Jekyll and Mr Hyde
and Other Stories
R. L. STEVENSON
An exciting selection of gripping tales from a master of suspense **£3.99**

Modern Short Stories 2:
1940-1980
Thirty-one stories from the greatest modern writers **£3.50**

The Day of Silence and
Other Stories
GEORGE GISSING
Gissing's finest stories, available for the first time in one volume **£4.99**

Selected Tales
HENRY JAMES
Stories portraying the tensions between private life and the outside world **£5.99**

£4.99

£6.99

AVAILABILITY

All books are available from your local bookshop or direct from
Littlehampton Book Services Cash Sales, 14 Eldon Way, LinesideEstate, Littlehampton, West Sussex BN17 7HE. PRICES ARE SUBJECT TO CHANGE.

To order any of the books, please enclose a cheque (in £ sterling) made payable to Littlehampton Book Services, or phone your order through with credit card details (Access, Visa or Mastercard) on 0903 721596 (24 hour answering service) stating card number and expiry date. Please add £1.25 for package and postage to the total value of your order.

AMERICAN LITERATURE IN EVERYMAN

A SELECTION

Selected Poems
HENRY LONGFELLOW
A new selection spanning the whole of Longfellow's literary career **£7.99**

Typee
HERMAN MELVILLE
Melville's stirring debut, drawing directly on his own adventures in the South Sea **£4.99**

Billy Budd and Other Stories
HERMAN MELVILLE
The compelling parable of innocence destroyed by a fallen world **£4.99**

The Scarlet Letter
NATHANIEL HAWTHORNE
The compelling tale of an independent woman's struggle against a crushing moral code **£3.99**

The Last of The Mohicans
JAMES FENIMORE COOPER
The classic tale of old America, full of romantic adventure **£5.99**

The Red Badge of Courage
STEPHEN CRANE
A vivid portrayal of a young soldier's experience of the American Civil War **£2.99**

Essays and Poems
RALPH WALDO EMERSON
An indispensable edition celebrating one of the most influential American writers **£5.99**

The Federalist
HAMILTON, MADISON, AND JAY
Classics of political science, these essays helped to found the American Constitution **£6.99**

Leaves of Grass and Selected Prose
WALT WHITMAN
The best of Whitman in one volume **£6.99**

£5.99

£4.99

£4.99

AVAILABILITY

All books are available from your local bookshop or direct from
Littlehampton Book Services Cash Sales, 14 Eldon Way, LinesideEstate, Littlehampton, West Sussex BN17 7HE. PRICES ARE SUBJECT TO CHANGE.

To order any of the books, please enclose a cheque (in £ sterling) made payable to Littlehampton Book Services, or phone your order through with credit card details (Access, Visa or Mastercard) on 0903 721596 (24 hour answering service) stating card number and expiry date. Please add £1.25 for package and postage to the total value of your order.